MW00444378

Ink in Her Blood
The Life and Crime Fiction
of Margery Allingham

Literature Advisory Boards

Studies in Modern Literature

A. Walton Litz, Series Editor
Princeton University

Consulting Editors

Joseph Blotner
University of Michigan
George Bornstein
University of Michigan
Jackson R. Bryer
*University of Maryland
at College Park*
Ronald Bush
California Institute of Technology
Keith Cushman
*University of North Carolina
at Greensboro*
Richard J. Finneran
University of Tennessee at Knoxville
Daniel Mark Fogel
Louisiana State University
Carolyn G. Heilbrun
Columbia University
Paul Mariani
*University of Massachusetts
at Amherst*
Thomas C. Moser
Stanford University
Linda Wagner-Martin
University of North Carolina at Chapel Hill
Patricia C. Willis
Yale University Library

Nineteenth-Century Studies

Juliet McMaster, Series Editor
University of Alberta

Consulting Editors

Carol Christ
*University of California
at Berkeley*
James R. Kincaid
University of Southern California
Julian Markels
Ohio State University
G. B. Tennyson
*University of California
at Los Angeles*

Studies in Speculative Fiction

Robert Scholes, Series Editor
Brown University

Challenging the Literary Canon

Other Titles in This Series

*The Witch and the Goddess in the
Stories of Isak Dinesen:
A Feminist Reading*
Sara Stambaugh

*Transcending Gender:
The Male/Female Double
in Women's Fiction*
Joanne Blum

*Charlotte Perkins Gilman:
The Woman and Her Work*
Sheryl L. Meyering, ed.

*Toward a New Synthesis:
John Fowles, John Gardner,
Norman Mailer*
Robert J. Begiebing

*Form and Meaning in the
Novels of John Fowles*
Susana Onega

Ink in Her Blood
The Life and Crime Fiction of Margery Allingham

by
Richard Martin

U·M·I Research Press

Ann Arbor / London

Cover design: Shayne Davidson

Copyright © 1988
Richard Graham Colin Martin
All rights reserved

Produced and distributed by
UMI Research Press
an imprint of
University Microfilms Inc.
Ann Arbor, Michigan 48106

Library of Congress Cataloging in Publication Data

Martin, Richard, 1934-
  Ink in her blood.

  (Challenging the literary canon)
  Bibliography: p.
  Includes index.
  1. Allingham, Margery, 1904-1966. 2. Novelists,
English—20th century—Biography. 3. Detective and
mystery stories, English—History and criticism.
4. Crime and criminals in literature. I. Title.
II. Series.
PR6001.L678Z76   1988   823'.912 [B]   88-27789
  ISBN ʋ-8357-2028-4 (pbk.)

British Library CIP data is available.

Für
Dagmar
. . . Du weißt schon

Margery Allingham in 1955

Contents

Illustrations

All photographs, except where otherwise stated, are reproduced with kind permission from the collection of Joyce Allingham.

Preface

In recent years whenever I told people that I was collecting material for a biography of Margery Allingham, the reaction—when it was not simply, "Who?"—was, "Why on earth Margery Allingham?" This question has not been difficult to answer, but its very existence has revealed how comparatively unknown a writer is, who, after all, has consistently had an unusually large number of her twenty-seven books in print for the last twenty-five years.

In reply to my questioners I explained that I have been reading Allingham novels since, at the age of seventeen, I was introduced to them by my mother, who, significantly or not, was born, like Miss Allingham, in 1904. I would continue that I have always been addicted to detective and crime fiction, and to her "off-beat" books in particular. In deciding to write a biography of a favourite author of my leisure hours, I saw a marvellous opportunity to combine research work and pleasure. I have not been disappointed. When I began, I had no idea what sort of person Margery Allingham had been, nor was I even sure that there was any material available for research. I need not have worried. Margery and her parents, particularly her father, were people who made a point of living out their lives on paper and never throwing anything away. In addition to the diaries, notebooks, letters, manuscripts, and publications at Margery Allingham's home in the Essex village of Tolleshunt D'Arcy, hundreds of letters have been made available to me by libraries, and by Miss Allingham's friends and relatives.

The mere existence of a person and her papers still does not warrant a biography. During her lifetime Margery Allingham was consistently mentioned in the same breath as Agatha Christie and Dorothy Sayers, she was named one of the ten best living writers of crime fiction, had ten of her books published simultaneously by Penguin, and sold altogether some three million copies of her works. Several biographies of Sayers have been written, and one very full one of Christie, as well as her own autobiography. Is it not then time for more to be known of Margery Allingham? Moreover, I am convinced that from a literary standpoint, Allingham's books are of considerably greater interest than the works of the other two women, and that she, as much as if not more than anyone else, was responsible for the development of the tradition of the contemporary sophisticated mystery story carried on by such writers as P. D. James and Ruth Rendell.

However true this all may be, was Margery Allingham's life so remarkable and so interesting that the telling of it is as important as the reading of her books? This has been for me a crucial question. The writer of biography inevitably recreates the life and personality of his subject; the person about whom one began slowly to collect information develops into one's own image of that person, and it is this image which dominates the biographer's mind and imagination. When I started on the project, the novels and stories Margery Allingham wrote already existed for me and implied a certain type of mind and dedication. However, the actual woman—who suffered from ill health, experienced financial and domestic problems, loved her husband, and found comfort in her house and garden—still had to be created.

The more material I gathered, the more people I spoke with who had known Allingham, the more I immersed myself in her letters and diaries, the more I became convinced that the life I was in the process of inventing had a peculiarly representative quality about it. Allingham was a middle-class Englishwoman committed not only to a professional writing career, but also to an outwardly conventional marriage and a small circle of professionally successful middle-class friends. The period they all lived through—the cynical twenties, the turbulent thirties, the Second World War, postwar reconstruction, the Welfare State, the new affluence of the early sixties—witnessed immense changes in almost all spheres of English society. Although conservative by upbringing and temperament, Margery Allingham was acutely sensitive to the potentialites and implications of a changing world and its attitudes.

During the time I spent researching Allingham's life, I reread all of her novels several times. Each rereading increased my respect for her writing, for the skilful mastery of narrative strategies, for her ability to exploit the various established forms of crime fiction, transforming them into novels which transcend the narrow limits of the subgenre. This accounts in part for the structure of the narrative that follows. I begin by attempting to pinpoint certain essential features of the traditional mystery story—"conventional to the point of being rigid" (Allingham 1953, 7)—with which Margery Allingham began her career. There follows a general overview of her work together with a summary of her own ideas about the genre—despite her disclaimer to her American agent Paul Reynolds that, "The truth is of course that I have *no* theories on mystery writing!"(Letter, 07.12.1948). From then on biographical chapters alternate with critical accounts of her major novels, linking her artistic progress with her experience of life and social change.

I have only dealt with major novels, omitting her earliest work, *Blackkerchief Dick,* written when she was seventeen, *The Case of the Late Pig,* a none-too-successful attempt to use Albert Campion as a first-person narrator, and *Black Plumes,* Allingham's one non-Campion mystery. Nor have I discussed *Cargo of Eagles,* since, although planned by Margery Allingham, it was completed after her death by her husband, Philip Youngman Carter. Apart from occasional brief references I have not mentioned the four novellas and the more than fifty short stories she wrote. The case I wish to present is for Margery Allingham, the novelist—hence the omissions.

She herself differentiated between two sorts of writing she was conscious of having done: writing purely for commercial reasons, in order to support herself, her husband, and her household for some twenty years; and the writing she really wanted to do. Margery Allingham explained this in her preface to the omnibus book, *Mr. Campion's Lady:*

> Right-hand writing is the story one tells spontaneously at the party. Left-hand writing is the one which one is made to tell by somebody else. The difference is that in the one case there is only oneself and the audience. But in the other, a third mind has intervened and it usually belongs to an extremely able, remarkably informed, highly self-opinionated professional editor not at all like oneself. . . . In right-hand writing one can coax the life out of oneself on to the dead paper in any private way one pleases. But in left-hand writing one must discipline the imagination and observe the rules and remember the idiosyncrasies and, above all, bow the knee to the fashion of the day. (Allingham 1965, 8)

This description of Allingham's writing is equally true of the central feature of her life. As a writer, she differentiated between self-pleasing spontaneity and the discipline involved in observing the rules. As a woman, Margery Allingham was someone whose training and class allegiances suggested an adherence to conformity, tradition, and established codes of behaviour; yet, again and again, there seem to be times when she could envision breaking with such pressures and limitations. If outwardly she "bowed her knee to the fashion of the day," there was a sense in which she sought, for her own satisfaction, "the private way."

Acknowledgments

Without the wholehearted support and encouragement of Joyce Allingham, this book would never have been written. From our very first meeting in 1983, Joyce has been unbelievably generous both in making her sister's and other family papers available to me, and in the way in which she has uncomplainingly and painstakingly answered literally thousands of questions. During the course of my work on this project, Joyce has become a very dear and valued friend, whose warm hospitality, good sense and infectious cheerfulness my wife and I have come to appreciate deeply.

In the course of my research, very many people patiently answered my queries, made letters and photographs available, and graciously gave their time to sharing their memories of Margery Allingham with me. Since to acknowledge specific debts would take up unwarranted space, I must simply say a heartfelt and all-too-inadequate thank you to: Sheila Archibald, Mary Brown, Hugo Brunner, Audrey Cameron, Beatrix Carter, Christina Carter, Charles Champlin, Michael Christiansen, R. L. Clarke, T. E. B. Clarke, Beryl Crawley (for the Allingham genealogy), Monica Dickens, Professor L. W. Forster, Christina Foyle, Noel "Bill" Gee, Francis Goodman, Gloria Greci, the late A. J. Gregory, M. R. Gregory, Noel Gregory, Jasper Grinling, Lawrence Hughes, R. Hammond Innes, H. R. F. Keating, Rev. Dr. Marcus Knight, J. Le Fleming, Sir Robert Lusty, Kenneth D. McCormick, Margaret McLaren, Dr. J. G. Madden, Dr. Russell Meiggs, Professor J. E. Morpurgo, Barbara Noble, Dr. D. M. Owen, Michael Parker, Paul R. Reynolds, Valentine Richardson, Walter Shewring, Sir Eldred Smith-Gordon, Elizabeth Stevens, Donald Swann, Olivia Swinnerton, Josephina de Vasconcellos, Keith Waterhouse, and Graham Watson.

The following institutions and firms kindly made material available, without which adequate documentation would have been impossible: Associated Newspapers Group, the Beinecke Rare Book and Manuscript

Library of Yale University (the William McFee papers), BBC Written Archives Centre, The British Library Newspaper Library, the Butler Library of Columbia University (the Paul Reynolds papers), Cambridge University Library, Messrs. Chatto & Windus, the Daily Express, the Greater London Record Office and History Library, Messrs. William Heinemann, the John Rylands University Library of Manchester, the Perse School for Girls, Cambridge, the University Libraries of the University of Arkansas (the Frank Swinnerton Papers), the University Library of Bristol University, and the University of Keele Library (the papers of Lord Lindsay of Birker).

This record of debts of gratitude would be incomplete without acknowledging the patient support of my long-suffering wife, Dagmar, an indispensable companion and source of strength along the way.

1

The Nature of Crime Fiction

*The most essentially modern (if, also, one of the most odd) forms
of literature the language has yet produced.*
Margery Allingham

Margery Allingham was not only a consummate writer of detective
fiction, she was also an accomplished novelist in her own right. Rather
than preface my study of her life and writings by placing her in the
context of the history of the detective story and its multidirectional
development within the twentieth century, I prefer to relate her work
to certain significant aspects of the genre. In this opening chapter, therefore, I shall, after considering the history of critical attitudes towards the
idea of the potential literary status of detective fiction, turn to two major
aspects of crime fiction: the relationship between reader and author,
and the insistence of the detective novel on its own fictionality, its own
artificiality. Finally, in order to introduce some order into the discussion
of Allingham's development, I shall briefly discuss the question of generic terminology.

Whether the detective story belongs to the world of literature or
not, whether the thriller may be considered a novel at all, whether crime
fiction partakes of the status of artistic fiction, are all questions which
have been raised during the past one hundred years by writers and
critics with a serious interest in the genre. They are, however, largely
irrelevant questions (one might as well label *A la recherche du temps perdu*
a love story, or *Moby Dick* an adventure yarn). It is not a matter of
whether all detective stories, all novels of mystery and suspense, de-
serve to be regarded as literature. What is important is the status of
individual novels and the readiness of readers and critics to perceive
why such works of fiction may have literary potentiality.

A brief survey of the positions taken in the consideration of the literary merits or demerits of the detective story reveals little more than certain swings in the pendulum of critical fashion, and yet it is salutary to note with what consistency that pendulum has swung and just what arguments have been employed to defend the varying points of view.

As early as 1868, the critical reception of Wilkie Collins's *The Moonstone* revealed the broad parameters of the controversy. The London *Nation* described Collins's novels as "curiosities of literature" which served "none of the recognized purposes of the novel," defined as the reflection of nature and human life, and the teaching of moral lessons in a serious way. By contrast Collins's works "appeal to no sentiment profounder than the idlest curiosity" (Page 1974, 174). The critic disallowed the realism of *The Moonstone* and reduced it to little more than a book-length puzzle. How different was the response of the anonymous reviewer on the other side of the Atlantic who, reviewing *The Moonstone* for *Lippincott's Magazine,* praised it as "a perfect work of art" admirably told in a forceful style. In particular he emphasized the organic construction of the novel: "to remove any portion of the cunningly constructed fabric destroys the completeness of the whole" (Page 181).

It is astonishing to note that this singling out of what I shall later refer to as the "orchestration" of the detective story as contributing to the truly artistic value of *The Moonstone* underlined a quality that has been virtually ignored by serious critics of the genre in the subsequent one hundred and twenty years. Attention has consistently been concentrated on the centrality of plot, at the expense of the more vital aspect of the combination or interaction of discourse and story, in the significant detective stories of this century.

To return, however, to the survey of opinions: At the beginning of the twentieth century there was, for G. K. Chesterton, no doubt as to the status of detective fiction: "Not only is a detective story a perfectly legitimate form of art, but it has certain definite and real advantages as an agent of the public weal" (Chesterton 1901, 4). These advantages Chesterton saw as the ability to express something of "the poetry of modern life" understood as the changing character of the city, and the ability to so romanticize the regulatory activity of the police force as to convey a sense of the criminal as a traitor to civilized society.

By the 1920s and the first flourishings of the so-called Golden Age of the detective story, writers and critics were less certain about the artistic status of the genre. While E. M. Wrong defended the detective story from the charge that it could never be art by suggesting that though detective stories were not realistic, realism did not hold a monopoly on art (Wrong 1926, 20), Dorothy Sayers, already an established practitioner, stated categorically that the detective story "does not, and by hypothesis never can, attain the loftiest level of literary achievement"; a failure which she put down to its inability to explore human passion (Sayers 1928, 37). In apparent agreement, an American professor of English literature, Marjorie Nicolson, discussing the popularity of detective stories among academic readers, attributed this very popularity to the fact that it was, in the late twenties, the only form of fiction "in which it is still possible to tell a story," and, while seeing detective fiction as a form of escape, defined this as "escape not from life but from literature" and her revolt and that of her colleagues as a revolt "from an excessive subjectivity to welcome objectivity" (Nicolson 1929, 485–86). This would seem to be another way of stating that detective fiction tells a story, and presents a puzzle for the reader to solve on the basis of the factual clues presented by the author.

There are characteristic changes in Dorothy Sayers's attitude as expressed in the introductions she wrote to the second and third volumes of *Great Short Stories of Detection, Mystery and Horror*, which she edited for Gollancz in the early thirties. In 1931 she came close to revising her earlier opinion when she noted approvingly the eagerness on the part of writers and critics to make the detective story "increasingly a real part of literature" (Sayers 1931, 12). In the following three years, however, she seems to have been guided by her own academic primness, and the approaching rejection of a genre she was, because of her own virtuosity, leading—to use Frank Swinnerton's phrase—"into dust" (Swinnerton 1938, 323). In her third introduction, Sayers once more took up the question of the relationship of the detective story to literature, and in the tart tones of the stereotypical schoolmarm, pointed out that literary language was not necessary for the detective story, which would be served better by clear, grammatical, and unpretentious English (Sayers 1934, 13). Thus, for Sayers, was the question finally resolved: the detective story should not attempt to put on airs.

With the exception of Marie Rodell's handbook for would-be mystery writers—"Mystery fiction is frankly commercial" (Rodell 1943, 1)—the 1940s ushered in a more reasoned appraisal of the detective story. Roger Caillois insisted on the total difference between the serious novel and the detective novel on the basis of their different attitudes to human nature: the first takes human nature as its basis and its subject, while the second only reluctantly admits human nature because it must (Caillois 1941, 11). Nevertheless, he wisely saw the reverse to his own argument and pleaded for a critical stance which would, "look for the sense in which it [the detective novel] represents . . . the most naive and the most primitively novelistic of all forms of the novel" (12). This seems to be one way of pointing both to the relationship between the detective story and the earliest forms of imaginative narrative, and to the necessity for making statements on the basis of selected texts rather than somewhat wild generalizations about a whole generic category.

Joseph Wood Krutch, after noting that in the mid-forties the detective story was the "most popular of all literary forms"—a remark which is both paradoxical and begs the question—enthusiastically came to its support since, at its best, it was both "one of the most detached and soothing of narratives" and also "impeccably classical in form" (Krutch 1944, 41–45). Admittedly, none of those remarks state clearly whether Krutch admitted the detective story to the canon of literature, but the general tone of approval coming from a respected literary critic is symptomatic of much academic response to crime fiction during the last forty years. At the same time, there is a strong whiff of "escape literature" in the air, in spite of the saving grace of the classical form, which, after all, Dorothy Sayers had already noted (Sayers 1928, 37).

The following decade added nothing but further confusion to familiar arguments. While established and respected authors championed the detective story—"melodrama is perennial and must be satisfied" (Eliot 1951, 460); "the immense and varied achievement of detective writers" (Maugham 1952, 110)—it is interesting to find a practitioner of the genre, Cyril Hare, stating that the detective story could never be literature since literature "is a delineator of human character," and the detective story deals with far too limited a cast of people (Hare 1959, 63–64). The insistence on the limited and limiting nature of detective fiction, which is seen as adversely affecting its presentation of reality, was echoed by K. M. Hamilton who saw "a measure of artificiality" as essential to the detective story, thus robbing it of the "emotional truth" of literature (Hamilton 1953/4, 105). The appeal to realism is a persistent note in the criticism of detective fiction; often it is seen as the touchstone for literary qualities and is thus symptomatic of many of the regressive tendencies in literary criticism of the fifties and early sixties. At the same time, however, its exploitation of realism is also adduced by detective fiction's defenders as a positive quality. Julian Symons may be taken here as an authoritative and representative voice of the latter position; in pointing out that "a regard for realism" was a requisite for the crime novel, Symons defined this quality as a way of treating "relations between human beings and not . . . an exact description of people and places" (Symons 1959, 128–29). That is, the true realism of the post-1945 detective story was to be a psychological rather than a physical realism. This led Symons to the almost grandiloquent conclusion that at its best "the crime novel is a modern version of an old morality play" (133)—which introduces moral realism as a third variant.

Symons's pluralistic realisms seem to lead to Geoffrey Hartmann's later characterization of the limitations of the detective story: "not that it lacks realism but that it picks up the latest realism and exploits it" (Hartmann 1975, 225).

As one might have expected, the sixties produced the greatest number of supporters for detective fiction's claims to literary status, from Boileau and Narcejac, who insisted that the genesis of the detective novel was no different from that of the novel (1969, 184), or Raymond Chandler: "the mysteries that survive over the years invariably have the qualities of good fiction" (1962, 64), to Dame Ngaio Marsh's businesslike statement in her autobiography, "I have always suggested that in an age of much shapeless fiction the detective story presents a salutary exercise in the technique of writing. It is shapely. . . . Economy as well as expressiveness in words must be practised" (Marsh 1981, 294). The emphasis on technique and language ushers in, not so much an argument based on the craft of writing, as a more acceptable set of standards than the somewhat worn criteria of moral realism and breadth of human characterization. Even so, the recognition of the detective story's dependence on formal criteria continued to be linked to its lack of realism. Geoffrey Hartmann talked of a "voracious formalism" which doomed the detective story "to seem unreal, however 'real' the world it describes" (225). Yet it is this very "unreality" and "formalism" which are exploited by Allingham in the name of realistic detective fiction, and which force us to observe the dichotomy between discourse and story, thus provoking the desire to pay closer attention to the fabric of her narrative.

During the sixties (in accordance, to some extent, with the decanonization of the times) a number of German critics turned their attention to detective fiction. Helmut Heissenbüttel suggested that the detective story was an exemplary story working according to a certain scheme and thus concerned with other matters than the traditional novel. Even so he came to the somewhat unexpected conclusion that "the detective novel appears to be one of the most open forms of contemporary literature" (Heissenbüttel 1966, 371; my translation), which suggests recognition of the amazing imaginative space that the limited genre could still offer. Meanwhile Peter Fischer returned to the hackneyed realism question, only to maintain that the detective story owed its sense of society and the world to its adherence to realism (Fischer 1969, 195). This remark reveals the way in which critics of the late sixties and early seventies—particularly in Western Europe—employed the detective story to confer a deeper social relevance to their own study of popular artistic forms. Only Ulrich Suerbaum showed an unwillingness to clamber onto the bandwagon and sceptically noted that the genre had failed, in the course of the twentieth century, to produce a single work which had been critically accepted as a great novel. Further, he pointed out that the popular form had had little or no influence on serious literature (a statement which seemed to ignore certain contemporary developments in both England and continental Europe). The most positive judgment he came to was that the detective novel was nothing more than a lengthened literary short form, which accounted for the development from mechanical puzzle to psychological mystery (Suerbaum 1967, 361–62, 370).

I shall conclude this survey of an almost fruitless discussion by citing two final examples, which point the way to a sane balance, and make it possible to enter upon a serious consideration of detective fiction without being under the obligation either to prove its literariness or to announce allegiance to one or other school of thought concerning its generic merit.

In a brief chapter, "The Typology of Detective Fiction," Todorov took up the question of the literary status of the detective story, and pointed out: "As a rule, the literary masterpiece does not enter any genre save perhaps its own; but the masterpiece of popular literature is precisely the book which best fits its genre. . . . To 'improve upon' detective fiction is to write 'literature,' not detective fiction" (Todorov 1977, 43). This observation pointed in two directions: at the critic and at the writer. The critic is implicitly exhorted to judge each work on its individual merit, whereas the ambitious writer is encouraged to ignore the imagined limitations of a genre by, if necessary, rejecting the genre label. Ultimately it all boils down to the observation that a good detective novel is not necessarily a good novel, whereas a good novel can share some of the themes and elements of the detective story. A final extension of these recommendations was contained in a letter written by the crime writer (a label he accorded himself) Nicholas Freeling to the editor of the *Times Literary Supplement* in answer to a review article which had included a characterization of the detective story as "light literature" (Anon. 1965, 280). Freeling wrote: "We are all murderers, we are all spies, we are all criminals, and to choose a crime as the mainspring of a book's action is only to find one of the simplest methods of focussing eyes on our life and our world" (Freeling 1965, 391). The scope and basic interest of the detective story, the crime novel, the mystery is defined: one way of calling attention by means of language, literary form, and narrative to human nature and its situation both individually and collectively.

More than any other variant on the basic novel form, the detective novel makes specialized demands upon the reader while offering him or her a particular form of pleasure or satisfied desire. Boileau and Narcejac acknowledged this in their study of the *roman policier,* when they emphasized that the detective story only achieves its full potential when the reader is completely fascinated (132–33). It is this very special relationship which exists between reader and text and, by extension, between author and reader, that accounts for much of the literary significance of the detective story and which is capable of revealing a further dimension of importance.

Early critical considerations of the reader of crime fiction sprang from assumptions about a particular, socially definable readership. Austin Freeman deduced from the intellectual satisfaction the genre offered, that the true connoisseurs were men of the intellectual classes—theologians, lawyers, and the like (Freeman 1924, 11). This view was still shared some twenty years later by Marie Rodell; and even a decade later the target group was still seen as the educated and successful (Bremner 1954, 251). When, however, in 1971, Colin Watson's book-length investigation of the readership of detective fiction appeared, this one-sided version of the truth was, to some extent, corrected. Watson not only placed the reader of detective fiction solidly in the middle classes, but also pointed out that the "majority of these readers . . . were women— the middle-class wives and mothers and daughters whose task it was to select and bring home a fresh supply of the family's reading matter" (Watson 1971, 29). The needs of this mildly prosperous middle-class readership, which found its satisfaction in the detective story, were defined as stimulus, diversion, relaxation, and reassurance (71), the last of which had been repeatedly adduced to account for crime fiction's continued popularity and hold on the reader (Strachey 1939, 14; Symons 1972, 18).

Chesterton, who was very much aware of the detective story both as game and as joke or toy, held that the reader "is conscious not only of the toy but of the invisible playmate who is the maker of the toy, and the author of the trick" (Chesterton 1964, 20). This view was further developed by Marjorie Nicolson, in her focus on the attempt to solve the puzzle of the text, to "a battle royal between the author and the reader" (489), while Dorothy Sayers expressed the author's point of view in the milder observation that the reader's "co-operation is all-important" (1931, 22). It would appear that the majority of critics and writers have been aware of the simple requirement expressed by Margery Allingham that "the tale must hold the reader's attention" (1949, 94). This form of relationship has been formulated in more sophisticated terms as the author's ability "to manipulate reader response to the ends of pleasure" (Porter 1981, 5). It is all the more surprising, therefore, when other critics suggest that the detective story expects the reader neither to exert his intelligence nor to make more than a minimum emotional effort (Hartmann, 220; Storr 1961). Furthermore, there has been widespread uncertainty as to how this is to be achieved and what demands are being made upon the reader. Even Umberto Eco's painstaking examination of the narrative structures in Ian Fleming's James Bond stories comes to little more than a generalizing conclusion: "In fact, in every detective story ... there is no basic variation, but rather the repetition of a habitual scheme in which the reader can recognize something he has already seen and of which he has grown fond." (Eco 1965, 113). However, Eco comes closer to a more seminal truth when he writes, "The author seems almost to write his books for a two-fold reading public, those who take them as gospel and those who see their humor" (Eco 1965, 115). The postulation of two types of implied reader—the one who consumes in order to reach final reassurance, and the one who reads for the intellectual pleasures afforded by both plot and narrative—offers a starting point for serious investigation. Yet in effect this is only a shift in focus when seen in conjunction with Marjorie Nicolson's recognition of "this very interaction of specialized authors and readers" (490). It is alarming to realise that, in over fifty years of critical attention to the genre, there has been so little consideration of the specialized reader implied in the texts of detective fiction.

In his book, *The Delights of Detection*, Jacques Barzun saw that the "enjoyment of detective stories requires a superior sophistication" based on the fact that the reader is always aware of the fictionality of the tale he is being told (Barzun 1961, 149). Similarly Leroy Panek noted that the Golden Age writers "did not try to absorb their readers in the actuality of a fictional world" (Panek 1979, 20). In both cases it is the self-referential nature of the detective story which is being hinted at, in order to explain the need for a particular type of experienced reader to appreciate the game in which he is being implicitly invited to participate. It is this, too, which George Dove was concerned with in his suggestion for a new area of detective story criticism: "There *is* a special relationship not found in any other kind of writing and reading of fiction. ... The writer's role is ... to lead the reader through a mythos of life and death, violence and redemption, without the reader's suffering hurt or distress" (Dove 1977, 205–6). This lack of distress results from the continued awareness the reader has that he is participating in fictive action. Any number of instances of detective novels highlighting their own fictionality can be brought forward to support such views. On the one hand, the reader may be more or less absorbed in a plot of greater or less credibility, on the other, he is accompanied throughout by the knowledge based on his reading experience that puzzles will be solved, the Manichean ethic satisfied, the detective-hero will survive all perils and prove himself once again to be indestructible. Whatever convolutions the story may contain, its end point—as that of the fairy story—is certain. The uncertainty, the variation, the ultimate intellectual pleasure is contained in the narrative discourse, which is offered the reader for his or her delectation.

The special relationship noted between author/text and reader in detective fiction is based on certain well-defined factors: (1) The author needs the reader to share in the mystification-puzzle-solution pattern; (2) The reader seeking the reassurance of the popular art form needs the text; (3) The text continually implies a reader whose reading experience of the genre is such that he can share ironies, recognize genre-specific stereotypes, and anticipate developments.

To a degree so obvious and so recurrent that it attains significance, detective story writers of the Golden Age either draw attention to the complete fictionality of what they are writing, or suggest that the events they narrate bear a relation to the traditional narrations of detective fiction. The most blatant, and probably best-known example occurs in John Dickson Carr's *The Hollow Man*, in which his detective, Dr. Gideon Fell, proceeds to lecture his companions on the situation "which is known in detective fiction as the 'hermetically sealed chamber.'" He points out that he is an inveterate reader of such books, and when one of his listeners asks why they should discuss detective fiction, replies: "Because . . . we're in a detective story, and we don't fool the reader by pretending we're not" (Carr 1935, 186). So much for the realism of crime fiction. This, too, would seem to point to the uniqueness of the genre both in its time and as popular literature. The refusal to accept the illusion of reality, together with the open encouragement to the reader to stand aloof from events and regard them as fiction, are part and parcel of the artificiality of the intellectual puzzle that characterized so much detective fiction of the period.

Similarly, in Ngaio Marsh's first novel, *A Man Lay Dead*, the question of the incongruity of realism in detective fiction is thematized in the following dialogue:

> "They say the Yard is never wrong in its inferences, though it sometimes fails to get its results. Do you believe this?"
> "My only information is based on detective fiction," said Nigel.

"So is mine," Rosamund laughed. . . . "And nowadays they make their Yard men so naturalistic that they are quite incredible." (Marsh 1934, 106)

Marsh's character still seems to be caught up in the disappearing model of the detective as eccentric, in contrast to the author, whose Roderick Alleyn develops into a model of normality. Marsh, in her earlier fiction, often deliberately drew attention to the obtrusive conventions of the genre, as in the following extract in which Inspector Alleyn is talking to his assistant: "I don't somehow feel it'll be a left-luggage affair. . . . They've been given a little too much publicity of late years. Limbs and torsos have bobbed up in corded boxes with dreary insistence . . . throughout the pages of detective fiction" (Marsh 1938, 182). The way in which such passages function reveals something of the particular relationship between author and reader in the world of detective fiction. For the experienced, intelligent reader such a remark allows him or her to enter into a privileged "insider" compact with the author, emphasizing the ambiguous relationship that really does exist: the challenge (to solve the puzzle before the denouement) and the pact (between specialists in the field).

A variation on the pattern is the occasional comment which emphasizes that the crime of the detective story is different from the real thing, or that the detective story is more wholesome and morally reassuring than more serious works dealing with murder and related crimes. In J. C. Masterman's *An Oxford Tragedy*, an Austrian professor of law, visiting the college where murder takes place, announces, "I said that I read detective tales, and so I do, but that's only as a kind of relaxation. What fascinates me, yes at times obsesses me, is the real crime—the murder that has actually been committed" (Masterman 1933, 32). The particular irony of such a remark is that, of course, the "real" murder that takes place in Masterman's story is not part of the relaxation of detective fiction, since the thrust of the remark is to underline the very authenticity of the narration, even though it is obvious to the reader that *An Oxford Tragedy* is "only" a detective tale. This needs, however, to be seen in the particular context of the narrational strategy deployed in the book, which is ostensibly told by a narrator of strictly limited vision: "If I am to tell the whole truth it can only be the truth as I saw it, and you, for your part, must resign yourself to seeing it through spectacles which you can neither polish nor remove" (7).

The purity and attraction of both detective story and thriller, seen as melodrama, are upheld by none other than one of the great early masters of the genre, Edgar Wallace. In his mid-twenties collection of stories centered on the mysterious Mr. J. G. Reeder, solver of crimes and protector of order, there occurs the following passage in which Reeder holds forth on the virtues of melodrama as opposed to the "sordidness" of great tragedy: "In melodrama even the villains are heroic, and the inevitable and unvarying moral is 'Truth crushed to earth will rise again'—isn't that idealism? And they are wholesome. There are no sex problems, unpleasant things are never shown in an attractive light— you come away uplifted" (Wallace 1925, 66). While not such an obvious instance of self-reflexiveness, such praise of a genre so closely related to that which Wallace himself practised is clearly intended to remind the reader of the deliberate exaggerations and artificiality (as in melodrama) of the detective story, which are seen as central to the ideological convictions of the author.

This insistence upon the positive, idealistic aspect of detective fiction is given an unusual twist in C. P. Snow's one venture into the genre, *Death under Sail*. Here Sergeant Birrell, who is presented throughout as an unpopular, over-officious, negative character, becomes the mouthpiece for an encomium on the detective story, which is only marginally ironical:

> Don't you see that the investigation of crime is one of the greatest romances in the world? Don't you see how wonderful it is? . . . Years ago they used to write ballads about war and brute force and lust. . . . Now they write detective stories in which all of men's energies are concentrated on seeking out the wrong. Don't you see what a change it is? If you look at it properly, detective stories are a sign of civilization. (Snow 1932, 43–44)

The reminder to the reader that he or she, by being drawn into the search for a solution to the puzzle, is not only motivated by vulgar curiosity, but by the same overwhelming romance of morality, is a clear exploitation of the specialized relationship between author and reader.

Although these forms of self-reference seem to be particularly common in interwar detective fiction, in Allingham's novels it reaches a greater level of sophistication. Remarks that characters make within the framework of apparently normal fictional dialogue have a direct bearing either on the narration of the novel or on the thematic concerns of the story, or even upon Allingham's whole authorial activity, as in the throwaway line, "There's a pattern in these things, and once you've seen it you've seen it" (Allingham 1965, 108). In general, it may be observed that a characteristic feature of detective fiction is that, in varying degrees, it continually calls attention to its own unreality, in order to cement the very real complicity between author and reader and to reinforce the extra-textual reference of the enterprise.

Throughout the foregoing sections I have referred, with somewhat cavalier bravado, undifferentiatingly to the detective story, detective novel, detective fiction, or crime fiction; the multiplicity of labels and possible definitions needs to be considered carefully, in order to arrive at some contractual agreement before turning to Margery Allingham's own versions of the genre. Serious criticism has tended, in the first instance, to differentiate between the *thriller* and the *detective story*. In his well-known essay, "The Guilty Vicarage," W. H. Auden saw the thriller as basically engaged in "the ethical and eristic conflict between good and evil, between Us and Them" (Auden 1948, 147). To this existential conflict is added the focus on exciting action (Hare 1959, 57–58; Todorov 1977, 47), or the idea that it "simply tells us *how* an act of violence was committed, and what happened afterwards" (Symons 1965, 423). It has also been suggested that the classic thriller is bound in time—or in spirit—to the Edwardian era of established British supremacy (Panek 1979, 11) and glorifies the hero in a struggle with a master criminal (Buchloh & Becker 1973, 77–79). According to such definitions, Allingham's early novels (*The Crime at Black Dudley*, *Mystery Mile*, *Look to the Lady*, and *Sweet Danger*) are all thrillers.

There would also seem to be widespread agreement about the basic features of the detective story or detective novel: whereas the thriller reader asks, "What happens next?," the reader of the detective story asks, "What happened last?" (Hamilton 1953/54, 102). That is, we are concerned with reconstruction and retracing by means of clues and information, and not with the action itself. At the centre of the detective story is the investigation of a crime by a person who is specialized in such work (either professionally or as a gifted amateur), with the aim of solving the puzzle of the perpetrator of the act, and of bringing the criminal to justice (Porter 1981, 5; Symons 1965, 423). On a more formal level, Todorov introduces the notion of the dual stories of the detective novel: "At the base of the whodunit we find a duality. . . . This novel contains not one but two stories: the story of the crime and the story of the investigation" (44–45). He goes on to point out that the story of the crime relates the true events ("What really happened"), whereas the second story explains how both narrator and reader came to a knowledge of this truth. In spite of its apparent sophistication, Todorov's theory still places the puzzle, the explanation of a mystery, the solution of a crime, the assignment of guilt at the center of the detective story, very much in tune with Symons's observation, "the detective story writer concentrates on the puzzle to the exclusion of reasonable behaviour" (Symons 1972, 175).

Nevertheless, around the mid-thirties new elements, or rather a new focus of attention, began to dominate some of the more successful and more innovative detective stories. This was noted by Mary McCarthy, who wrote in 1936, "The detective story writer today is . . . preoccupied with milieu" (McCarthy 1936, 382). The realization of this shift away from the centrality of the puzzle led other investigators to modify previously accepted definitions; in 1941, Howard Haycraft used the term "the novel of detection-cum-character" for post-1920s detective fiction, and related it to the expression "literary detective novel" as being a particularly British development in the hands of Allingham, Innes, Marsh, and Blake (Haycraft 1941, 183). Nicholas Blake attempted to formulate the development by contrasting the conventional detective story (*roman policier*), which put unreal characters in realistic situations, with what he called the "fashionable detective story" or "novel of manners," in which realistic characters were placed in unreal situations (Blake 1942, 403). Later critics, accepting the "detective-novel-as-novel-of-manners" formulation, defined this as a novel with a crime interest and added, as though aware of some missing ingredient, the term "psychological crime novel" with a stronger emphasis on the prehistory and preparation of the crime (Buchloh & Becker 1973, 73–77).

For some time it seemed that the term "detective" applied to story, novel, or fiction was a limiting label in view of both the increasing interest in character and milieu, and a growing narrative sophistication. Thus we find Julian Symons introducing the term "crime novel" to be applied to "a book written seriously" and which investigated "the springs of violence" (1959, 128, 132). Later he adopted Nicholas Freeling's phrasing and called the crime novel "a book which centres on a crime" in order to focus "eyes on our life and our world" (1965, 423). This is finally modified in Symons's book-length study, *Bloody Murder*, to the observation that the "crime novelist tends to make the story secondary to the characters" (1972, 175)—a remark which is not particularly helpful, since the strictly hierarchical relationship does not really obtain. Presumably Symons meant that the crime novel is a novel in which the story is invested more in the personality of the characters than in earlier detective fiction, and involves a greater foregrounding of the narrative discourse.

Of course, other terms and definitions have been used, in particular that of the "suspense novel" (Todorov 1977, 50); however, it is Margery Allingham herself who added confusion by the introduction of the broad term "mystery" with the variations "modern mystery" and "straight murder mystery." All of these terms have in common the idea of the rigid conventionalism of the detective story (Allingham 1963, 7), and the "implicit suggestion that there is a reason in all things" (1949,

94). This led her to arrive at a similar conclusion to Symons's when she wrote that:

> The mystery is, in a way, a modern version of the Morality plays of the Middle Ages. . . . As does the modern Mystery, they stated an elementary theory of Right and Wrong, Growing or Dying, in a cheerful, popular way, to a generation of ordinary people who were exposed to a great new flood of contradictory beliefs, cynical theories and some of the most demoralizing hazards civilized humanity has ever experienced. (1963,13)

Thus when discussing Allingham's novels, I shall be forced to use a range of terms marking a swift development towards the mystery or crime novel, for, as she herself put it, "They're not quite detective stories really. They're my own particular brand of novel" (Meras 1963).

2

Mystery and Margery Allingham

I regard my books as novels, not just as thrillers or detective stories.

Margery Allingham

Margery Allingham holds an anomalous place in the history of crime fiction. Whereas the works of a considerable number of previously lauded authors from the interwar years are virtually unobtainable, two dozen of her books are in print on both sides of the Atlantic. Nevertheless, the place and space she occupies in the critical works devoted to the genre remain severely limited. In view of the overwhelmingly positive occasional evaluations of her achievement, this critical neglect is puzzling. Eric Routley, a minister of the Congregational Church, was unrestrained in the praise he accorded Allingham in his "personal monograph" on detective fiction in the early seventies: "I doubt whether the detective story has ever reached a point of maturity higher than that to which Margery Allingham brought it. She seems to me to stand on higher ground than either Ngaio Marsh or Dorothy Sayers" (Routley 1972, 156).

Routley's estimation was based, in part, on what he saw as Allingham's investigation into and portrayal of "the dark mysteries of evil" (148); the equally positive judgments of other critics are not only based on thematic considerations. There seem, rather, to be three basic aspects of her work which have been put forward by Allingham's defenders: her portrayal of character, her sophistication and intelligence, and—of greatest importance—the quality of her writing. With respect to all three criteria, she is often seen in relation to her slightly senior contemporaries, Agatha Christie and Dorothy Sayers. Jens-Peter Becker is representative of those critics who, in praising her "plasticity of character" see only a difference of degree between Allingham's novels and those of

Christie and Sayers, but it is a degree which Becker sees as making her the most "loveable" of the three (Becker 1975, 29, 35). The emphasis on character-drawing is expanded by Panek to include a focus on "description and analysis" rather than on action, and he suggests that in Allingham's novels of the second half of the thirties the description of people becomes more important than the unmasking of the criminal. For him the postwar books achieve "the perfect blend of the thriller, the detective story, and the novel about people" (139, 142). The thrust of these views is towards a focus on the way in which Allingham aimed at an amalgam of the "serious" novel and the detective story form.

Earlier critics grouped Margery Allingham with Nicholas Blake and Michael Innes as the "young masters" of the new sophisticated detective story, which was regarded as a novel of manners. John Strachey was the first to express such a judgment, and to point out that much of the success of these writers could be explained by their choice of "a form which is rigid and limited" (13). As we shall see, the formal rigors of the detective story attracted Allingham for the very reason that they demanded new strategies of variation and innovation. Strachey, it should also be mentioned, compared Allingham favorably to Sayers as being "more sophisticated." A few years later, Howard Haycraft, while adding the name of Ngaio Marsh to the group of exponents of the "literary" detective novel, repeated Strachey's opinion and singled out Allingham for special praise (1941, 185). Some thirty years later, Julian Symons, in looking back on the critical commendation of the "young hopefuls" of detective fiction at the close of the thirties, noted that Strachey's choice was an intelligent one, "but in fact only Allingham was able to develop her talent further in the post-war world" (1972, 130). Nevertheless, in his discussion of both Allingham and Marsh, Symons was sceptical about combining ironical social observation with the writing of detective fiction (124–25). Here, it seems to me, lies the crux of the matter: as Todorov suggested, you either write a first-rate detective story within the limits of the popular form, or you transcend these limits and write a novel, which may or may not be significant *as a novel*, but will not be a detective story.

Margery Allingham poses a problem to the critics of the genre because she disturbs them by doing something which they are not, of necessity, prepared to allow her to do. One is reminded of Proust's comment on the individual genius of the actress Berma: "We have brought with us ideas of 'beauty,' 'breadth of style,' 'pathos' and so forth which we might at a pinch have the illusion of recognizing in the banality of a conventional face or talent, but our critical spirit has before it the insistent challenge of a form of which it possesses no intellectual equivalent, in which it must detect and isolate the unknown element" (Proust 1920, 45). In Allingham's case this "unknown element" is, as some critics have seen, the quality, not so much of her plots, themes, or character portrayal, as of the writing itself.

Haycraft characterized Allingham's language as "the fluid prose of a thoroughly adept and sophisticated craftsman" (1941, 185), whereas A. E. Murch noted that, in her novels of manners, Allingham's "writing is more studied, more 'precious,' than in detective fiction generally" (Murch 1958, 236)—the critical unease is obvious. It becomes clear that while Haycraft solved the problem by qualifying the somewhat prosaic word "craftsman" with the adjective "sophisticated" and Murch modified "studied" with the more negative "precious," both harboured the suspicion that what Allingham was writing was dangerously close to being "literary." L. A. G. Strong came out into the open by observing "Chekhovian adroitness" in one of Allingham's short stories (Strong 1959, 159), and by the beginning of the seventies there was no doubt in Colin Watson's mind when he announced that she "became a highly accomplished and unfailingly literary contributor to mystery fiction" (131). It is salutary to note that the person who most nearly put her finger on the distinguishing feature of Allingham's prose was not a critic but a fellow practitioner, Agatha Christie, who, two years after Allingham's death, wrote: "She has another quality, not usually associated with crime stories. Elegance. Elegance of style is unusual nowadays. Virginia Woolf, Elizabeth Bowen—not many others come to mind. How seldom are words used with aptitude, delicacy, point" (Christie 1968, n.p.).

On a number of occasions Margery Allingham attempted to formulate her own view of her aims and her achievement. She was, in her own phrase, "an instinctive writer," in the sense that much of what she wrote did not emerge from a clearly thought out thematic plan either of the book in question, or, more generally, of life in any intellectually philosophical sense: "I am by nature an intuitive writer whose intellect trots along behind, tidying, censuring and saying 'Oh my!' It has taken me a very long time to comprehend this and to allow for it" (1965a, 11–12). In this statement, Allingham is clearly referring to the painstaking discipline of her writing and at the same time accounting for the continuous maturing process of her work. Yet even the intuitive writer must begin somewhere; why then with the detective story? She herself saw the beginnings rooted in the enjoyment she and her husband shared in reading "lighthearted adventure stories" (Edgar Wallace and P. G. Wodehouse) in the mid-twenties. This enjoyment coupled with the natural urge to write was encouraged by the demand for what she referred to as "a literate and intelligent literature of escape" (1949, 43). Allingham defined the much maligned term "literature of escape" as an instrument of solace, "an escape from an intolerable hour." Above all she noted that "any kind of book can provide the necessary vehicle" (94). She drew no careful lines of demarcation between genre and genre, subgenre and subgenre, popular and serious, but rather laid a clear emphasis on a shared humane functionality, which she claimed for her work as for any other literary product. In fact, Allingham saw the modern mystery story within the framework of the application of this theory of escape literature to the crises and upheavals in Western society that began in the mid-thirties.

She said of her own books that they were novels "of the life of the time" in which a sudden death in mysterious circumstances often served to "make characters reveal themselves" (1949b, n.p.). Within such an undertaking mystery writing becomes "a kind of reflection of society's conscience" (1961, n.p.), writing which combines the telling of home truths with the business of entertainment. Not only is the modern mystery novel part and parcel of the universal literature of escape, but the crime writer is seen to be historically in the tradition of the entertainer with a social function, commenting, often ironically, on faults in the fabric of society.

Allingham's comments contain no clear indication of the particular attraction, for a writer of her convictions, of the detective story form and formula. In a talk which she gave in 1958, she traced the development of the "better detective story" to the American suspense novel, which she defined as "a true novel, but one which obeys the formula and the disciplines of the classic crime story" and went on to comment, "that's the way mine are going" (1958, n.p.). When later she defined her own version of the serious mystery as "the tale cut to fit the box," she was expressing that the attraction for her lay in the very rigidity of the form in an age "when every other kind of writing tends to be without prescribed form" (1963, 11, 7). It is interesting to note an identical attitude expressed by Ngaio Marsh: "The one thing that can always be said in favour of the genre is that inside the convention the author may write with as good a style as he or she can command" (1981, 227–28). The comparative lack of need for thematic or formal invention thus permits a focus on the writing itself—the very thing which so disturbed the early critics and the very thing which accounts for Allingham's ceaseless development as a novelist: "I have experimented steadily, developing, I suspect, rather like a painter, who grows tired of one technique quickly, and is always searching for a new one. . . . As far as I am concerned, one is just about as real as the other" (1963, 12).

Any attempt to give a broad overview of any writer's work is going to be limited to superficial categorization along the lines of genre specifics, major themes, and imagined observable developments. If then I persist in doing this for Margery Allingham, the reader should regard the undertaking as a preliminary attempt to achieve order, or, if one prefers it, to establish certain basic hypotheses about her endeavors.

Like many mystery writers and no few "serious" novelists whose active writing life was as long (forty-five years), Margery Allingham's output was extensive: twenty-six published novels (including two nonmysteries and three thrillers published under a pseudonym), over sixty short stories, four novellas, almost thirty published articles and broadcasts, as well as more than a hundred book reviews. I shall restrict my overview to those twenty novels of crime and adventure published between 1929 and 1968; all other work is, for now, incidental to my general evaluative purpose. As we have already seen, the nomenclature of classification is an area filled with traps and pitfalls; I would, however, offer the following preliminary categories for Allingham's work in an effort towards systematization: adventure thriller, serious detective novel, modern mystery, wartime adventure mystery, and crime novel.

The first grouping covers the period 1929–33 which opens with *The Crime at Black Dudley* (1929), in which a solitary murder is almost totally subordinated to the direct confrontation between a group of healthy, young, right-thinking amateurs and a sinister collection of Germanic crooks. At this early stage in her career, Allingham seemed uncertain whether to pursue the adventure-espionage tale or the story of a murder investigation. *Mystery Mile* (1930) is more clearly conceived, although the basic pattern is similar. Albert Campion, who in the earlier novel had been a young man who lived by his wits, appears as a self-declared adventurer pitted against the powerful leader of the forces of crime, known appropriately as Simister. With a certain amount of help from some young enthusiasts and a few country wiseacres, Campion triumphs in what he clearly perceives to be "a death game" between good and evil (1930, 340). The new element which Allingham injected into the novel was her familiarity with the East Anglian countryfolk and countryside together with an increased interest in the portrayal of character. The third of this early group, *Look to the Lady* (U.S. title, *The Gyrth Chalice Mystery*, 1931), is easily the least satisfactory, with its curious mixture of family legend, country superstition, gypsy lore, and the conflict between traditional virtue and money-grubbing nastiness. It does, however, introduce Campion's widespread network of allies and associates—on this occasion the gypsies—and the first of a number of female villains, murderesses, and common criminals, Mrs. Dick Shannon. All three early novels present a fundamental conflict between the organized forces of evil (crime on the large scale with many a hint of elemental wickedness) and those whose basic weapon is their conviction of being on the side of the right, the good, and the legal. In all three, disorder and crime invade rural peace and harmony, and can only be banned by almost foolhardy adventurousness.

Although chronologically not the immediate successor, *Sweet Danger* (1933) (U.S. title, *The Fear Sign*) belongs with this group, since it is, to a certain extent, a more sophisticated and also more playful reworking of *Look to the Lady* with some elements of *Mystery Mile* included. No murders are committed and there is a considerable subplot based upon an interest in black magic. However, the personality of Allingham's villain becomes clearer and less stereotypical; Brett Savernake, financier, business tycoon, and incorporation of barely legitimate greed, is possessed of megalomaniacal visions of his own powers and importance. This becomes a characteristic of almost all Allingham villains, so that the experienced reader, by decoding the information given, often arrives early at a presentiment of the criminal's identity. *Sweet Danger* expands upon the by now characteristic rural setting—the Essex-Suffolk village countryside in which the books were written—but is of particular interest for the way in which Allingham seems deliberately to force the adventure thriller in the direction of a parody upon itself.

Before embarking upon *Sweet Danger*, Allingham had already turned her attention to a possible new development within the strict limitations of the traditional investigation into a crime or crimes committed by an unknown figure. In *Police at the Funeral* (1931), Campion joins forces with the police, represented by the first of several close official friends, Inspector Stanislaus Oates, who appeared briefly in *Mystery Mile* and *Look to the Lady*. While the plot is ingenious—the murders being the almost fortuitous results of the acts of a man of unbalanced temperament who has committed suicide before the story begins—the presentation of milieu and character are preeminent. The grand manner of Great Aunt Caroline Faraday, widow of a late Victorian Cambridge academic, and the overwhelming physical presence of her house, Socrates Close, introduce the serious detective story, which Allingham went on to perfect in *Death of a Ghost* (1934). In both novels, the focus of the writing is upon getting character and setting just right, and in never allowing the mechanics of detection to dominate the text. Campion is presented as someone who detects neither by pure ratiocination or flashes of intuition, nor by the painstaking accumulation of information and clues: "He did not arrive at this conclusion by the decent process of quiet logical deduction, nor yet by the blinding flash of glorious intuition; but by the shoddy, untidy process half-way between the two by which one usually gets to know things" (1934, 145). The importance of the emphasis upon such a procedure is that, in spite of occasional authorial witholdings of information, Campion's method is not that of the master brain or super detective. Rather, he arrives at knowledge as the reader does, with the same information and by the same representative human processes.

Having placed her murders in two households oriented to the memories of the glories of a former age—the Faraday menage and the artistic world of the relics of the late John Lafcadio, R.A.—Allingham turned, for the remainder of the thirties, to a deliberate three-book plan which would scrutinize the well-defined worlds of publishing, the theatre, and haute-couture allied with moneyed leisure. The three novels which resulted are the modern mysteries, with their emphasis on contemporaneity and the delineation of milieu. *Flowers for the Judge* (1936) combines the criminal acts of an almost godlike publisher with the whimsical portrayal of past fantasies. At the center of the novel is, not so much the publishing business (except as a form of local color), as a study of conflicting personalities and their attitude to the role of past values in the contemporary world—a theme which continued to occupy Allingham for the rest of her life. The novel only partially succeeds because Allingham appeared to find it difficult to decide which of many potential stories should dominate. In *Dancers in Mourning* (1937), she reveals a much surer hand. The petty jealousies and conflicts of theatrical life off-stage are universalized into a portrayal of common human weaknesses. It is characteristic of the modern mysteries that the novel contains a number of lovingly elaborated individual portraits, in particular that of William Faraday of *Police at the Funeral*, who, relieved of the oppression of his mother's Cambridge home, is now Uncle William, whose shamelessly prevaricating memoirs have been transformed into a successful West End musical: "Uncle William sat back in his chair, the bright lights glinting on the double row of near-white curls at the nape of his plump pink neck. He looked worldly and benign, and somehow bogus" (1937, 15).

The minor characters are carefully drawn throughout the novel, as, for example, the eccentric, rose-growing Dr. Bouverie, whose therapy is largely based on straightforward common sense. Such concern reveals Allingham's sense of the necessity for establishing an identifiable fictional community. Murder enters into such societies both as a reminder that disaster may be the potential Janus face of success, and as the symbolic extension of human fallibility. In such a context, the establishment of the murderer's identity becomes the act which restores order to a world temporarily out of balance. So, too, in *The Fashion in Shrouds* (1938), the "normal" world that is established throughout the early part of the book is thrown out of gear by murder; yet the act of violence throws more light upon the society involved (and the inescapability of this involvement) than upon the act itself. The modern mystery is much more a portrayal of and investigation into aspects of contemporary society than it is concerned with crime and detection—the mystery is not so much that of the identity of a criminal as of human nature itself. The combination of violence and uncertainty are almost tangential to the focussing of intelligent speculation upon the workings of men's minds and of that peculiar combination of human beings that produces fragile communities of order within the larger social frame. Thus it is the eccentricities of those who can afford to set up a rich man's playground complete with private airport, or the esoteric disasters of design copying in the world of fashion which are foregrounded, rather than the sordid stabbing of an ex-model, or the death in a gilded aeroplane of an unlikeable colonial administrator.

The two final books of this period elude neat classification. *The Case of the Late Pig* (1937) is little more than a whimsical novella with incidental murders and is Allingham's only venture into first-person narration (Campion as narrator). It contains both a variation on the rural setting of *Sweet Danger* and the seeds of the disturbed country idyll which Allingham was to elaborate in *The Beckoning Lady* some eighteen years later. Furthermore, it is almost too playful in its machinery to be considered of any great importance. *Black Plumes* (1940) is another anomaly: the only mystery without Campion, it has many elements of the serious detective novels of the earlier thirties—a dominant old lady, the professional art world, a megalomaniac as murderer, some minor romantic interest, and an undercurrent of physically oppressive evil. The absence of Campion is, perhaps, the most interesting feature. It suggests that with the outbreak of war in 1939, Allingham was uncertain as to the role her detective could play as an escape from a real world whose capacity for evil appeared to outrun that of the imagined world of fiction.

Allingham's solutions to the problem of Campion's wartime role were significant for her later development: first, both she and Campion reverted in *Traitor's Purse* (1941) to the adventure thriller manner of the early novels. It is a tale based on the supposition that one method of bringing England to her knees would be by the mass postal distribution of forged currency throughout the country. Campion, hampered by temporary amnesia induced by a blow on the head, is forced into acting very largely in the dark; the master criminal—the director of a government research institute—is another of Allingham's characters with an amoral sense of their own importance. At the end of the novel, Campion and Amanda Fitton, who have been intermittently in contact since their first meeting in *Sweet Danger*, are on the brink of matrimony, and Allingham seems set to face the rigors of the more immediate business of winning, or at least sitting out, the war. The other novel of this period, *Coroner's Pidgin* (1945) (U.S. title, *Pearls before Swine*), is a reversion to the modern mystery. Allingham's investigation into the group dynamics and loyalties of the people surrounding a well-known society personality become daring RAF pilot turns into a preparatory study of the inevitable changes that society (and upper-middle-class English society in particular) was to experience in the postwar years. The novel is replete with deliberate references to earlier books and figures from them, which act as reminders of a world that is rapidly passing away. *Coroner's Pidgin* seems to have been pivotal in Allingham's career; had she followed the mode of *Traitor's Purse,* she would probably soon have been eclipsed—at least in popularity—by Ian Fleming. As it was she set the tone for the complex novels to come, which, without exception, are multifocussed examinations of the conditions of the post-1945 world.

Allingham's last seven books belong to the category of the crime novel—the narrative of contemporary life with a death and its investigation as unifying center of interest. Apart from the focus in *Tiger in the Smoke* and *Hide My Eyes* on the criminal rather than the crime and its investigation, these final novels represent a refinement and maturing both of the early adventure thriller and of the modern mystery.

With *More Work for the Undertaker* (1949) Allingham made a brilliant start in adapting the modern mystery of milieu to the scrutiny of the all-pervasive phenomenon of postwar change. At the center of the novel is a West London backwater and the decayed family of the Palinodes—a picture of what might have happened to the Faradays of *Police at the Funeral* in a changed world: "Every time the world goes thud they put their heads back in a book" (1949a, 230). It is significant that the murderer, by no means such a megalomaniac as in other Allingham novels, possesses one godlike characteristic which turns him to crime: Henry James (the novel is dominated by the book-reading Palinodes), manager of a small, old-fashioned bank, unsuccessfully attempts by his criminal acts to halt change.

Closest in theme and social focus to *More Work for the Undertaker* is a much later book, *The China Governess* (1962), which also endeavors to find possible continuities to link the postwar world with the earlier days of 1939. A story of a young man's search for his true identity and of the clash of wills and interests between those longing to preserve the traditions of the past and those working to overcome age-old privilege and traditional prejudices, *The China Governess* seems to treat murder as incidental. On the other hand, a great significance is given to the power of words and the role of language, with the result that the novel becomes an investigation, in criminal/detective guise, of the role language plays in creating the dichotomy of truth and fiction.

If these two novels, separated by twelve years, form a thematic unit, those which came between have extremely diverse interests: the attempt to penetrate the criminal mind and to portray the force of evil, or self-centered amorality, and, between the two a self-indulgent interlude of country peace and sophisticated foolery presented with a refinement of narrative orchestration. Ex-commando Jack Havoc of *The Tiger in the Smoke* (1952), with his philosophy "There aren't any coincidences, only opportunities" (1952, 149), marauds through the novel committing five brutal and virtually unmotivated murders before he is brought up against the persuasive but, for him, unacceptable commonsense Christian goodness of Canon Avril. Havoc's murderous attempt on Avril's life misfires, symbolizing the fallibility of his beliefs. Not only is the novel a compelling study of evil—particularly in its relation to the good—but it is interesting for the intertwining of stories and the resultant manipulation of changing narrational perspectives. *Hide My Eyes* (1958) (U.S. title, *Tether's End*) reduces Campion to a background figure (he appears in only four of the twenty-one chapters), and while foregrounding the charming liar and ruthless killer, Gerry Hawker—a totally civilian Havoc—the novel is, as the title suggests, an exploitation of the concept of limited moral vision and, by extension, of limited narrative perspective. Another of Allingham's concerns in *Hide My Eyes* is the theme of knowledge and the foundations of knowledge in an everyday setting.

In many respects the most original (and certainly the most charming) of Allingham's books, *The Beckoning Lady* (1955) (U.S. title, *The Estate of the Beckoning Lady*) is an accomplished interlude in the development of the crime novel. Strictly speaking no crime is committed: deaths which seem to be murders are virtually accidental, and the suicide of the fortuitous killer is an almost peaceful release. The true threat in the book, the ruination of an idyllic part of the English countryside by an international consortium planning to operate an illegal racecourse, is successfully averted, and is so vague as to be only marginal anyway.

In this book Allingham came closest to perfecting her own particular novel of manners, or rural comedy—a crime novel without a real crime. Moreover, it is the nearest she came to writing autobiographical fiction with the portrayal of a character very similar to Youngman Carter, her husband, and the sort of conjugal affection which leads to the comment, "Love isn't a cement, it's a solvent" (1955, 91).

Margery Allingham's last two novels, *The Mind Readers* (1965) and *Cargo of Eagles* (completed after Allingham's death by Youngman Carter and published in 1968) return, partially, to the thriller adventure formula with stories about research establishments, nationally important scientific secrets, extrasensory perception, traitorous activities, gang warfare, hidden gold, and secret service operations. However, both Campion's years—he ages with Allingham and the century—and the symbolic uses to which the material is turned, preclude the action-packed mode of the adventures of the early thirties. These two books are very definitely adult adventures. *The Mind Readers*, in which Allingham reutilizes the moral instance of Canon Avril, is ultimately a novel about communication, whereas *Cargo of Eagles* continues the reappraisal of social change begun with *More Work for the Undertaker*. In the final novel, Allingham showed a keen interest in the signs of modernity as she read it. Moreover, by foregrounding that form of intertextuality which forces the reader back on her previous works, Allingham focusses attention on the questions both of the role of an ageing investigator (Albert Campion) and of the crime novel, in a world in which evil is not only universal but also made to appear harmless because ever-present; one of the characters remarks upon "the basic human delight in doing evil" (1968, 66).

While Allingham willingly surrendered to many of the limitations imposed by the pattern of crime-investigation-solution, in much of her work the traditional detective story is disrupted and dispersed by the sheer interest in the structure of character constellations, which often results in distraction from the theme of murder or crime. LeRoy Panek goes so far as to suggest that all Allingham's novels have the same basic plot: Campion associates with people involved in the investigation of a murder; there are two groups of people—those who are friends of Campion's and people on the fringe; the murderer is a member of the latter group and "someone who murders because of his own bloated ego" (1979, 143). This observation is only partially true and does not make any particularly important contribution to the study of Allingham's work. A basic similarity between novels is only on the level of the elements of the story, whereas the real interest of her work *as a nov-*

elist—as mentioned already—is to be found on the level of the discourse (Christie's "elegance of style"), or even in the variations she rings upon established themes.

Variety becomes superficially apparent from a cursory investigation of Allingham's villains; of the twenty-odd criminals and killers, five are women and the men range from a master criminal posing as a boring art expert, a composer for musical revues, a country doctor, and an ex-soldier, to a canteen manager. The methods of killing employed tend to be limited: nine stabbings, seven poisonings, four varieties of blunt instrument, four shootings, an overdose of insulin, and a few minor variations. What I am suggesting here is that Allingham deliberately played down the criminal act and eschewed over-dramatic or over-inventive methods of murder. Rather, the focus, from *Police at the Funeral* onwards, was on the personality of the criminal, who almost without exception fits into Panek's formula of the "bloated ego," or, as I have already suggested, megalomania. Further, whereas the conventional detective story moves relentlessly from the discovery of the murder, through investigation, to arrest and often punishment, in Allingham's novels the fate of the criminal is by no means a foregone conclusion. In four books (*The Crime at Black Dudley, Dancers in Mourning, Traitor's Purse,* and *The China Governess*) we never learn what happens to the killer, six murderers die by accident, either while struggling with the younger Campion, or while attempting to evade arrest, four commit suicide, and only four are actually arrested. This is not to suggest that Allingham reveals any sympathy with her murderers, but rather that she appears to find the recounting of formulaic conclusions of little interest. Nothing is revealed about character in the process of retribution. Only Max Fustian in *Death of a Ghost* is shown at the moment when the balance of sanity is disturbed and he is revealed in all the pathetic enormity of his own self-destructive, insane egoism: "From the floor all that remained of Max Fustian smiled slyly at him with drooling lips. Mr. Campion stood very still. His anger dropped from him. In its place came the strange horror which is purely instinctive, a primitive horror of that which is not a right thing" (245–46).

It has become an unwritten law of crime fiction that an author, to be successful, or rather to ensure recurrent success, must have, as an immediately recognizable trade mark, a detective or amateur investigator with clearly defined physical features, habits, and personality. The eccentric as detective (Holmes, Poirot, Wimsey, Fell) was superseded by the professional, the intellectual, even the emphatically normal (Marsh's Roderick Alleyn and Innes's John Appleby), or, in the USA, by the man of action (Sam Spade and Philip Marlowe). Campion has something of all these but remains an essentially average figure; he is not so much the author's mouthpiece or alter ego as the reader's representative, someone who sees his metier as doing that which anyone could do: "after all, deduction is only adding two and two together" (1931, 105). Campion's world is, apart from the outer trappings of a private flat near Piccadilly, an unexpected manservant and a succession of fast cars, a world in which a knowledge of people and contacts with them predominate: "Mr. Campion's strange world of nods and hints and mysterious understandings among people who trusted each other" (1955, 155). Above all, Campion—like most other detectives of the period, both male and female—is by the very nature of his avocation a conservative, a believer in the traditional values of the society to which he chooses to conform, and which he devotes his energies to protect.

Even while Allingham was still preoccupied with the adventure thriller, she made it clear that Albert Campion was not to be regarded as a detective: "he's not a detective" explains Biddy Paget in *Mystery Mile* (220). Once Allingham turned to the serious detective novel she insisted that Campion was not a detective at all; detection, as he himself is made to say, is the work of the police (1931, 21; see too: "Man-hunting isn't my *métier*. It's a job for the police" 1934, 199). His role develops in the early thirties from that of a quasi-adventurer and helper to someone who offers his services in good causes. The first position is stated early in *Police at the Funeral*: "I'm a professional adventurer—in the best sense of the word" (21); the second is outlined in *Death of a Ghost*, where the reader is told that: "Campion, had taken up the adventurous calling of unofficial investigator and universal uncle at first as a hobby and finally as a career" (55).

In the modern mysteries, Campion investigates in order to help friends or people who apply to him for assistance; in the wartime adventure mysteries, he is either involved officially or gets dragged into a mysterious situation by accident. His role becomes even more anomalous in the postwar crime novels; directly involved—even commissioned—in *More Work for the Undertaker*, he plays little part in the direct solution of mysteries in the novels which follow, and is much more a friend who happens to be on the scene. Margery Allingham herself commented, "As a detective of the old polite school he has been forced underground a little in later years" (1958, n.p.). It is only with the return to adult adventure in the two final books that Campion is granted a more foregrounded part to play; a part which is defined in *Cargo of Eagles* as that of "a negotiator and unraveler of knots" (1968, 9). As with the criminal, so too with the investigator: it is not so much the action as the personality and mind involved which is of interest. Campion as a reader of signs, and thus yet another reader of the mystery, is much more important than any view of him as the infallible and relentless pursuer of wrongdoers.

One further aspect of Allingham's narrative practice, which is particularly significant to a serious appraisal of her work, should be brought forward here; since it operates quite clearly out of context as well as within the frame of an individual novel, it has its place within this general overview of Allingham's work. I am referring to those moments when her writing seems deliberately, or even accidentally, to refer back to itself and to the whole enterprise of the composition of crime fiction. For instance, in *Police at the Funeral*, Campion remarks during the course of his attempt to discover the truth about a series of mysterious deaths, "After all, an explanation, however unpleasant, is better than a mystery" (110). Here he is stating the principle on which detective fiction is based: rather the unsavory truth than no knowledge, or, phrased somewhat differently, Allingham's novels are intimately concerned with knowledge, the bases of knowledge, and the process of gaining it.

In *Death of a Ghost*, Inspector Oates is made uncomfortable by the realisation that "by his mere presence," Campion "transformed the most straightforward cases into tortuous labyrinths of unexpected events" (63). What appears to be a downright negation of the expected role of the "great detective," who brings blinding light into the obscurest darkness, is in fact Allingham's comment on the transparency of the conventions governing detective fiction: since the investigator must prove his powers, his very presence is an indicator that no event will be without significance and no problem too slight, no mystery too simple. As she states in a later novel, "Nothing is *nothing* to do with anything" (1945, 253). Campion, a semiologist of crime, is the person who "recognized the signs" (1962, 105), whereas Margery Allingham is the one whose task is to tell the tale, and to call attention to its fiction: "If you're going to say it, say it" (1965, 48).

This would also seem to be the place to raise one final nagging question, to which, as yet, no satisfactory answer has been found, and to which I can only suggest possible further lines of enquiry. In spite of Marjorie Nicolson's observation at the end of the twenties that the detective story was a predominantly male field (1929, 491), it remains a fact that the majority of the most distinguished practitioners have been and are women: Christie, Sayers, Allingham, Marsh, Josephine Tey, Gladys Mitchell, Highsmith, and P. D. James. What is the explanation for this phenomenon? Why have very able women writers deliberately chosen to write crime fiction, and why have they been so successful? It is quite amazing that, in the sixty years of serious criticism of the genre, virtually no attempt has been made to investigate, let alone solve, this problem. Admittedly A. E. Murch traced the women detective story authors back into the nineteenth century, from E. S. Drewry's *The Death Ring* (1881) to Elizabeth Gaskell's *The Squire's Story* (1853), yet summarized their skills and the success of their work as depending upon "a shrewd application of common sense" and "a quick eye for such informative details as sudden changes in household routine." The early women authors of detective fiction were seen as foreshadowing the "intuitional or psychological detectives of the twentieth century" (1958, 165–66). This limited scope and specialized skill theory is echoed in a broadcast interview that Margery Allingham gave in the same year as the publication of Murch's book, when she said of the nineteenth-century tradition of women novelists and the later authoresses of crime fiction, "I think the type is just a continuation of the original British authoress. We're not as a race very introspective, but we are extremely curious and interested in our neighbours and we get to thinking about them" (1958a, n.p.). This view is repeated in Allingham's Harrods talk at the end of the same year, in which she noted that women are natural detectives with a real interest in other people (1958, n.p.).

The notion that women are particularly adept at penetrating the human psyche as a result of some form of natural curiosity—unacceptable as it may seem as an explanation—continued to be the common view from the late fifties to the mid-seventies. Yet when the whole problematic of female creativity and the female imagination was taken up by feminist critics, little further was added except a reiteration of the idea of limited experience and the introduction of a somewhat nebulous idea of female ways of knowing. Elaine Showalter pointed to the strict separation between male and female experience in the nineteenth century and suggested that as women's share in common experience increased, women's fiction simply insisted on this form of knowledge. Showalter was, however, cautious enough to realize the difficulties in pinpointing and defining a specific female style, or inherent female qualities in prose (Showalter 1977, 257–58).

P. D. James, herself a distinguished writer of crime fiction, disappointingly had little light to shed on the problem in an article she wrote on Dorothy Sayers in the late seventies. She insisted on the essential limitation of women mystery writers, whom she saw as "chiefly concerned with malice domestic, the stresses, tensions, irritations and hatreds which can fester in a close community" (James 1978, 73–74), all of which may be true, but does not suggest any clear reason why such writers should turn to detective stories rather than to straight fiction. Finally, in 1981, another writer of crime fiction, Jessica Mann, devoted an entire book to female crime writing; it is all the more regrettable that the only solution she could come up with was an invocation of the element of fantasy. Writing of the Englishwoman's success as a writer of detective fiction Mann noted, "She writes something which is, for her, fantasy. . . . The English lady is producing a work derived in its most vital parts entirely from imagination. None of the mystery writers whose success has been lasting met with crime or criminals during her career" (1981, 54). Nothing could be more futile or less helpful; no one would dare to come forth with such a statement to account for the success of any male writer in the field of crime fiction. The criticism of detective fiction has singularly failed to produce a satisfactory explanation for women's choice of and preeminence in the field.

An attempt to put forward a general theory, and also to account for Allingham's personal interest and success in the genre, might start from a reminder about the British readers of detective fiction. On the one hand, they have been categorized as middle-class and female (Watson, 158), but they have also been seen as males belonging to that group of the educated and successful, who, in the interwar years and later in the fifties and sixties, were no longer able to deploy their talents and energies as in the nineteenth-century years of imperial expansion or the early twentieth-century period of colonial consolidation. For both groups, the detective story offered a surrogate for the exercise of energy and intelligence and an underpinning of a "sense of personal responsibility" (Bremner 1954, 251). If we add to this observation the common knowledge that the two groups from whom the majority of successful crime writers emerged in the late thirties were academics and women, we may note the bond between writer and reader. We are dealing—and particularly in the case of women—with two classes who were very largely denied active and influential participation in the events of the so-called real world, and who had thus been thrown back upon other reserves of strength and other outlets of expression.

In raising the question of why people (no matter what sex) write detective novels, Boileau and Narcejac emphasize the fundamental ambiguity of the genre in that it allows the reader to perceive two worlds in one: an imaginary reality and a real imagination. Given this, the readers who combine both the adult (of the real world) and the child (of fantasy), in reading detective fiction "cross a certain borderline, experience the inhuman, that is a world in which our points of reference are no longer valid" (188; my translation). Fantasy does play its role, but not in the vague and limited sense seen by Jessica Mann. In order to understand the function of the female imagination in crime fiction, one must first establish the nature of female reality, from which both author and reader may be freed by the play of the creative imagination. This limited experience of active, powerful and influential life finds its parallel and its means of expansion in the limited form of the detective story. The quality of limitation involved was described succinctly by Elizabeth Hardwick in an article originally written in the fifties: "Women have much less experience of life than a man. . . . Experience is something more than going to law school or having the nerve to say honestly what you think in a drawing room filled with men. . . . In the end, it is in the matter of experience that women's disadvantage is catastrophic" (Showalter 1977, 317).

I think that to this form of limitation one needs to add the limited acceptance of women in the literary world of the twenties and thirties, or even of the sixties. The role of women writers had been very largely established by the turn of the century as confined either to magazine fiction of the romantic or romance variety, or to varying forms of the domestic novel. When a certain degree of liberation, a certain widening of the field, was granted to women, the phenomenon which resulted was the stylish and innovative novel devoted to the recording of women's experience, such as the work of Dorothy Richardson or Virginia Woolf, or, in a more restricted area, Radclyffe Hall. There remained, however, that large group of articulate, creatively motivated, and skilled women writers, of whom Margery Allingham was one, who wanted neither to write of love and historical romance, nor of the contemporary experience of women, but simply desired to write fiction. It seems to me likely that literary-sociological research into the material and professional situation of the woman writer in the first half of this century could provide an extremely cogent reason for the "escape" into the mystery and crime novel with the possibilities that it offered "to see not only the elementary problem but the curious symbolical way in which it can be used" (1958, n.p.). The detective story, as a mode of fictional expression, offered itself to the woman writer both as a challenge to create something new out of a fixed form, and as a vehicle for expressing styles of vision and statements of opinion which, in the form of a straight novel, would have come up against the traditonal male critical bias of publisher and reviewer combined. Margery Allingham herself saw this retirement to a position of comparative literary unimportance as having immense benefits: "The Mystery is an art form whose discipline has been beneficial and which has always kept us free in our very unimportance. We have the privilege of Court Fools. There is very little we dare not say in any company in any land" (1963, 13). One need only compare this with Elizabeth Hardwick's statement quoted above, to begin to understand why women took to writing detective fiction, why they adopted the crime novel as their almost predestined form of expression.

In addition to any general theory accounting for women writers' choice of the detective story, individual biographical information may be expected to provide further enlightenment. Hence, partly, the present attempt to place Margery Allingham's fiction within the context of her life. This endeavour proceeds on the assumption that, although her writing was probably the most interesting thing she ever did, her life, her character and personality, her experience of the world, her feelings and the opinions uttered outside the context of her fiction, reveal valuable aspects of the totality of work and author. This is not, of necessity, to deny the truth of this comment by Agatha Christie: "I think I am rather glad that I knew her only by the words that come with such art from her pen. Her whole intriguing personality seems gathered together there" (1968, n.p.). A careful study of Margery Allingham's life on the basis of her letters and diaries, as well as other nonfictional material, and the testimony of her friends and acquaintances, will help to decide how much of the "intriguing personality" belongs to the page as "art"—an escape from personality—and, perhaps, how much *more* intriguing was the personality of the Margery Allingham whom Agatha Christie never knew.

3

The World Was Still a Promise

There certainly is something remote and fantastic about one's own childhood, when the world was still a promise.

Margery Allingham

On June 3, 1903 in St. James's Church, Gunnersbury—not far from where nowadays the Chiswick flyover carries the M4 motorway into central London—two first cousins were married: Herbert John Allingham, journalist, and Emily Jane Hughes, a photographer's daughter. A year later Margery Allingham was born. From these bare facts I shall attempt to weave the first strands of the fabric which is to become the pattern of her life.

The Allinghams were Londoners: Herbert's parents James William and Louisa had spent the early part of their married lives in Walworth and Lambeth, moving out to Brentford at the end of the 1870s. Here, they were near William's sister, Emily Jane, who had married William Walter Hughes in 1878. In later years, this marriage does not seem to have been very happy; Hughes was a heavy drinker, and his wife was often forced into mollifying impatient sitters by posing as his assistant, taking a picture with an empty camera, and then, when her husband was sober, requesting the sitter to return to the studio for a second attempt since the plate had unfortunately been spoilt. In 1879 their first child, also christened Emily Jane, was born, and grew up with a gift for trimming hats and writing romantic stories.

Herbert and Emily's mutual grandparents had both died long before their grandchildren's marriage; William Allingham (described at various periods of his life as a "landed proprietor" and a "manufacturing chemist") had died in 1874 at the age of seventy-one, only two years after his much younger wife Elizabeth Jane. Both of them had lived their entire lives in the Kennington district of South London (not far from the

Elephant and Castle), where Elizabeth Jane had brought eight children into the world. The homemade legend, whereby this branch of the family was descended from a mysterious William Allingham of Ireland and his gypsy-born cook is certainly not true; it was probably born of the desire to be associated with the well-known Irish poet William Allingham (1824–89). The truth, however, is unorthodox enough: William was the eldest son of a liaison between John Allingham, an attorney with offices in Clerkenwell, and a certain Charlotte Duncan. Allingham's legal wife Martha (d. 1857) had already given him three sons when William was born in 1803. Although he had at least four other children by Charlotte Duncan, there seem to have been amicable relations between the two groups of offspring. This is indicated by the fact that one of the provisions of John's will (he died in 1835) was that his books were to be divided between his three legitimate sons and the two eldest of the Allingham-Duncan boys.

Herbert does not seem to have been greatly affected by the irregularities of his great-grandfather's domestic arrangements, nor is there any reason for him to have been; after all he was only seven when his grandfather died, leaving him with no further contact to a generation beyond that of his parents. His father, William, who had begun his professional life as a compositor and commercial clerk, had by the end of the century cofounded one of the early advertising agencies, J. C. Francis & Co., which also published a number of journals, including the *Christian Globe*, of which he was editor. William's brother, John, edited and published several papers for boys such as *Boys' World* and *Our Boys' Paper* in the 1870s and 1880s; he made his name as the author of the very popular "Ralph Rollington's Schooldays" which had innumerable sequels, so that John Allingham eventually adopted the hero's name as his pseudonym (Lofts & Adley 1970, 37). Herbert's first story, "Barrington's Fag" was published in one of his uncle John's papers in 1886.

Herbert was educated at Ardingley College and Cambridge University, where he matriculated in 1883, with the intention of entering the church. He was a noncollegiate student, the normal status for underage students (he was after all only sixteen) and for those who were not able to pay the high college fees. In 1888, he took the examinations for the general B.A. degree, the final qualification which the vast majority of nineteenth-century students attempted. In view of his wide interests in later life, it is worth mentioning that the general B.A. examination included papers on the Acts of the Apostles in Greek, a Latin classic, a Greek classic, algebra, elementary statics and hydrostatics, an essay in English, and some questions on Shakespeare and Milton. After graduation, Herbert changed his mind about ordination and went into journalism, a choice which, given the careers of his father and uncle, was not altogether surprising. He eventually became editor of the *London Journal*, but retired soon after his marriage to devote himself to freelance serial story writing for a number of publishers including the Amalgamated Press, John Lang, and Thomsons (Lofts & Adley 1970, 36–37). He was, in Youngman Carter's words "one of the last of a race of giants who made fortunes for others in the formative years of the pulp press" (Carter 1982, 31). The payment for these stories was Allingham's sole source of income; he worked hard and constantly until his death in 1936, keeping a meticulous account of the number of words he wrote each day, which were then added together to give weekly, monthly (over 26,000 in March 1918), or yearly totals (352,850 in 1927). When, in a letter to Frank Swinnerton, Margery Allingham was later to write, "I think he was the most impressive personality I ever met. I adored him" (01.01.1938), she was giving expression to one of the keys to her own development. She probably owed more to her father than to anyone else, with the possible exception of her husband. Herbert's death in the mid-thirties, was an immense loss to her.

In 1909, when Margery was five, Herbert decided, partly for the sake of his family (Margery's brother, Philip, had been born in 1906), partly for the peace and quiet from which he could benefit himself, to leave Broughton Road, West Ealing for the countryside. Having re-signed his editorship, there was no routine job to keep him in London; he could visit editors and agents on weekly trips to town. The search for somewhere within comparatively easy reach of London led him to the small Essex village of Layer Breton outside Colchester, where the vicar was a former Cambridge man, Rev. Bixby Garnham Luard. The Allinghams rented the Old Vicarage on the edge of the village; it is clear from a surveyor's letter to Allingham two years later that there was no bath with running water in the house and that it was altogether in poor repair. Margery, a normally imaginative child, peopled the meadows around the house with fairies, and seems to have run fairly wild during the first two years there. A dozen or so years later she looked back on this time in a poem entitled "Layer Breton Meadow"—a place "where the fairies played"—and marked the passing of the years in the lines,

> I would not go into that meadow now
> Lest all I found when pressing back the bough
> Of that old oak was long rank grass grown wild.
>
> (Notebook, 1923/24)

In the Meadow at Layer Breton, ca. 1909

There were always a lot of visitors to the house at Layer Breton, mainly members of the family and close friends of Herbert's such as Richard Starr, who wrote fiction for boys and comic pieces about Irishmen, as well as over fifty novels in a long lifetime (he died in 1968 aged over ninety), or George Richard Mant Hearn, who was principally a writer of fairy stories, but who also painted the occasional picture. One of Herbert's oldest friends was the novelist William McFee, who had run away to sea at the age of seventeen. During the First World War, he served in the Royal Navy, and later settled in the United States. On his visits to England he often stayed with the Allinghams and was a favourite correspondent of both Margery and her father. On a typical day at Layer Breton Herbert would be working on his current serial, his wife, Em, would perhaps be writing one of her magazine stories for girls, and there might also be visits from Uncle John and grandfather Allingham. Herbert later wrote of his daughter "she was a writer because her people were writers" (Letter to McFee, 03.09.1927). This was the setting for the first significant moment in Margery's life:

> When I was about seven, my father . . . decided I should stop trying to become a portrait painter and settle down to follow in his footsteps. So he presented me with a small study in our big, old-fashioned, white-walled house on the Essex marshes, a dangerously full, pint bottle of ink, a ream of lined paper, pens, and—bless his practical heart—a plot. From this distance my impression is that I wrote that same fairy story five hundred and forty-five times in the next twelve months. (Allingham 1949)

The procedure was similar to that which Herbert knew from his experience of editors: it was they who determined the characters and the basic plot of the stories, which he then "worked out with the same academic interest that he gave to a chess problem" (Carter 1969). Whatever the success of Margery's first efforts, she never looked back, and writing became one of the principle activities of her childhood. Herbert's recipe seems to have been quite simple: "He reckoned that if I still couldn't write after he'd taught me the technique, I must be half-witted. . . . He argued that success was a matter of tapping the emotion that lay within you" (Duncan 1960).

Since the biographer, nosing through diary revelations and rereading personal letters enjoys a form of posthumous intimacy with his subject, he also adopts familiar forms of address. Margery Allingham's family and friends shortened her name to Marge—and so shall I. In 1911, shortly after her initiation into the craft of writing, it was decided that seven-year-old Marge's education should be taken in hand, and she was

While at Endsleigh House School, Colchester, ca. 1916

sent as a weekly boarder to Endsleigh House School in Colchester, which was run by the Misses E. A. and L. M. Dobson, who presented Marge with a Bible on their retirement in July 1917. (Unfortunately they, like so many after them, could not spell Marge's name correctly and inscribed their gift to "Marjorie Allingham".) The Dobsons were succeeded by Dora Griffin and a Miss Sharp, neither of whom seem to have been very popular with Marge. At the school she received a sound grounding in the basic subjects; the school bill for 1918 records tuition in English, mathematics, French, German, Latin, science, and class singing plus such extras as drawing, dancing, and gymnastics. Marge, who gained the nickname "Inky," showed enthusiasm for amateur theatricals and little else. She wrote home that she had acted in a pierrot show and was so absorbed that she forgot to stammer—an affliction from which she had suffered throughout childhood. In November 1918, her father decided—maybe under pressure from his daughter—to remove her from Endsleigh House and send her to the academically superior Perse High School for Girls in Cambridge. The Misses Griffin and Sharp seemed to have taken umbrage at this sudden decision; Marge's report in a letter to her father is worth quoting if only for its precocious style:

> Miss Sharp has been furious with me ever since. Now that I am leaving her rotten school she seems to have lost all interest with me except to find fault; she doesn't exactly flare up and row, but she says catty things, perfectly unnecessarily, and it makes me feel simply mad, but of course if I said anything to her there would be a wearisome row and it isn't worth it, so I preserve an aggravating beam. (04.12.1918)

In the middle of the First World War, when Marge was thirteen, the Allinghams had returned to London, renting a top floor flat at 7 Hurlingham House, Blomfield Crescent, Bayswater; this was at the Harrow Road end of the Westbourne Bridge over the railroad tracks into Paddington Station, and close to the Grand Union Canal and Little Venice. It is not certain what exactly motivated the move, but Marge's suggestion that her father "gave up trying to keep up our big old house" (1941, 23), is a likely explanation, since Herbert was often in financial difficulties. The family kept on a rented holiday apartment on Mersea Island, just off the Essex coast south of Colchester, which was to be the scene of many a family holiday and outing over the next decade.

In January 1919 Marge, now a large fourteen-year-old with wide eyes and lustrous long brown hair, was sent to the Perse school, boarding at Sarum House, a school property in another part of the town not far from the railway station. Some eighteen girls boarded under the watchful eye of Rose Luard—a relation of the Allinghams' landlord at Layer Breton—who taught history and singing and was a strong and beneficial influence on her girls. Marge had heard in advance from a young mistress at Endsleigh House that she would probably be frightened of the headmistress, "she's so ugly but she's really awfully decent." In fact Miss Kennett was an academically distinguished mathematician with degrees from Cambridge and Dublin. Marge seems to have thrown herself into the activities of the school, taking a lively interest in English literature, the school magazine, and the debating society. In addition, she wrote and produced little plays for her fellow boarders to perform. Alice Narborough, a slightly younger contemporary of Marge's at Sarum, was later to write of her: "I shall always remember with pleasure her brief period at the Perse and particularly of course at Sarum House, where she was extremely popular, and of course very mature *yet* she tolerated us silly little schoolgirls and wrote fascinating plays and got up at 6 A.M. to rehearse" (Letter to J. Allingham, 03.07.1966).

Herbert Allingham was watching the progress of this unusually mature girl of fifteen carefully; he was an acute, if not entirely unbiassed observer, who confided in a friend his belief "that the child has talent," and announced his intention to try to keep her at school as long as possible. His fears that "in a year or two she will take her life into her own hands and poor pa will have to grin and pretend he likes it" (Letter to Edith Heald, 10.11.1919) were by no means unfounded. On January 10, 1920, Marge announced her decision that, since she did not feel she was getting anywhere, she wanted her father to take her away from the Perse. Rose Luard's evaluation of Marge at this period, that she "needs more education . . . if she is to do good work in the future" (07.07.1920), fitted in with Herbert's estimate of his daughter: "She has brains and she has acquired a lot of out-of-the-way knowledge, but I feel she wants some systematic course of study. She is a curiously sane girl—writes romantic plays yet hates all fads, makes jam, designs frocks, chaffs her mother and cajoles me" (Letter to W. McFee, 19.08.1920). Marge at the close of her formal schooling thus appears as a mixture of sensible young lady, competent housewife, and imaginative writer—a combination which was to survive, virtually unchanged, for the remainder of her life.

Marge left the Perse in July 1920, at the end of the summer term—two months after her sixteenth birthday. As yet there were no clear indications of what she wanted to do, nor was Herbert going to hurry her. In October, grandfather William died, and Herbert seems to have turned very much to the unoccupied Marge for companionship. The two of them walked in Kew Gardens, went a number of times to the Old Vic theatre to see performances of Shakespeare, and then on November 27 they attended a recital given by students of drama and elocution at the Regent Street Polytechnic. There is no record of the program or of Marge's reactions, but shortly after this she and her father agreed that she should enrol at the school. She was at this time "a nervy, big-boned, excitable child . . . quick to rage or laughter, self-conscious, over-aware and altogether about as restful as an unbroken mule" (Allingham 1963b, 40). Herbert's motives in agreeing to the idea of the Poly seem to have been his belief that a course of elocution would cure Marge's stammer rather than add positively to her education. For this he had other plans.

On January 11, 1921, Marge attended the Poly for the first time, experiencing it as "very scaring" but "not really bad." She found herself in the "General" class, which was compulsory for all students attending the department of speech training. On the first evening each participant had to get up and read from a book of poems, then their performances were commented on critically. Marge recorded that out of sheer nervousness, she recited without a stammer; this was the final cure: "Whenever it appeared again I brushed it off contemptuously as a vanquished enemy" (1963b). The end of the stammer still left the problem of Marge's further education. This was remedied by sending her to a private tutor, Barbara Harper, a fellow of the pioneer establishment for the higher education of women, Queens College, Harley Street, who had been recommended by Miss Luard as "a very clever, cultivated and charming person" (Letter to H. J. Allingham, 07.07.1920). Marge read and studied major works of English literature with her twice a week for the next two years. Although (apart from diary records of her visits) Marge left no account of the tuition with Miss Harper, it would not be over-imaginative to suggest that the close study of the major English texts with someone who clearly was a champion of the education of women must have contributed both to Marge's fierce independence, and to the ease with which she was later to exploit her mother tongue.

The first year at the Polytechnic consisted mainly of classes in elocution, based on the learning and recitation of dramatic monologues and poems. Marge soon became impatient and began composing her own material. One piece, in which she acted the part of a peasant girl whose highwayman lover was about to be executed, revealed her histrionic talents: "She got up and became . . . a peasant woman watching the execution of her lover. It was heart rending" (Note by Betty Carter, 20.11.1983). The success of this effort encouraged Marge to continue, and her notebooks of the period are full of somewhat mawkish verses and heavy dramatic orations, most of which were abandoned. It was not until the winter of 1921–22 that she finally attempted a full-length play—a verse drama, *Dido and Aeneas*—for her classmates to perform. *Dido* was presented with a modicum of success on June 1, 1921. Marge was not only the author: she also played the female lead, designed the costumes, and produced the play. There was a scattering of reviews in the London papers, one of which suggested that "Miss Margery Allingham should be heard of again when she gets a little older" (*Referee*, 02.07.1922).

It was characteristic of the fullness of Marge's first year of freedom from formal schooling, her first as a girl enjoying what must have seemed to her to be adult privileges, that while she was writing *Dido*, she was also working on her first novel. The origins of this book went back to the summer holidays of 1921, spent at the house in Seaview Avenue, Mersea Island. On the evening of August 3, Marge, her brother Phil, their father, and G. R. M. Hearn were left together after other visitors had left. "We found the time drag somewhat and Margery suggested that we should amuse ourselves by 'trying the glass.' This was a kind of parlour game which Margery had brought home from school two years earlier. During those two years she had only played it once or twice, the subject not interesting her." "Trying the glass" referred to tumbler-turning, in which a common tumbler was inverted in the middle of a circle of pieces of paper on which the letters of the alphabet had been written. The participants then each placed a finger on the glass and asked questions. Apparently of its own accord, the tumbler moved here and there across the surface of the table indicating letters which, when noted down, formed words and sentences.

The Mersea experimenters kept a fifty-one-page record (from which the above quotation was taken) of their sessions, which took place at intervals until August 13; they appear to have contacted the spirits of a number of people who lived at Mersea in the late seventeenth century, many of whom engaged in the usual smuggling activities of the time. Read with hindsight, it is pretty clear that Margery's inventive imagination played a leading role (or at least a helping hand) in the occult games. Be that as it may, on returning to London, she sat down and began writing the book that would be her first published novel, *Blackkerchief Dick*. It was finished in early April 1922, and sent by Herbert Allingham to the well-known literary agents, A. P. Watt & Son, who agreed to try and find a publisher for it. They were successful; the novel was published in England by Hodder & Stoughton in August 1923, and by Doubleday Doran in the United States two months later. In the introduction, which he wrote for the American edition, William McFee

Photograph of Marge Sent to William McFee in 1922
(Courtesy of the Yale Collection of American Literature, Beinecke Library, Yale University)

noted that "there is one notable feature about this novel . . . and that is the clean and workmanlike characterization." I do not intend to discuss *Blackkerchief Dick*—it is a novel which Marge preferred to forget in later years, and which is remarkable solely for the youth of its creator—but the emphasis on the young author's skill at delineating character, and the praise for her craftsmanship (two features which were to become mainstays of her writing in the years to come) are significant. There were a few kind reviews and then silence, but Margery Allingham had made her debut as a writer of promise.

She now had two successful achievements behind her—*Dido* and *Dick*—and meanwhile had begun to write commercially as well. Marge's aunt, her mother's younger sister Maud Grace Hughes, who had married the journalist Edward Wood in 1916, devoted herself wholeheartedly to the popularization of the new entertainment medium, the cinema. In 1919 she had founded *Picture Show*, the first film fan weekly, which was immensely successful. Her publishers, the Amalgamated Press, decided to support a new venture, so in 1921 she launched *Girls' Cinema*, a blend of short stories based on current films, gossip about the stars, beauty hints, fashion notes, horoscopes, and a problem page—all for twopence a week. In November 1921, Aunt Maud commissioned Marge to write a film story; she was pleased with the result, and from then on Marge wrote regularly for *Girls' Cinema* until the magazine folded in 1935. This work was her first, and at times sole source of regular income. Between November 1921 and December 1925, she wrote about ninety film stories which earned her an average of two hundred pounds per annum, or about the equivalent of the yearly wage of a railway clerk (Stevenson 1984, 122–23). When in 1925 Maud Hughes began a third magazine, *Joy*, aimed at young working girls, Marge was one of the regular contributors of verse and stories. A remark in her diary in February 1925 is, however, significant of the direction that her writing was to take: "Maud very enthusiastic about my share in *Joy*. Felt very bucked about it (but must not leave my love, the solemn stuff)."

Life for Marge during these first five years of the twenties was not all work and study; among other things she was to make the acquaintance of a young man, whose mother's second cousin, Florence Fisher, had married Herbert Allingham's younger brother Arthur. Aunt Flo, who did a lot of Herbert's typing, was a frequent visitor to both families and carried tales of the young man's artistic accomplishments to Hurlingham House and of Marge's precocious successes on stage and in print to the other family. In October 1921, Philip Youngman Carter, his sister Betty, and their mother, Lilian, came to call; Marge wrote in her diary, "Pip came, not much of a chap." Pip, who had left Christ's Hospital (school) earlier that year, had just started studying art at the Regent Street Polytechnic, having rejected the possibility of trying for an Oxford scholarship. After some initial uncertainty and a visit to the Carters at Watford, Marge decided to accept the young man; at the beginning of November she recorded, "Pip came and I read his verses aloud." The two were the same age, seventeen. He continued to visit Marge throughout the following winter, but in the spring of 1922 the visits began to tail off. Marge does not seem to have been ready for any form of flirtation, nor did she share in her girl friends' dramatic sentimentality, which she found completely incomprehensible ("Heard Miss S.'s love story. Dear oh me, I must be a very uncommon freak"). Pip had to be content with sharing books and poetry and the occasional visit to the theatre.

Before she could accept anything more than intellectual friendship with a member of the opposite sex, Marge needed the emotional impact of romantic involvement with another girl. This was provided by a slightly older fellow-student at the Poly, Angela Doubleday ("Charles"). On her eighteenth birthday Marge wrote in her diary: "Charles came all the way up from Streatham to bring me some flowers. . . . I love her more than anything just now. I think she likes me. It is funny that one woman should attract another so much."

Angela Doubleday clearly reciprocated Marge's feelings, and the relationship was to last for about eighteen months before Marge began to become aware of Angela's weaknesses, and tired of her. It was an attraction of opposites. Marge was heavily built, brown-haired, and, as a photograph of May 1923 shows, ungainly but with dreamy eyes and an attractive mouth; Angela "was a tall very fair haired hungry-looking girl." In *Dido and Aeneas*, Angela played the part of Aeneas to Marge's Dido, and in January 1923 they acted together in a production of Euripides' *The Trojan Women*. Referring to this production, a fellow student and close friend of Marge's has commented, "Marge had a large part and so did Angela . . . and time and again the two of them were to be found in a passionate clinch in the wings" (M. Brown, letter, 08.12.1985). That year Angela spent part of the summer holidays with the Allinghams at Mersea, where she showed signs of being something of a bore and a complainer. By the following spring their relationship was not merely over, it was virtually forgotten; in March 1924 Marge noted in her diary, "Saw Charles, can't think what I ever saw in her." Nevertheless the sudden release of emotion inside her, the discovery that she could inspire devotion, even passion, as well as offer it, seems to have broken down much of Marge's reserve in her subsequent dealings with men.

At the height of the "Charles" affair, Marge was amused by her grandmother thinking that she was going to marry Pip, yet, as the relationship with Angela cooled, Marge became more attracted to him, possibly because there was more that she could share with him intellectually: "I like him in a way. He is honest-hearted if a bit conventional on top." These reservations about Pip's latent conventionality are interesting; her suspicions of this element in his character were born out in later years when he easily succumbed to the attractions of conservative affluence. However, once the publication of *Blackkerchief Dick* was behind her, Marge was more concerned about the future of her writing career than about romance.

She had left the Polytechnic at the end of the summer term 1923 with a number of certificates but no final qualification, and faced freedom uncertainly. Herbert Allingham suggested that she write a book revealing the thoughts and ideas of her own generation. He made this suggestion on the basis of the conviction, confided to his diary, that Marge "has a spark of genius in her. At any moment she may do something big" (13.01.1923). The moment was not yet to come. In December 1923, Marge and her father rented a cottage in the village of Lyminge, not far from Folkestone in Kent, in order to do some undisturbed writing. The image of Marge as the devoted disciple of her father, getting down to work with a partly ascetic, partly romantic gesture of retreat from worldly pleasures, was probably one that she had of herself at the time. She was, however, realistic enough to continue writing film stories for Aunt Maud.

The book that emerged from this period of retreat and devotion to her vocation was completed in March 1924. It was called *Green Corn* and was destined for failure. In it she had set herself the task of explaining her generation with neither knowledge of anything but her own small segment of it, nor the necessary distance to gain an understanding of what she did know. The novel recounts the last year at school of a Marge-like heroine, and her early years at an institution closely resembling the Poly. Unlike *Blackkerchief Dick*, it is not even particularly well written; as G. R. M. Hearn wrote to her later in the year, "It is too old for a school story and too young for a grown-up one" (21.10.1924). The manuscript was submitted by Watt to various publishers without success; in July Marge took it back. The withdrawal, which the stay at Lyminge while writing the first part of *Green Corn* represented, was prolonged after the return to London. In January 1924, Mrs. Allingham

Marge with Her Father, Herbert Allingham, in the Late 1920s

found a studio which Marge could share with her father at 21 Delamere Terrace, three blocks from Hurlingham House, overlooking the canal. A major element in this retreat from the amusements of society was to put Pip at a distance. Although she was attracted to him, she felt that her chief priority was her work, so she sent him away for an initial three-week period at the beginning of 1924, noting in her diary, *"I won't love him."* Her resolution reveals Marge in a determinedly antitraditionalist stance; after all, this was a period when a nineteen-year-old, middle-class English girl was expected to be thinking of heterosexual romance culminating in marriage, not of her career.

Although superficially unmoved by the rejection of *Green Corn,* as was shown by her immediately commencing a new novel, *The Lover* (fortunately never finished), Marge's resolution to devote herself to her "art" was shaken. Withdrawal from the social pleasures that other members of her generation were enjoying in the mid-twenties was not paying off.

Early in March 1925, Marge became interested in a freestanding building in the garden of Hurlingham House. Investigation revealed that it contained one huge room with two alcoves; she decided that this would make an ideal studio where she could both work and live apart from the family. She rented the building for a nominal sum, turned the alcoves into a bedroom and kitchenette, and furnished the enormous room as work and living space. This was to be the centre of Marge's creative and social life for the next year and a half—the least productive period of her life. Even though she wrote virtually nothing apart from her pieces for Aunt Maud, the studio became the setting for a process of social maturing and the establishment of one of the roles she would always play best—that of the perfect hostess.

Marge gathered a small group of close friends around her with whom she talked, played, sometimes worked, and always laughed. One of the group, Mary Orr, a Poly student, who had gone on the stage, has characterized the studio as the place where they all would gather to "talk, put the world to rights, dream our dreams for the future and laugh away the time" (M. Brown, Reminiscences, typescript, 1985). On the whole, "the gang," as Marge called them, were typical products of the age: the impetus for their actions was the search for enjoyment, all thoughts of a secure future with a safe job and responsibility they decried as stuffy and middle class. Marge shared the general restlessness, in the sense that she could still not be sure in which direction she was going, and longed for something to do with the talents that she was sure she possessed.

Another member of the group was Marge's younger brother Philip,

"Phil," who was nineteen at this period and a disappointment to his father. He had not got into Tonbridge School at thirteen, and had gone on to fail the entrance examination to Worcester College, Oxford. When Marge took over the studio, Phil was working halfheartedly in the family advertising agency run by his uncles Ernest and Philip. Herbert Allingham was worried about his son but did not despair of him; in his diary he wrote: "He is restless and unsettled . . . has proved his grit. He should do well *if the women leave him alone.*" It was, however, more a case of Phil being the great womanizer than the passive victim of female wiles. He was a wild young man, the proud owner of a two-seater GN cycle car, in which the gang often went haring off to the coast at weekends, "coming back in the dawn light," as Mary Orr remembered, "driving round Marble Arch shouting 'Top of the morning to you' at rather surprised and amused policemen."

In May 1925, Phil introduced Marge to a friend of his, Reggie Goode, who had something to do with cars. He was quite unlike both Pip and Angela Doubleday: ginger-haired and very big, there was something bovine about him, something earthy and even common. Marge seems to have deliberately chosen this young man as the complete antithesis of everything connected with her withdrawal from the world, or with her previous emotional involvements. Reggie was neither artistic, nor creative, nor did he share any of Marge's intellectual interests. It seemed as though she was going out of her way to emphasize the distance she was trying to put between herself and her recent past. Soon she was recording that she was very fond of Reggie, and by July Marge was certain that she was in love with him, but feared that it would all come to nothing, like her past experiences. There is never any indication in her diary about Reggie's feelings or confidences. Certainly Marge approached the relationship with great care: "I am really in love with him. I feel I would chuck up everything and look after him, which is of course absurd" (Diary, 30.08.1925).

However absurd she felt a sacrifice for Reggie's sake might be, the relationship continued until the summer of 1926, when the two parted after an emotional farewell. Reggie brought Marge little but his companionship in having a good time; in particular he helped her in her attempt to revoke her earlier decision to cut herself off from social contacts and emotional adventures. The creatively sterile year 1925 had shown her what she could achieve socially as the rallying point for a number of amusing friends—but it did not satisfy her. Nor did it satisfy Herbert Allingham, who, on his fifty-eighth birthday, wrote in his diary, "Margery has done no serious work this year." He was, however, gracious enough, and, as it proved, perspicacious enough to add that he believed she was "thinking and subconsciously making plans" (18.12.1925).

Shortly after the General Strike of May 1926, Pip Carter moved out of his mother's house in Watford and took an attic flat in Neal Street in the then slum district of Seven Dials with a former school friend, Alan Gregory ("Grog"). There they lived the lives of what Gregory referred to as "bohemians with an air of respectability." "The Hovel," as they christened their apartment, was anything but romantic: "There was neither water nor inside sanitation and the only domestic device was an elderly gas stove which, if a penny was placed in the meter, in the manner of its pestiferous kind, lit at any point where a match was applied. Fiercely garrulous tomcats haunted and hunted the stairs, adding their natural scents to those of . . . cooking and infidel decay" (Carter 1982, 45). Pip and Grog earned their living from numerous odd jobs all connected loosely with their artistic skills: from designing the lettering on wine and pillbox labels to thinking up pictures and captions for rude postcards. Occasionally Pip was fortunate enough to get a lucrative commission for a book jacket. Neither of them, however, had any form of steady employment, nor could they command the sort of regular income that Marge was getting for her work for Aunt Maud and the Amalgamated Press. The two men were living carefree, careless lives in London—young men freed from the restraints of home life. "The Hovel" was for Pip what Marge's studio had been for her: a chance to make creative use of independence.

As a schoolboy Pip was remembered for being "slightly detached from the rest" with "a dry wit and a sense of satire" (Rev. Dr. M. Knight, letter, 31.12.1985). It was this developed sense of humour that continued to attract Marge. She had made several attempts to come to terms with Pip in the period before the move to the studio, but had come up against what seemed to her his sentimental wish to marry her. This she had rejected outright, and Pip had played little part in Marge's social life with the "gang," and none at all during the episode with Reggie Goode. Marge's ability to fall in love unreservedly with Goode, and not with Pip, seems to indicate that in Pip's company she was afraid to let herself go, just because she was genuinely attached to him. He would seem, however, to have had a powerful advocate in Marge's father. Early in October 1926, Herbert Allingham went to see Marge at the studio and "talked Pip." Less than a month later, Pip received an invitation to dine at Hurlingham House. Events moved slowly. Early in January 1927, a very different Marge from the nervously impetuous young student of the early Poly days called at the Hovel to take tea with

Pip. She was noticeably fat and there were still occasional traces of a stammer, but she was much more self-assured. Dressed in simple well-cut self-made clothes, "she wore her hair in a coil over one ear, and in the other she had an unusual ear ring" (Betty Carter, 20.11.1983).

The Allingham family had by this time moved again. Herbert's financial position having improved, thanks to having sold a serial story in the U.S., he had decided that a return to the country would do the family good and restore to them the peace and quiet that they could no longer find in postwar London. "I like London in all its familiar moods but not so much when it is trying to behave in the manner of a giddy young thing" (Letter to W. McFee, 1919). The Allinghams' choice fell on the former parsonage at Letheringham, some three miles from Wickham Market, in a remote and sleepy part of Suffolk. It was a pleasant red-brick house at a quiet road junction and surrounded by a large well-laid-out garden. Herbert described it in a letter to McFee, "the nearest pub is a mile away. . . . Nothing to do but work, read and potter about the garden" (01.01.1928). The move took place in December 1926, with Marge, who had taken a few lessons a month before, driving her parents in the Allinghams' newly acquired Morris from London to Letheringham, where she joined them in the new home.

On March 30, 1927 Marge went up to town from Letheringham leaving her parents busy writing. The following Thursday, April 4, Herbert Allingham received telegrams from Marge and Pip separately, announcing their engagement. The next day a letter came from Pip's mother advising Herbert not to let Marge marry her son because of his difficult character. Allingham sat down at once to reply to Lilian Carter, whom he had known and been very fond of in his undergraduate days at Cambridge. Recalling their common past experiences he wrote: "It so fell out that we both found happiness apart from one another but to-night I like to feel that perhaps the qualities in you and me which made us sympathetic with and understand one another were transmitted to our children and have been the means of bringing them together" (06.04.1927). Marge herself was somewhat more prosaic in her account of the matter to William McFee: "I have got engaged to be married (in the 'nice respectable' way you're so down on). Dear, dear what a business it all is—I had no idea it was so formal an affair. I do not think you would approve of my sweetheart but he is a worthy young man and not at all likely to beat me" (July 1927).

Philip Youngman Carter and Margery Louise Allingham were married on September 29, 1927 "in the costers' church of St. Giles in the Fields" (Allingham 1963b); the bride was given away by her father, Phil

Allingham was best man, and Mary Orr one of the bridesmaids. Neither engagement or wedding seem to have been occasions for sentiment, or for anything else but merriment. Pip and Marge had known each other for six years, during which they had never been anything but very good friends. Although Pip had on a number of occasions attempted to put their relationship on a more emotional footing, Marge had always resisted. It now seemed that the decision to marry should be interpreted as a public declaration of their determination to work creatively together in the same home, rather than an announcement of love and devotion. Some twenty years later Marge wrote,

> At the time of our marriage . . . neither of us possessed very much save our talents, and our older friends and relatives were, to be discreet, mildly skeptical as to the wisdom of the step. Fortunately . . . this alliance, so lightly undertaken in the midst of the first postwar slump, proved to be the most intelligent thing we ever did. We began to collaborate at once in an atmosphere of cheerful inconsequence and a world of young friends. (Allingham 1949)

I think there can be no doubt that on both sides there was much more emotion invested initially in the relationship than Marge was, perhaps, willing to admit. Both her understatement to McFee and the hindsight assessment seem deliberately to play down any admission of feeling, let alone passion or sexual attraction. Nevertheless, her refusal to base marriage purely—even mainly—on emotional involvement proved to be a wise move as far as her professional writing life was concerned. At the same time, Marge's positive evaluation of married life in terms of collaboration and friendship could well have been a convenient rationalization of certain deficiences in an otherwise efficiently successfully partnership.

Two weeks before the wedding, Marge and Pip had rented the flat that was to be their home for the first four years of their married lives, 1 Middle Row Place, Holborn. The whole area was badly bombed during the Second World War, so that Middle Row Place no longer exists; it was a tiny cul-de-sac next to 325 High Holborn (the old Birkbeck Bank), between Southampton Buildings and Staple Inn Buildings, "as you left High Holborn by a passageway leading into Middle Row Place, there was a door on the right . . . which opened onto a steep flight of stairs direct from the courtyard. This led up to the bookie's office and Marge and Pip's flat" (Joyce Allingham, letter, November 1985). Pip remembered one memorable day when he and Marge won a quarter's rent from the bookmaker, "but within the year he went bankrupt and we took over the whole floorspace" (Carter 1969, xii). The flat was surrounded by high office buildings, and the printing works of some of the nearby Fleet Street newspapers were undeniably close; Marge recalled that the flat "shook like a powerdrill morning, noon and night from the vibrations of the printing presses beside and below it" (Allingham 1963b).

It was characteristic of the particular nature of their relationship— collaboration and "not the outcome of 'a grand passion'" (H. J. Allingham in a letter, November 1927)—that after only a week of married life, Marge and Pip were joined by a third person in the shape of Pip's friend of his "hovel" days, A. J. "Grog" Gregory, who was to stay with them for the next thirteen years. Later Marge was to say that Grog came to tea one day and never left. He was two years younger than Pip, whom he had known at Christ's Hospital; after leaving school, he had had some training at the Slade School of Fine Art in London and had then joined forces with Pip. Slim, fair-haired, and somewhat vague, he was a natural sportsman with a good eye, a music lover and easy-going fellow who, nevertheless, seemed incapable of fending for himself. He was easily integrated into the Carter menage and soon made himself useful by typing Marge's manuscripts, doing some of the lettering for Pip's book-cover designs, and producing the beautifully drawn maps and endpapers which became a recognizable decoration of Marge's thrillers. As she herself put it in later years, "the only solution we found for Grog . . . was to make a job to fit him and take him over like a baby while preserving his self esteem" (Letter, September 1938).

Thus was Marge established in creative married life; her father was soon able to report that, "they are very happy in their little home" and that Marge was "meeting lots of interesting people, working, and having a full life" (Letters, November and December 1927). All seemed set for success. Pip's sister, Betty Carter, commenting in later life on the marriage, put her finger on a possible key to its success: "They had an inbuilt communication which passes my own understanding" (Letter, November 1983).

4

When First We Practice to Deceive

The detective story writer is a web spinner by profession, a deceiver with a licence, but since all licensed bodies are subject to certain rules the author of the successful puzzle story is compelled to deceive without cheating.

Margery Allingham

Marge's debut as a writer of detective fiction came two months before her marriage: on July 18, 1927, the *Daily Express* announced that the first instalment of a new detective serial story, *The White Cottage Mystery* by Margery Allingham, would be published later that week. Readers were informed that the editor had "locked the final chapters in a safe" and they were "invited to submit their own version of how the story will end." A prize of twenty-five pounds was offered for the solution which came closest to Marge's own. Although *The White Cottage Mystery* is neither important as a novel nor as a detective story, it initiates Marge's career as a writer of crime fiction. After her failure to repeat the brief success of *Blackkerchief Dick* with *Green Corn* and subsequent efforts, she was all the more willing to pay attention to a remark made by G. R. M. Hearn extolling the freedom of the pure action story. She was well aware of the popularity of the thriller; after all, the late twenties marked the zenith of "by far the best-known and most widely read low-brow writer" of his time (Graves & Hodge 1940, 144)—Edgar Wallace. Marge welcomed the idea of trying her hand at a genre which was limited by strict rules, whose restraint, however, was negligible compared with the dreadful strait jacket of keeping bitterly serious when one was not that way inclined (1963, 10).

Her natural lightheartedness is not that apparent in *The White Cottage Mystery*, but she profited from the popularity of the genre and her dedication to good writing—the serial was sold to Jarrolds, who published it in book form the following year. It is worth noting here that *The White Cottage Mystery* reveals Allingham's understanding of the genre as being one way of probing the intricacies of contemporary life. She shows a serious concern with crime both as an observable symptom of social evil, and as an unavoidable social unpleasantness involving the entire community:

> The whole of our civilization is one network of little intrigues, some harmless, others serious, all going on in the dark just under the surface. A crime calls the attention of the community to one point, and the searchlight of public interest is switched on to this particular section of the network. The trouble is that the light does not fall upon one spot alone, but shows up all the surrounding knots and tangles, making them out of all proportion by their proximity to the murder. (Allingham 1928, 43)

The preoccupation with the contrast between the peaceful surface of community life and the sudden uprearing of crime and wickedness runs throughout Allingham's work, and is a particular hallmark of her early adventure thrillers. Marge justified her choice of the genre to a critically skeptical William McFee: "It's a fine detective story, a good painstaking piece of craftsmanship. . . . If a lady can't write a detective story or any other story to buy herself a trousseau, when can she write one?" (Letter to McFee, August 1927). The cool awareness of the relationship between skillful writing and commercial success is characteristic of Marge's business sense, which was to be of sustaining value over the decade to come.

In March 1928, Marge announced gleefully to McFee, "I've started another with more blood and action and SINISTER HAPPENINGS in it" (Letter 10.03.1928). This was to be *The Crime at Black Dudley*, which was completed by the end of July 1928 and published the following January. The blood in the novel is mainly confined to the murder, early in the story, of Colonel Coombe, the invalid uncle of a young ascetic poet, Wyatt Petrie, the last of the historic Petries of Black Dudley in Suffolk. It later emerges that the Colonel has lived a double life for years and was the planning brain behind a number of daring crimes. Coombe's employer, a mountainous German master criminal, Von Faber, stops at nothing in the attempt to regain possession of a set of plans stolen from Coombe's body after he was stabbed during a playful reconstruction of an ancient ritual played by Petrie's young house guests. Youth, enthusiasm, ingenuity, and the knowledge of being in the right triumph over the evil machinations of Von Faber, but the mystery of Colonel Coombe's murderer still remains unsolved. It is finally revealed that

Petrie himself, driven by revenge for the criminal corruption of a girl he once loved and by his sense of family honor, was responsible.

The Crime at Black Dudley is notable in the first instance for the introduction of Albert Campion, the protagonist of Allingham's subsequent books. Although he is included in a character list for the novel in a notebook of the period, Marge was to comment later that he appeared suddenly in the story, and that she gave up work on the book for a week in the endeavour to lose him (Allingham 1935). The main problem seems to have been his facetious humour, yet in the notebook he is characterized as, "a Bright Young person. Rather foolish looking young man with a rabbity face and inoffensive manners;" a synopsis of the plot states that "Campion was employed by someone who wanted papers." Introduced into the novel as an agent for a rival power to Von Faber, Campion is revealed as an ingenious professional who puts his talents at the disposal of the forces of good. He is characterized by a protective inoffensiveness, an air of lunacy, and irritating speech mannerisms, which are seen to be his "chief stock-in-trade" (1929, 120).

Campion certainly became the recognizable trade mark of Allingham's books, but *The Crime at Black Dudley* also introduces a number of characteristic features of her fiction, which are, to my mind, of greater significance. For example, at one point George Abbershaw—the character Marge originally intended to be the hero—and one of the girls in the party, Margaret Oliphant, locked in a room by Von Faber, establish contact with a servant, Mrs. Meade, another captive, who reveals a knowledge of some of the events so far hidden to the others. Her story of the behaviour of the crooks after the discovery of Colonel Coombe's murder makes it clear that they were not responsible. A narrational comment follows: "Mrs. Meade's story had deepened the mystery instead of destroying it" (105). This is one of the earliest instances of the way in which Allingham's narrative tends to comment upon itself, and, in so doing, to echo the reactions of the reader. The reminder that if the professional criminals are not responsible for the murder, then the murderer must be one of the young house guests, both confuses the reader and arouses his curiosity. Similarly, earlier in the book, Abbershaw, whose perspective controls the narration, becomes the reader's representative within the fictional setting. Immediately before the discovery of the murder we read, "There was something going on in the house that was not ordinary, something that as yet he did not understand" (29), or soon after the discovery: "He felt convinced that there were more secrets in Black Dudley that night than the old house had ever known" (38). On both occasions, Abbershaw is made to articulate thoughts that the reader instinctively shares, and at the same time the very articulation compels the reader to read on. A similar acknowledgment of the reader's presence occurs near the end of the book, when the crooks' plan to set fire to Black Dudley and immolate the young residents is thwarted by the providential arrival of the local hunt; Allingham herself voices the reader's incredulity when one of the characters is made to say, "What a miracle. . . . What a heaven-sent glorious miracle. Looks as if our Guardian Angel had a sense of humour" (150). This awareness of the reader and his reactions, and the simultaneous articulation of this awareness, acts as a reminder of the artificiality of the narration, of the fictionality of the novel.

This way in which the narrative draws attention to the tradition of detective fiction serves to foreground the author's awareness of the reader. In *Black Dudley* there are few instances of this technique which in later works was to become increasingly noticeable. However, it is significant that Campion, once the excitements and adventures are over, returns to the question of Colonel Coombe's murderer and asks Abbershaw: "Are you sleuthing a bit in your own inimitable way? Is the old cerebral machine ticking over? Who and what and why and wherefore, so to speak?" (159) The list of interrogatives corresponds exactly to the basic questions of the detective story: the identity of the murderer, the nature of the weapon, and the motive. Such remarks are to be seen as signals to the attentive reader, who is immediately made aware of the obvious reference to the classic detective tradition.

In his account of *Black Dudley* in a series of articles on Albert Campion's role in Allingham's fiction, B. A. Pike unwittingly puts his finger on another important feature of the novel when he notes: "The principal villain, 'the most dangerous and notorious criminal of modern times' is, incongruously, 'the living image of those little busts of Beethoven which are sold at music shops'; the Colonel's vintage car, 'one of the pioneers of motor traffic,' proves to be set mysteriously 'upon the chassis and engine of the latest . . . Rolls-Royce';" (Pike 1975–76, 2). Taken together with Amanda Fitton's later remark in *Sweet Danger*, "Appearances matter an awful lot" (1933, 73), this observation underlines Allingham's concern with the contrast between superficial appearances and the submerged facts, the evil lurking beneath the harmonious surface. The way in which such a central theme is carried over into what Pike refers to as the "felicity of detail" in the narration is a measure of the sophistication of Marge's early writing.

After the success of *Black Dudley*, Malcolm Johnson, the managing editor at Marge's American publishers Doubleday Doran, suggested that she write a novel centred on Campion (Allingham 1958a); this was the origin of *Mystery Mile*, which was finished by the early autumn of 1929. Like its predecessor, the new novel was largely written during long stays at Marge's parents' house at Letheringham in the spring and summer of the same year. I mention this detail since it seems to account, at least in part, for the rural setting of the book (Mystery Mile is a village on a virtual island in the estuary of the River Orwell) which contains a number of references to the locality (e.g., Hadleigh, Woodbridge, Ipswich, Debenham, and the repeated mention of Suffolk itself). The nature of Marge's collaboration with Pip on *Mystery Mile* is revealed in some notes found on a page of Alan Gregory's sketch book. Here the major plot elements of chapters 15 to 21 are outlined together with a selection of salient details. The notes are all in Pip's handwriting. This would suggest that the actual mechanics of the story were worked out together, or as Marge herself put it: "In the main, I should say that two-thirds of the ideas and half the jokes were . . . his" (1949, 94). What remained solely Marge's contribution was the nature of the narration. Writing of the novel on its appearance in the spring of 1930, the reviewer of the Philadelphia *Record* commented that in a mystery story Marge saw "something bigger and more complete than just a plot on which to hang a casual narrative" (Anon. 1930). It certainly represents a considerable advance on the rough and tumble of *Black Dudley*, while continuing to deploy some of the techniques introduced in the earlier book.

There can be no doubt about the theme of *Mystery Mile*, it is stated quite unequivocally near the beginning: Campion—"a sort of Universal Aunt" (1930, 220)—explains to the young American, Marlowe Lobbett, that the master criminal Simister "may be a devil . . . anything you like, but he's as real a power of evil as dope is" (215). From then on, "it's a death game" (340) between good and the forces of evil, which once again lurk beneath the surface of the civilized and familiar; when finally Ali Fergusson Barber, the art expert and social bore, reveals that he is Simister, we read: "The genial, rather stupid old gentleman had vanished, and in his place there looked out at the young man at the table something mocking and incredibly evil hiding within this monument of flesh" (365). Marlowe's father, Judge Lobbett, who has come to England after repeated violent attempts to put an end to his crusade against Simister and his possible exposure of the villain, puts his affairs in Campion's hands. The subsequent adventures and final physical confrontation between Campion and Simister, alias Mr. Barber, ending in the horrifying death of the master crook in the soft mud of the Essex saltings, proceed at almost breakneck speed. Campion—"not quite a private detective" (245)—is still something of a mystery figure. This is thematized in Biddy Paget's words, "You don't know Albert" (230), early in the book. Hints are given to his former illegal activities in the company of the unspeakable Thos. T. Knapp; Campion is further described as being "comic about women" (220), and ends as the disappointed lover of Biddy, who has chosen Marlowe instead. In both respects Marge pays homage to two tenets of the traditional detective story: the detective should be a figure of mystery and even eccentricity, and there should be no love interest to mar the suspense. To the anxious Isopel Lobbett's comment that he does not know how worrying it can be to be in love, Campion replies, "That's all you know young woman" (317)—the only reference he makes to his own emotions.

An important aspect of *Mystery Mile* is Allingham's exploitation of the narrational theme of knowledge in the form of salient facts and details: knowledge is either withheld from or shared with the reader at significant moments in the narrative. When, for example, Campion organizes his precautions against a surprise attack on the village, he enters into consultation with George Willsmore, one of Marge's intuitively wise old countrymen. We read, "They remained deep in conversation together for some time" (228); with the result that the elaborate warning system of watchers and whistlers comes as a surprise both to the fictional characters and to the reader. This pattern is varied when information is withheld from both Campion and the reader when Judge Lobbett initially refuses to disclose the nature of the evidence of Simister's identity which is in his possession, "I daren't and won't confide in any of you youngsters" (246). The interest-rousing function of such a statement is obvious, and yet it needs some further pondering to realize that it also functions as a means to draw the reader further into the imprisoning fictional narrative by treating him as one of the participants in the action. Only at climactic moments is information finally and fully shared with the reader (and with fictional characters); Campion, for example, is eventually forced to reveal that he was responsible for Judge Lobbett's disappearance by the unexpected publication of an accidental photograph of the judge in a newspaper (341). A more subtle variant of the technique is when the author imparts information in the form of a hint which the fictional characters do not understand, but which the reader could work out for himself. While Campion and the others are attempting to imagine who Simister could be—after having been saddled with the presence of Mr. Barber for large sections of the tale—Campion theorizes that "our little Sim . . . is probably some well-known and respected person, like the Premier, or Mr. Home of the Home and Colonial" (351). This comes close to the actual clue to Simister's identity: a children's book of *The Arabian Nights* containing the story of Ali Baba. Allingham seems at pains not to cheat, to take the reader into her confidence, or at least to give him or her a fair chance to solve the mystery with all the facts—and a number of hints—available.

In *Mystery Mile* narrative as theme begins to become particularly and consciously important. After Biddy Paget's unpleasant adventures during which she was kidnapped, chloroformed, interrogated, and mildly tortured by Simister's men until Campion and the others came to her rescue, the young people return to Campion's flat. At this stage only Biddy is in possession of the full story of what happened to her, so that explanations are expected from her position of knowledge. Campion initiates the revelation by narration: "The time has come . . . when we gather round Biddy and hear the worst. . . . Imagine we're a Sunday paper. Spare us nothing. Not a single gruesome detail" (337). The unexpected turn from the simple statement of obvious fact to the almost heavy-handed humour, which depersonalizes and objectifies past suffering is clearly deliberate. Marge prepares the reader not only for a new narrative perspective, but also for a set piece of formal narration, which has more to do with the reader than with the fictional situation. The characters are carefully assembled around Biddy as a sort of substitute audience, rather like a collection of lay figures standing in for the real human beings (the readers) at whom the narrative is aimed: "They had drawn round the girl, who was lying propped up on the Chesterfield. Marlowe sat on the back of the couch, Isopel on the floor beside her, Campion straddling a chair before her, and Giles and Lugg on either side of him" (337–38).

One stock-in-trade of the mystery writer is, of course, the clue; in Allingham's fiction clues take the form of signs; signs which have to be delivered and read with care. Early in *Mystery Mile* the reader is forced to sidestep from the main plot by the unexpected suicide of the elderly rector, Swithin Cush, knowledge of whose greatest secret (that he had never been ordained) was revealed to him by the itinerant palmist Anthony Datchett, one of Simister's minor employees. No sooner has Cush left the young people to carry out his gruesome task than messages arrive: Biddy receives the command, "Tell Albert about our longest walk," and Campion is given "a single ivory chessman, the red knight" (253). Both clues are eventually explained. Biddy recounts her memory of the "longest walk" which ended at "a belt of quick mud"; Campion forces her to examine her recollections, and asks her how she knew that it was quick mud: "Oh, there was a board up, you know. . . . The board said 'Danger'"(258). The message calls upon the recipient to revisualize a common sign which becomes particularized as soon as it is seen as relevant to a specific present situation. Campion's red chessman is more esoteric: a pun on the name of the place where he eventually hides Judge Lobbett, Redding Knights. In a similar manner Campion and the others are faced with Lobbett's suitcase full of children's books, which hide one book, which itself hides the single story, Ali Baba, which in turn hides Simister's identity. Objects become intentional signs and thus clues in the mystery. As such, they demand to be read, but only the specialized reader can do so. In this case the specialized reader is not solely the professional investigator, Mr. Campion, but anyone in possession of the necessary experience and prior knowledge.

Since Allingham takes over a character, Campion, from a previous novel, there are, as one might expect, references back to that book. The Simister of *Mystery Mile* hints at Campion's employer in *Black Dudley;* similarly Guffy Randall of the former novel is used as a reference to the possible veracity of a rumour in the second (235). At one point, Campion mysteriously announces that the only source for certain information is "the best old Sherlock of them all—old W. T." (286), who is none other than Marge's detective W. T. Challoner of *The White Cottage Mystery.* This habit of repeating place names (Black Dudley is referred to during Campion's final confrontation with Simister), and reutilizing characters and events from past novels becomes a regular feature of Marge's fiction. Admittedly other writers of detective stories refer to their earlier books, but usually only in the form of aside reminders— Watson recalling one of Holmes's former cases, or Hastings reminding Poirot of a past triumph. In Allingham novels such intertextual references have more complex functions. In the main, however, they are used to impart a sense of continuity, and at the same time to strengthen the link between author and regular reader by creating a sense of familiarity based on recognition.

Mystery Mile was completed shortly before Marge's parents left Letheringham for the more modest Dairy House at Shelley, southwest of Ipswich on the Suffolk-Essex border. The house is a remote, somewhat gloomy early-twentieth-century building, not much larger than a suburban detached residence, isolated from the village proper, which can be reached by footpaths through the meadows along the banks of the River Brett. Here Marge and Pip spent Christmas 1929. Marge was already at work on her next book, *Look to the Lady.* It was finished in June 1930, and published the following January. The period of its composition remains a blank, since neither Marge's nor her father's diary for 1930 exist, nor are there any letters extant. The novel itself was the Doubleday Crime Club's "Book of the Month" for March 1931, which elicited an ecstatic "Oh my! oh my! oh my!" from Marge (Diary, 28.02.1931). In many respects, however, it is the weakest of this early group of novels: the plot is a mixture of ancient family tradition (the legend surrounding the Gyrth chalice), international crime in high places (the mysterious society of highly positioned men of blameless reputation who order and finance the theft of priceless art treasures), witchcraft and rural superstition, ruthless violence, and Albert Campion.

Campion appears once again in his role as "universal uncle and policeman's friend" (409), with a kindly, facetious manner. When the reader tires of his incessant chatter, Marge is there to placate him in the words of one of the characters, who admonishes Campion, "Stop showing off" (493). Employed to prevent the anonymous syndicate from stealing a priceless Anglo-Saxon chalice, Campion moves to the village of Sanctuary where he joins forces with Val and Penny Gyrth—representatives of the clean-living, right-thinking, young gentry familiar from *Black Dudley*—aided and abetted by an elderly American historian Professor Cairey. Uncertain as to the identity of the syndicate's agent and possessed only of the assurance that once the agent is killed, and thus prevented from carrying out his task, there will be no further danger, Campion goes into action. After numerous subplot diversions and further mysteries, the agent is revealed as Mrs. Dick Shannon, a hard-riding, ruthless, but bankrupt horsetrainer, who is not afraid of sailing close to the wind of illegality. Campion's public school chivalry is upset at the thought of having to engineer the death of a woman, but conveniently Mrs. Dick falls to her death while attempting to steal the chalice.

The main plot is once again concerned with the thwarting of the evil beneath the surface of rural calm; much is made of that contrast in this novel: "The underlying horror which seems always to lurk somewhere beneath the flamboyant loveliness of a lonely English countryside in the height of summer, a presence of that mysterious dread, which the ancients called panic, had become startlingly apparent" (500). Repeatedly when danger is imminent or mystery and horror increase, Marge prefaces the next stage of the adventure with a description of the apparent beauty and calm of the surroundings: "The view from the window, half obscured by the leaves of an enormous oak, led the eye down the steep green hill-side to where a white road meandered away and lost itself among the fields which stretched as far as the horizon. The scene was incredibly lovely, but the young people were not particularly impressed. Penny was pale. She seemed to have grown several years older since the night before" (431–32).

In spite of its somewhat disappointing quality, *Look to the Lady* is of some interest as a novel which takes signs—that is, anything which may be perceived as standing for something or someone else—and the reading or misreading of them, as a theme. In the course of the swift-moving adventure, Campion prevents Penny from trying to transport the chalice to London for safekeeping and thereby running the risk of being robbed en route. "Penny sat staring at him in bewilderment. 'It's not fair of you to look so idiotic,' she said involuntarily. 'People get led astray'"(460).

Allingham emphasizes in Campion's outward mannerisms the misleading nature of appearances, which in turn leads into the theme of the misreading of signs. At the very beginning of the narrative, the reader is confronted with the naming of names, the character of handwriting, and the supremacy of recipient over message. Val Gyrth, temporarily estranged from his father, and penniless in London, comes across "a battered envelope lying face up among other litter" (391); the envelope bears his name and the address of the sender, but is empty. Sender and receiver are thus temporarily given priority over any message as signs in themselves, which, when read aright, lead Val to the person who will communicate with him. When he goes to the address on the envelope, he discovers the sender's representative, Campion's mountainous manservant, Lugg, who speaks to him in code: "I see . . . *you take the long road*" (394), a phrase which Campion later repeats (401) as a test of Val's integrity (the words being a signal used by Campion's opponents). These few instances establish a thematic context in which Campion becomes, of necessity, a professional sign reader for the very reason that he is ignorant of a major element in the mystery: the identity of the agent employed to steal the chalice (412). This in turn is presented to him in the form of a sign, which Campion's informant misreports as the name "The Daisy," which is taken to be a nickname (485–86). Later, when questioning Sanctuary's local witch, Mrs. Munsey, Campion learns that Mrs. Dick Shannon's first name is Daisy (518); thus misreading is corrected, not by further interpretation of a sign, but by the simpler expedient of offering additional, extraneous information.

In the course of the novel, Campion (whose own name is a barely disguised sign, having its possible origin in the old French word for champion) himself employs signs in the hope that they will be received by adept readers. At one point he rescues Val Gyrth from the enemy who have kidnapped him in a manner reminiscent of Biddy Paget's adventures in *Mystery Mile*; Val is then discovered close to Professor Cairey's house at Sanctuary with a flower in his buttonhole: "Penny snatched it. . . . 'Don't you see what it is?' she said, her voice rising. 'There's hundreds of them in that field where you woke up. It's a white campion. There's only one person on earth who would think of that'" (539). In a similar manner Campion entrusts Penny with a sign for the leader of his gypsy allies, Mrs. Sarah, in the form of "an old-fashioned hair ring" which reveals the sender's identity to the old lady: "'Orlando!' she said with evident delight"—referring to one of Campion's many *noms de guerre* (533). Here, then, we have a series of signs all designating the same person, Campion; the flower as a means of informing friends that he is near at hand; the ring guaranteeing that the bringer is his representative; and the name by which he is known only to the initiated.

As might have been expected, the references back to the earlier novels increase: the brass plate on the door of Campion's Bottle Street apartment (probably an insider's pun on Vine Street, Piccadilly) (400), his leaving the scene of action at climactic moments (535), or the use of names such as Abbershaw and Lobbett (462, 495). However, one feels that these references are of less significance than they were in the previous novel, and simply come naturally to the author. All in all, *Look to the Lady* presents us with the perfect example for Marge's own account of the composition of the three early thriller adventures: "One collected as many colourful, exciting or ingenious inventions, jokes, incidents or characters, as one could lay hands on and simply crammed them into the box as tightly as they would go" (1963, 11). Or, in the words given to Mrs. Cairey in the novel: "I never dreamed I'd have so much mystery going on around me" (498).

Although *Sweet Danger* (1933) appeared only after *Police at the Funeral* (1931), as far as plot and theme are concerned, it belongs quite decidedly to the group of adventure thrillers. The comparison made by *Time and Tide*'s reviewer: "the author is as skilful in construction and characterization as Miss Agatha Christie" (Sunne 1933, 290), unconsciously drew attention to the impact which Marge's experiment with the serious detective story had had on her writing. This was underlined in the *Sunday Times*' comment that *Sweet Danger* was "a book for the connoisseur of detective fiction" (Gillett 1933). The novel was in fact written virtually parallel to the second straight novel of detection, *Death of a Ghost*: "I paused in the middle of one to write the other. . . . I have always felt that they were my best efforts" (Letter to Frank Swinnerton, 08.06.1937). *Sweet Danger*, though clearly a return to the mode of the earlier adventure thrillers is sustained by a greater refinement of technique. Marge wrote to Doubleday's London representative Mary Leonard: "We are hard at work on SWEET DANGER now and are very keen on it. It promises great fun" (Letter 05.04.1932); the "we" emphasizes the cooperative undertaking with Pip, and the fun is characteristic of the lightheartedness both of the collaboration, and of the fictional material.

Early in the novel a throwaway line of Campion's characterizes the plot: "It's not a simple story" (1933, 26). The nature of the complexity is expressed within the authorial narration towards the end of *Sweet Danger*: "something slightly absurd, slightly magnificent, and mightily romantic" (245–46). Within the frame of these two involuntarily self-reflexive comments, the plot of the novel develops. It is almost absurdly romantic and blatantly artificial: the search for three proofs of the hereditary right to the Balkan minikingdom of Averna, together with the necessity of thwarting the ruthless efforts of Brett Savernake, a megalomaniac tycoon, to obtain them. The setting is the Suffolk village of Pontisbright (the original name of the Essex village of Chappel where Marge now lived), replete with superstitious locals, canny countrymen, and a lunatic doctor who practices black magic. The novel is often remembered as introducing Campion's later wife, Amanda Fitton, now eighteen years old, "at a stage of physical perfection seldom attained at any age" (62) and with remarkable skills with anything mechanical or electrical. The book closes with a sentimental scene in which the wounded Amanda—she has been shot by Savernake—asks Campion to wait about six years until she is ready for him, a request which produces a most untypical reaction in Campion: "His face was expressive, a luxury he scarcely ever permitted himself" (251). It is evident that the author(s) must have had a lot of fun with the convolutions of the plot and the great set pieces of action, but the main interest of the novel lies in the refinement of the narrative discourse.

From the moment when Campion apologizes for narrating the full story of the hidden kingdom of Averna to his friends with the remark, "I'm sorry to trot out all this history" (27), Allingham reveals once more her awareness of the reader. Sometimes this awareness leads her to withhold information; for example, on one occasion, the reader is temporarily excluded from possession of the knowledge shared by Amanda and Campion. They are arranging the technical details for the broadcasting of the ringing of a great bell, which will acoustically reveal the hiding place of one of the proofs being sought. Amanda then says, "I don't think you've got any idea the sort of noise this, . . ." but Campion hastily interrupts her, " 'Signal,' said Mr Campion quickly" (197). In the fictional context—the two are alone—there is no need for him to silence her; the only reason can be to conceal information from the reader, and thereby force him to share in the mystery, to become more completely encircled by the narrative.

A typical exploitation of authorial awareness of the reader comes at the end of chapter 15 of *Sweet Danger*. The drum hiding the first proof—the deeds signed by Henry IV written on parchment used as the drum's underhead—has been somewhat unorthodoxly obtained by Amanda from the museum where it was housed. Initially the reader, together with Hal Fitton, Amanda's brother, witnesses her return to Pontisbright. We are told of Hal's anger at his sister's behaviour, his appropriation of the drum, and his imprisonment of Amanda in the granary as a punishment. Hal then takes the drum up to his room in the mill. There follows a sudden change in the narrative perspective: "From where he stood Hal had a wide view of the surrounding country" (172)—a view which Allingham proceeds to exploit, bringing the characters present on the scene into focus: Lugg, Mary (Hal's older sister), and then Campion's returning associates. When, however, Hal takes these young men to look at the drum, "the bracing cords had been slashed through, and the underhead had been removed" (173). While they are trying to understand what has happened, there is a noise from the yard below, and when they look out of the window they see Amanda breaking open a wooden packing case. I have paraphrased these last four pages of the chapter at some length in order to give a clear impression of the sequence of events. The author appears deliberately to mislead the reader into drawing the conclusion that Amanda is responsible for savaging the drum and appropriating the parchment. Who else could have done it? Campion has disappeared from the scene, apparently bribed by Savernake to organize a counterrevolution in South America; the enemy is out of sight; no suspicious strangers have been seen. In fact Allingham is exploiting the detective story reader's sensitive readiness to draw inferences from information presented. She also knows that such a reader will—contrary to his experience of the genre—always tend to choose the obvious and easy answer on the basis of the clues and hints the author doles out to him. This passage reveals not merely an acknowledgment of the reader's existence, but also Marge's acute understanding of the workings of his or her mind in response to the invitation of the text.

This is born out by an instance of the playful way in which her characters' utterances can be made to reflect upon the thriller and its readers. Faced by the riddle of the drum as part of the Averna proof, Guffy Randall comments: "We'll get to the bottom of it, you'll see. I'm only afraid the thing may be too easy" (100). His remark indirectly states both the expected pattern of the detective story—the linear development towards the final solution—and the experienced reader's principal criticism—that the puzzle is too easily solved. It is, perhaps, not accidental that the one quality of Randall's which is explicitly mentioned is his "heaven-sent gift of curiosity" (11), which, of course, makes him an ideal detective story reader, or, as fictional character, the born observer of events and chaser after puzzles. Allingham makes full use of such opportunities to indulge in reflections on her own narrative throughout *Sweet Danger*, as, for example, when she comments on the first visit of Campion and his friends to Pontisbright Mill: "From the moment they approached the front door, an air of faintly hilarious unreality descended upon the whole proceedings" (59).

In *Sweet Danger* narration has undergone some refinement since the earlier novels; Marge makes greater use, for example, of shifting perspectives. I have already pointed to the example of the moment in chapter 15 when events are narrated from Hal Fitton's "wide view." In the penultimate chapter 22, when Campion engages in hand-to-hand combat with Savernake (reminiscent of the confrontation with Mr. Barber in *Mystery Mile*), the narrative begins from the authorial standpoint, but then focusses in on Savernake's point of view. He believes that he has succeeded in drowning Campion in the mill pool and climbs on to the bank: "As he paused to look down a faint sound disturbed him from the shadow . . . and he stood listening. But as nothing else occurred to arouse his suspicion he continued on the task he had set himself." The reader, alerted by the clue "a faint sound," is prepared for the appearance of one of Campion's allies, but then, together with Savernake, he is deceived into following the probable linear development of the main action. Immediately Allingham again switches the narrational perspective: "Flattened against the wall in the shadow of the shed, Amanda stood trembling, hardly daring to breathe . . . for the first time in her life, she was almost paralysed with fear (233)." Instead of the arrival of help, we are presented with an observer whose paralysis we of necessity share. Then Amanda takes up an active role, gaining possession of the box which contains the final proof, and is hit by Savernake's bullet just as she reaches the safety of the mill. Once again perspectives change as the observer loses consciousness: "'Amanda!' Campion's voice was strained. 'For God's sake get out of this. . . . 'And then in a new tone: 'Hullo, I say, Amanda, are you hurt?' . . . an exclamation escaped him and he set her down gently against the wall . . ." (234–35), in order to impel the action to its inevitable conclusion.

As in *Look to the Lady*, Campion, faced with the appalling fate of his enemy, who falls through the mouldering boards of a platform over the metal paddle wheel of the mill, attempts to help the villain: "'Hold on,' he said. 'I'm coming.'" (236). This is just one of many reminders of earlier books which occur in *Sweet Danger*. One way in which such references may function is by setting in motion a process of association which will impart further information to the reader. From the beginning of the story Campion has been followed by one of Savernake's minor minions, "Peaky" Doyle, who is ultimately employed to break into the Pontisbright mill. Campion reveals to his friends that Doyle is not unfamiliar to him, and when they question him about this, Campion replies: "We don't know one another well . . . . We met in the house of a mutual friend in Kensington. There was a fight going on at the time. Mr. Doyle hit me over the head with a life-preserver" (111). This is a clear reference to the operation in which Campion and others rescued Biddy Paget from the hands of Simister's gang in *Mystery Mile* (328–31). By referring the reader back to the earlier novel, Allingham immediately characterizes Doyle as dangerous, mean, and connected with big crime—information which is not vital, but seems to be inserted as a bonus for the careful reader.

Allingham's four adventure thrillers reveal a development in her narrative technique which far outruns the skill of the characterization and plotting. These elements are not vital in this form of the genre, which depends almost entirely on action and timing. It is, therefore, all the more significant, considering the direction which her writing was to take, that by the early thirties Allingham had developed strategies of narration as diverse as the exploitation of the awareness of the reader and his reactions, self-referential comments upon the narrative, deliberate highlighting of the artificiality of fiction, and the manipulation of intertextual references to previous books. In addition she showed herself perfectly capable of using the simple thriller as a vehicle for expanding abstract themes such as the nature and function of signs and codes. Thus Marge's decision after the completion of *Look to the Lady*, that it was time that she "should attempt a slightly more serious story" (1949, 94), does not come so unexpectedly.

5

The Only Reasonable Way

I was born into a family which sincerely believed that writing was the only reasonable way of passing one's life.

Margery Allingham

From her marriage in 1927 to the outbreak of the Second World War in September 1939, Marge's life was shaped by the sheer hard work of continuous production, rather than by exciting events or momentous incidents. The progress and development, the discoveries and excitements, are nearly all intimate and personal; above all they belong to an internal, mental, and emotional life which only too often others could not observe or share. In the following overall view of the period, it is people's characters that count rather than their actions, Marge's intellectual development rather than things she did in the outside world. A closer look into these years involves sharing Marge's thoughts about herself, her work, her relationships, the very reason for her existence. There are even times when we shall be confronted with her feeling of the emptiness behind the incessant activity: "There are hideous moments when I get the unhappy conviction that I'm a sort of demented beaver—a lunatic animal working itself to death to make something it not only doesn't need but doesn't particularly like" (Letter to R. Meiggs, 01.04.1937).

Although she once characterized herself as a "prodigiously slow worker" (Letter to the editor of *Red Star Weekly,* 18.04.1934), in the twelve years from 1928–39, Marge wrote eleven novels, four serials (three of which appeared in book form under the pseudonym Maxwell March), thirty-six short stories, four articles, and reviews of almost one hundred books. This was in addition to the weekly film stories for *Girls' Cinema* until its demise in September 1935. Most of this activity was based on the pragmatic realization that she needed to sell her writing to finance her life with Pip, who had no regular work throughout this period. The responsibility of being the sole breadwinner in a household that, from August 1934, consisted of four adults plus the domestic staff needed to take the burden of housekeeping off Marge's shoulders, was often almost more than she could bear. Time and again her diary records her own fears about the desperately urgent need for money—fears which were never apparent to those who lived close to her. Yet at times she still managed to stifle her emotional reactions and take an objective look at the situation: "I am of that type of woman who is three parts uncivilized (and who therefore feels everything intensely) and one part pure cold analyst who feels nothing at all and notes everything with intense interest" (Letter to R. Meiggs, 12.08.1938). It was the cold analytical side of Marge which enabled her to deal with the frequent financial crises by attempting to relativize the role of money: "Money is not a sacred thing," she wrote to a friend. "As long as one realizes that the stuff has to be manufactured . . . I cannot see that it is particularly important" (Letter to R. Meiggs, March 1938).

As well as frequent short visits, Marge and Pip spent two months of 1928 and three months of 1929 at her parents' home at Letheringham. On the second occasion they actually swapped homes with the Allinghams and were able to enjoy the Old Vicarage on their own with Alan Gregory. Herbert Allingham had noted the fact that there was nothing much else to do there "but work, read and potter"—a view which is supported by the following account of the village which appeared in a local paper at the time: "The very fact that it seems to exist in all that choice beauty born of a quiet past and undisturbed by the more compelling sounds of today, seems to give it an air of aloofness and a certain pleasant attraction" (*Suffolk Chronicle and Mercury*, 08.06.1928). Walking round the garden at Letheringham, Marge and Pip discussed and planned much of *The Crime at Black Dudley* and *Mystery Mile*. It was here, too, that large parts of the two novels were written. When in October 1929 the Allinghams moved to Shelley, the Dairy House naturally became the younger couple's country retreat; here they spent the first three months of 1931 planning and arguing about the new "serious" novel, *Police at the Funeral*.

Given the conduciveness to creation that they had experienced in the country over these three-and-a-half years, it is not surprising that Marge and Pip began to look around for their own country home. This they found in the Essex village of Chappel, some five miles west of Colchester, dominated by that magnificent monument to Victorian railway architecture, the viaduct of the Stour Valley branch of the old

Working with Philip Youngman Carter ("Pip") in the Garden of the
Old Vicarage at Letheringham, ca. 1929

London and North Eastern railway, with its thirty-two one-hundred-foot high arches. Marge had known the village for as long as she could remember. Her aunt, Grace Russell, a former chorus girl, had been given a cottage there by Dickie Cheffins, a businessman who had been very fond of her. In 1924, just after Grace's marriage to Charles Russell, her uncle William Walter Hughes died and her aunt (Marge's grandmother) came to live with them. The Allinghams had been frequent visitors to Aunt Grace's home, Pope's Hall, since the early days of the century; they now had a double tie to Chappel.

Viaduct Farm House, the rambling house that Marge and Pip rented, has a Tudor heart with additions built at various times, in particular the late eighteenth century. Viewed from the road as one comes down the hill from Great Tey, the house blends into the great oaks and willows along the banks of the river Colne, which runs behind it. To the left, the triple chimney echoes the arch motif of the viaduct. The house is almost at the end of a rough track leading off the main road, past the small church, and looks out over meadows which slowly rise up the hill. At the end of the track is the great, black-painted, wooden mill, which appears as Amanda's home in *Sweet Danger*. From the mill, as a local journalist was to note in 1935, there is "a delightful view of the Colne. . . . It was a picture for an artist to paint" (Jefferies, 1935). The house itself had no running water and no electricity, but the rent was only fifty pounds a year. Thus it was that on September 29, 1931, Marge, Pip, and Grog, together with the dog Neb, which had followed them home one evening from Leicester Square tube station, arrived in Chappel, "that incredibly happy valley" (Letter to R. Meiggs, June 1937).

The three-and-a-half years spent at Chappel established the pattern of Marge's life for the remainder of the decade. What spare time she could find was spent in cooking, needlework, and interior decoration. Otherwise she and the two men worked in "an incredibly untidy studio, which looks like an old-fashioned playroom, and is littered with books, masses of paper . . . and scraps of material" (Anon. 1934). In this room, on the ground floor to the right of the front door, Pip would sit drawing at one window, while Marge dictated her latest chapter or story to Grog from the fireside sofa. Work dominated, particularly once Marge had discovered a new source for augmenting the family income: serial thrillers for the mass-circulation magazine *Answers*. In January 1933, she began writing "Other Man's Danger," for which she was to be paid five hundred pounds. Although this sounds a sinecure, writing for *Answers* seems to have been somewhat akin to torture. The editor and his two deputies expected Marge to write a section of the tale, submit it, and

With Pip and Alan Gregory at Viaduct Farm House, Chappel, ca. 1932

The Mill at Chappel (Pontisbright)
The Home of Albert Campion's Future Wife, Amanda Fitton, in
Sweet Danger.

then appear at conferences consisting of critical bombardments and instructions as to the story's future development. However, Marge's basic writing habits, as Alan Gregory described them, never varied:

> She used to shut herself up and write it all out by hand, having walked round the garden with Pip, discussing how the plot would go on. During which time Pip would probably be doing one of his book jackets. . . . Then Marge would be ready with another chapter, so at that point I would take it down from dictation straight on to the typewriter, making possible suggestions about where phrases could go and so on, and at any rate we got that first typing done. Then she would go away and look through it. . . . Then would come the fair typing . . . altering the things she wanted to; then I could make the fair copies for the publisher. (Interview, 11.10.1983)

The only events that were allowed to interrupt the pattern of almost continuous work were the visits of friends and relatives, a weekend party, and an occasional cricket match in the meadow outside the house. The common factor to all these diversions was people; Marge could throw herself into the entertainment of others with immense enthusiasm, she was "a wonderful hostess, very large in a long flowing gown . . . but being able to carry off her size because of her handsome, kindly face and majestic presence" (Noel Gregory, letter, 30.12.1985). The dominant feature of the parties during the thirties was fancy dress; the Saturday evening festivities were given a theme: a Victorian party, a French party with the house decorated as the Café des Ordures, a Salvation Army party. If such goings on seem a trifle childish nowadays then the fault may well lie with us; as Marge herself realized, "It is dreadfully kiddish but it takes the edge off the locals and permits one to wear anything one has about" (Letter to R. Meiggs, 08.07.1937). She was able to plan her leisure activities with a certain pragmatism, seeing the practical social advantages behind the playfulness.

The parties were not particularly large, usually about sixteen including host and hostess, and the core group of guests remained basically the same. Among others there would be Robert St. John Cooper, a successful journalist, who was an editor on the *Daily Express*, a close friend of Pip and Alan Gregory—"very much one of the 'circle'" (N. M. Gee, letter, 07.11.1983). His wife, Philippa (née Gee), was later to get a divorce and after some time to marry Grog; she was a competent artist, a graduate of the Slade. Leslie Cresswell was an older friend of the Regent Street Poly days. Having been invalided out of the Royal Engineers during the First World War, he became a technical artist for the Temple Press magazine *Motor* and "one of the finest artists in this field" (Anon. 1979). "Cressy," a tall gangling man with gray hair, seemed somewhat out of place at these festive frolics, but Marge valued

A Party in the Early 1930s
Standing, left to right: Bunny Wright, Alan Gregory, Marge, Ronnie Reid, a friend, Littley Wright. Sitting: Pip, Philip Allingham, Winnie Bristow (Maud Hughes' assistant). At front: Joyce Allingham.

Marge and Pip at "The Half-Nelson," the Carters' House Bar, in the 1930s

him as someone who was "easy to talk to" (Diary, 21.05.1934); in later years she was often to rely on him for companionship. Other quite frequent guests were Phillippa Gee's brother Bobby, a commercial photographer; a local farmer and sheep-breeder, Frank Girling, who was a friend of the artist Alfred Munnings; the Rushburys—Henry who was to become an R.A. and Keeper of the Royal Academy and his flirtatious wife Birdie; and two somewhat vague brothers, Bunny and Littley Wright, a banker and a journalist, "yobby little men but not so awful as many of their type" (Diary, 24.06.1934). From time to time Philip Allingham, who, in 1928, had finally given up all attempts to adapt to the constraints of conventionality, and had gone on the road as an itinerant salesman or grafter, would appear with one of his fairground friends. The parties served the function of enabling these hardworking professional people, who were slowly becoming successful, to let off steam for a while. The games they got up to appear schoolboyish but, in such a context, comprehensible. One of the guests recalls an evening when, "Bobby St. John Cooper arrived late, tight, and without a costume. He was stripped naked and this bearded figure was lowered through a trapdoor in the ceiling exclaiming, "Be still and know that I am God," whereupon the vicar swept his wife off in high dudgeon" (T. E. B. Clarke, letter, 21.01.1984).

A similar carefree spirit seems to have pervaded the annual cricket matches between a team made up of Pip's house guests and the local Chappel team. Marge saw the institution of village cricket as epitomizing "the very English secret of combining individualism with co-operative effort" (1941, 31), and the particular version which Pip instituted was a game to be taken with extreme seriousness, although it was to gain a playful context. One hot day one of the Carters' friends, Edward Terrell, Recorder of Newbury since 1935, arrived in a sunhat of his wife's. After an afternoon of mocking and joking, the hat was burned and the ashes put in a container, which was kept as a trophy at the winning side's pub from year to year until the end of the decade.

The nature of such activities reveals that they were not a central part of Marge's life, but rather a peripheral relaxation from the important business of writing and earning her living. The friends that mattered to her were those with whom she could talk rather than play, those who gave her either a testing ground for her own ideas or who were able to widen her horizons and share her own intellectual aspirations. During the Chappel years this role was played more by her father than by anyone else. Since the early twenties, he had shared a love of the theatre with Marge and had kept a constant watch upon her writing. Allingham's own work had been based on a very similar necessity to make money to support himself and his family—a task which he carried out with dedication, craftsmanship, and optimism: "I must cut down expenses. I am always saying that, I know. . . . Behold in me the Aged Optimist," he wrote to McFee (01.01.1928). In later life Marge revealed that: "In the depression period, when both my father and I were rather badly hit, we used to send twenty pounds back and forth to each other without any request or comment. If I needed it, the money would arrive. And if he required it, I would have such a violent impulse to send it to him that it was quite irresistible . . ." (1964, n.p.).

Herbert Allingham was a handsome man with a scholarly appearance, and he inspired warm affection in those who knew him well: "Doubtless God might have made a better person, but doubtless he never did," was the tribute of his lifelong friend Hearn (Letter to M. A., 10.04.1934). Once, however, Marge had emerged as a successful novelist, he must have realized that there was little more he could do for her professionally, although he continued to read her manuscripts and to comment critically upon them. Marge seemed to need his approval of what she was writing, and also to need the strength and determination that he radiated. The realization of his physical deterioration, and the spectacle of his dying was a catastrophe for Marge: "Feel disaster has overtaken me. One of the two supports of my world is going" (Diary, 03.01.1936).

During the two months of January and February 1931 Marge wrote ten film stories for her Aunt Maud and went through the anxieties attendant on the publication of *Look to the Lady*. More important, however, she completed her first straight detective story, *Police at the Funeral*, which was written in nine weeks flat. Hiding her excitement behind a facade of facetious solemnity, she wrote to Mary Leonard, "We are rather pleased with the new story . . . which is, we think, a distinct improvement on our earlier efforts, being less wild and more plausible as befits the dignity of our advancing years" (Letter, 01.03.1931).

No new novel was begun before the move to Chappel, which coincided with the commission to write her first thriller serial for *Answers*. That took Marge until March 1932, by which time she had begun *Death of a Ghost*, which, together with *Sweet Danger*, was to occupy her for the rest of the year. This attempt to write two very different novels side by side resulted from her interpretation of the poor sales of *Police at the Funeral* in America. To Mary Leonard she admitted that it seemed as though she had failed to "capture the higher-browed mystery fan" and had therefore decided that for the American market (which was more lucrative than the British) "the first thing for me to do is to write two

'Mystery Mile' stories immediately." Since *Death of a Ghost* was promised to her British publisher, Heinemann, for the fall, Marge wryly
remarked that "if Johnson gets the thriller in July, I shall be lucky (and
half dead)" (Letter, 01.04.1932). As it was, *Sweet Danger* was not finished until the end of the year and not published until March 1933,
leaving the remainder of that year to complete *Death of a Ghost*. There
was hardly any period throughout the thirties when Marge was not at
work on more than one project at the same time; the climax was reached
between January 1936 and December 1937, when she produced four
novels and twenty short stories. Was it irony or self-justification when,
the following spring, she talked of "work for its own sake" as "all there
really is of lasting comfort in life" (Letter to R. Meiggs, March 1938)?

In spite of this frenetic activity and increasing critical recognition,
Marge's entries in her diary often reveal traces of acute uncertainty and
doubt, culminating in the statement, "Sometimes I wonder why I do it
all," which leads automatically to the tortured self-questioning, "Where
am I going, what am I getting?" (Diary, 12.11.1934). At the heart of such
remarks is the feeling, reminiscent of the mid-twenties, "I'd like to live
a little" (Letter to R. Meiggs, March 1938). At the same time she was
aware that the responsibilities of providing for Pip and herself, plus
Grog and the servants, did not allow her to throw everything up and
do what she wanted. Behind Marge's frustration lay a contradiction of
which she seemed only partly aware. Her novels of the period portray
a number of successful professional women: a senior secretary, Miss
Curley in *Flowers for the Judge*, two actresses, Slippers Bellew, in *Dancers
in Mourning*, and Georgia Wells, in *The Fashion in Shrouds*, and a top
fashion designer, Val Ferris in *Shrouds*. However, the conception of the
position of such women in marriage tends to be extraordinarily conventional (Val, for example, is expected to give up her career and devote
herself to her husband, which she accepts without a moment's
thought). Admittedly Campion's future wife, Lady Amanda Fitton, is
an accomplished engineer, but, in *Shrouds*, she is still single. Linda
Sutane, in *Dancers*, who is a neglected wife, but devoted mother, self-
effacing, young, and gentle, is presented as Campion's ideal. Marge,
on the other hand, gives the impression of feeling that she had been
forced into the role of a forerunner of the actively employed woman of
our own times, devoted to her profession, earning sufficient money for
an entire household (which included two dependent men), and thus
occupying a position of traditional male power. Her problem lay in the
growing unwillingness with which she assumed this role, and in her
suspicions that the goals to which it led were—because they were out
of line with tradition—neither important, nor of necessity, desirable:

"Feel put upon but have uncomfortable feeling that it's my fault. Have either taken on more than I can chew or else am trying to do a he-woman's job and am trying to do it nicely and in a feminine fashion" (Diary, 5.5.34).

The awareness of her own femininity, and the attempt to live up to an ideal of womanhood that had little to do with the demands being made upon her, led to much of the frustration in Marge's life during the period. Nor was the other support of her life after her father, Pip, always particularly sustaining. Marge had very clear ideas of what marriage meant to her though she did not have any illusions. For her it had little to do with passion and sentiment: "The parties undertake to live under the same roof and by so doing they unavoidably constitute a home" (1936, n.p.); that which governed life "under the same roof" was not intellect or even rationality, but "manners, guts, the seven virtues and horse sense" (letter to R. Meiggs, 31.12.1936). Reality at Chappel looked somewhat different; time and again Marge records rows and fights with Pip. The subject was nearly always the same: "kid v. car really" (Diary, 01.06.1934). Such quarrels grew out of Pip's wanting to do or procure something very expensive, not at all necessary, and entirely for himself, as in the case of the car. Marge, who was very fond of children, realized from the first that Pip did not share her feelings; after one of their periodical rows, she wrote: "We ought to have some joint project. A kid? I'm afraid it's not in his line" (Diary, 23.01.1934). The local doctor, James Madden, who was a lifelong friend of the Carters from his arrival in the district at the end of 1934, has confirmed that it was Pip's refusal that ultimately stopped Marge from having children. Apart from Pip's opposition, it would probably have been highly impractical, at least during most of the thirties, to have added children to the household. Quite clearly, even with servants in the house, the traditional expectations of a mother's role (which Pip, among others, would have supported) would have been a hindrance to Marge's writing and thus to her ability to make money to maintain that style of life to which Pip was now accustomed. On the surface the picture emerges of a woman being prevented from fulfilling the function traditionally expected of her by society because of the selfishness of her husband and the pressures of professional life. One should, however, note that in spite of her fondness for children (at least during her last twenty years), Marge never articulated a personal wish for one of her own apart from the cryptic hints in her diary. It may have been that she used Pip and the demands of her work as rationalizations to excuse her own lack of desire. Maybe, too, she supplied Campion and Amanda with a son, and used children, teenagers, and young adults as major figures in *Hide My*

Eyes, The China Governess, and *The Mind Readers* to experience vicariously the cares and pleasures of parenthood. These can, however, only remain suspicions.

Pip had been cultivating a taste for the life of a country gentleman, riding, shooting, attending dinners and hunt balls and mixing with the county. These were activities which did not appeal to Marge, nor was she, after a long day's work, in any position to enjoy staying out to the early hours of the morning. Pip took no notice, and spent many a night in the company of others, arriving home shortly before Marge was ready to begin a new working day. Marge complained, "He doesn't (or won't or can't) see that he ought to behave a bit like a married man, since he makes me look so bloody cheap if he doesn't" (Diary 11.10.1934). In spite of differences and ructions, there seems to have been no diminution of Marge's fundamental happiness with Pip nor of their genuine affection for each other: "Very fond of the old boy. When the Colchester folk leave us alone and he doesn't catch their suburbanity, he's very nice, and anyway I do love him" (Diary 05.02.1934). The possible contradictions in her experience and the undemonstrative nature of their affection led Marge to attempt a more explicit account a few years later: "Carter and I really *love* each other. . . . It's bread and butter stuff. . . . It's unexciting but filling and makes one grow. It's not sick making or undignified or tragic or ugly ever and *can't* be. You only get it by giving it" (Notes to a letter from R. Meiggs, August 1938). Marge reveals here an infinite capacity for patience and a very sane understanding of the nature of change in human relationships. Whatever else Pip may have been, he enabled her to fulfil herself within the limits which she imposed.

On April 17, 1932, Herbert Allingham recorded in his diary the death of Dr. Salter. John Henry Salter had been a friend of the family's, and particularly of Marge's mother, since their Layer Breton days. Born in 1841, he had studied medicine at King's College Hospital London and taken up his first practice in the Essex village of Tolleshunt D'Arcy at the age of twenty-three in October 1864. He had never left. Dr. Salter was a man of many parts and a more than local celebrity. As a breeder of retrievers he had become a judge of dogs with a worldwide reputation, which had taken him as far as Russia, where he was the guest of the Czar and a friend of the Grand Duke Nicholas. He was a famed rosegrower and judge for the Royal Horticultural Society, a dead shot, a fine boxer, and a good horseman (Day 1974, 476–78). Marge had known the "Old Doc" all her life, accompanying her mother on regular visits to D'Arcy House, his Georgian residence in the center of the

Dr. John Henry Salter, the Previous Owner of D'Arcy House

village. Emmy Allingham was obsessed with Salter, the typical elderly, virile, Victorian male, conscious of being attractive to members of the opposite sex; she was convinced that she meant more to him than anyone else, and that when he died he would leave her his house and garden. Mrs. Allingham's hopes were founded on the sand of her own deluded estimation of their friendship. After Salter's death she wrote a lightly fictionalized account of visiting his grave in which she says: "For twenty-five years he had been the ruling factor in her life—her husband was part of herself, but did not come into the picture at all. . . . The attributes the Doctor stood for her husband ridiculed" (Unpublished ms.).

When Salter died and did not fulfil what Em understood as his part of the bargain, she had a severe nervous breakdown and spent May and June 1932 in a nerve hospital in Northampton. After her recovery, Em still had difficulty in understanding how Dr. Salter could have forgotten what she felt to have been his promise to her; this provoked her to write to Herbert, "The more I see of men the more I approve of women taking a hand in the affairs of the country" (Letter, June 1932). Fate proved to be partially on her side; in July 1934 Dr. James, one of Salter's executors and the inheritor of D'Arcy House, was killed in a motoring accident together with his wife, and the house was put on the market. After much discussion and weighing of the pros and cons, which lasted from early September until mid-November, the Carters, with the financial support of Marge's parents and Pip's mother, finally bought D'Arcy House for just over one thousand pounds.

The origins of the village of Tolleshunt D'Arcy go back to pre-Conquest days; in 1000 A.D. it was called Tollesfuntan, in Domesday Book it appears as Tolesfunte. The land was held until the fifteenth century by the Tergoz family and then, in 1441, a certain Robert Darcy of Norman origin obtained the land (Ekwall 1960). In 1931 the population of the village, pleasantly situated on an eminence near the estuary of the Blackwater, was 748. D'Arcy House is as rambling as Viaduct Farm House, with an imposing red brick Georgian facade looking out on the village maypole at the junction of the routes to Tiptree, Maldon, Tollesbury, and Colchester. The interior accommodation—virtually unchanged during the fifty years from the Carters' purchase until its sale (in 1985) by Marge's sister, Joyce—extends over three floors, with an elegant dining and sitting room, cosy breakfast room and kitchens on the ground floor, an immense landing across the entire length of the house at the rear of the first floor, which Pip, Grog, and Marge used as a studio, and several good-sized bedrooms in the front; on the third floor are a number of smaller rooms for servants or guests. Undoubtedly the great attraction of the house must have been the vast well-stocked and lovingly cared-for garden with lawns, trees, shrubs, bushes, roses, an immense variety of flowers, and a central avenue of the famed D'Arcy Spice apple trees, to say nothing of a huge meadow next to house and garden, and a paddock across the road from the front door. It was a terribly tempting but also terribly daunting prospect; not only was there the actual purchase price to consider but the potentially high running costs—and all for a household with only one regular breadwinner. Nevertheless, as Marge wrote to Mary Leonard: "The family is more excited I find when the financial ice is thin. It's like old times and the excitement of being alive all returns" (Letter, March 1935).

The party which moved to D'Arcy some time in May 1935 consisted of Marge and Pip, Grog, the housemaid Christina Carter (who had come to Marge in 1934 and is still at D'Arcy), and Mary Orr, "Cooee," who had returned from a brief career on the stage to help Marge when servant problems became acute at Chappel. Another period of Marge's life was ending, although at that time it could not be seen with the clarity of hindsight that provoked her friend to write of the move from Chappel: "I rather think we were all happier there than at D'Arcy . . . we were certainly younger and just lived joyously for each day . . . it couldn't stay like that, but . . . we left something of our youth there and it was never quite the same as we all grew up" (Letter from M. Brown, 08.12.1985).

Death of a Ghost had been published during the last year at Chappel, and had done much to establish Marge's reputation. The book had sold well and had had first-class reviews: "One of the best detective stories of today, written by a master of the craft" (*Sunday Chronicle*, 04.03.1934). In the spring of 1934, Marge could report that "Heinemanns have been pleased and my past sales have been equalized already. . . . So we all feel very pleased with life" (Letter to Malcolm Johnson, March 1934). She had already started a new serial for *Answers*, "Rogue's Holiday," which was finished early in July. Film stories occupied most of the rest of the year apart from the short story "Publicity," which was sold to the *News Chronicle* in November. Some time around Christmas, Marge got the idea for a new set of three novels to be centered on various professions, which would allow her to comment on various aspects of modern society. Feeling that the professional world she knew best was probably the world of publishing, she decided to start there. From the beginning the title was fixed; she wrote in her diary, "Started Flowers for the Judge. . . . Very pleased with story, have a hunch it's going to be good" (17.01.1935). The confidence lasted; two months later she wrote to Mary

D'Arcy House, Tolleshunt D'Arcy

Leonard that she was pleased with the way the book was developing, "It's a better *detective* story than I usually get" (March 1935). A month later she was reading the first thirty thousand words to her father, before sending the manuscript to Malcolm Johnson at Doubleday's.

The book was probably finished towards the end of the summer of 1935, before Marge began her third and last serial for *Answers*. In sending the manuscript to Johnson, she reacted sharply to his earlier criticism, which she felt was directed at tailoring the book too carefully for the Crime Club market: "This story I've sent you is a novel not a thriller. . . . I would like to say here and now that under Margery Allingham I shall write the sort of book I believe in and no other. Maxwell March is a first class hack. Margery Allingham thinks of her reputation" (Letter to M. Leonard, n.d.) The asperity is indicative of Marge's understanding of her own work; she had abandoned thrillers with *Sweet Danger*, and the classic detective story with *Death of a Ghost*, from now on she was a novelist who happened to write about crime. Her uncle, Edward Wood, was not far off the mark when he wrote to Marge after reading *Flowers:* "I can see you at the fork of two roads. Are you going to leave the detective thriller and concentrate on the brilliant writing?" (Letter, 04.03.1936). Now that the hack work of film stories and *Answers* serials was coming to an end ("Shadow in the House," the final "Maxwell March," was finished in March 1936), there was no doubt in Marge's mind as to the aims she had set herself: "Fiction is my art, my profession" (Letter to R. Meiggs, n.d.).

Herbert Allingham died on January 10, 1936 after a short illness during which the tension between Marge and her mother became almost unbearable, "Emmie talking of her own extraordinary virtue and my sinfulness all . . . the time" (Diary, 09.01.1936). Mrs. Allingham was to shift from bad-tempered vindictiveness to religious fervor throughout these days, and Marge lived in horror of the prospect of her mother wanting to come and live at D'Arcy—a fate she managed to avert. Marge was by no means the only one to mourn the loss of her father; G. R. M. Hearn, who had remarked shortly before his death, "I shall never know or like a man again like I do him" (Letter, 02.01.1936), now wrote, "I do not think there will be a day of my life when I shall not remember him. I loved him very much and always shall" (Letter, 13.01.1936). Looking back on Allingham's death almost two years later, William McFee commented: "Since the old man died, Marge, I have missed his letters so much. For so many years he and I corresponded and it left a terrible gap in my life. . . . So you must take his place" (Letter,

31.12.1937). Marge felt the gap acutely and was to fill it first with work, and later with new friendships, which would supply something of the guidance she had always expected and received from her father.

The year 1936 was one of immense creative productivity for Marge. For most of it, she amused herself with one of the least successful of her novels, *The Case of the Late Pig*, which, she told Frank Swinnerton, had been written "really to recover me from my father's sudden death and grim little funeral. . . . There is nothing I find so comforting as a thundering piece of bad taste enjoyed in secret" (Letter, 01.01.1938). Not perhaps a very positive judgment of the novel, but an apt one. Of greater immediate satisfaction was Marge's discovery of a new source of income, which also implied quality: the *Strand* magazine under the editorship of the remarkable Reeves Shaw—"he taught me about as much as my father had done" (1965, 10). Marge wrote six *Strand* stories in 1936, as well as two for the *Evening News*, and two for the *Standard*. She was no longer earning money as a hack, but as the sought-after writer of quality short crime stories, even if they were written with a main eye on the financial reward. However, this form of success brought problems of its own, which Marge summarized: "The whole thing is complicated by my work improving and me suddenly getting paid for quality instead of quantity. At Chappel I could dictate a 7,000 word film story to Grog from a sick bed with a temperature of 102, but I can't do a *Strand* story like that" (Letter to R. Meiggs, March 1938). However true that may have been, the sheer quantity of Marge's output for the year is still amazing, particularly when one considers that in December 1936 she was to begin her most ambitious novel to date, *Dancers in Mourning*.

Work on the new novel went at the same breakneck pace with which she had written *Police at the Funeral* six years earlier; by January 5, 1937 Marge had completed 63,000 words and in anticipation, Pip was already designing the jacket; another 17,000 words were written in the following nine days and by January 23, she was rewriting the last chapter. Marge was very confident about the book, "Bloody good story though I say it. *I like it.* Whoever doesn't is barmy" (Diary, 23.01.1937). The following day it was finished: "Dictated the whole of the last portion of the book to Grog. Up till 1.30 a.m. Quite an emotional finish. Like old times again. We're *very* sanguine" (Diary, 24.01.1937). Fortunately this confidence was shared by Dwye Evans of Heinemann, who was enthusiastic. By the beginning of April the book was in the proof stage: "Heinemann are purring over me which is a mercy." Of the book she wrote, "I think it's all right. It's more of a book and less of a simple tale than my previous efforts" (Letter to R. Meiggs, 01.04.1937). Marge sent a copy to a new friend, the novelist and critic Frank Swinnerton, whom she had met the year before when he had invited her to a dinner to meet (among others) the crime writers H. C. Bailey, E. C. Bentley, and Freeman Wills Crofts. She was clearly still somewhat overawed by her first contact with the "real" literary world and added a somewhat mawkish postscript to her brief covering note: "Don't think I'm asking for a review (I know you don't touch thrillers anyway). This is a personal thing because I think you or Mrs. Swinnerton might be entertained by it. . . . Thrillers are for fun anyway—to read, I mean—aren't they?" (Letter, 29.05.1937).

It is perfectly clear that Marge did not think of *Dancers* either as a thriller or just as fun, but her respect for the literary establishment seems to have got the better of her. Swinnerton's response was most gratifying; he acknowledged receipt of the book with the phrase, "You are now my favourite author" (31.05.1937), and when he had read it, wrote a two-page letter in his minute script praising *Dancers*. He singled out the "felicity of the writing" for special mention, explaining, "one never knows what the next page, or paragraph, or sentence may hold in . . . surprise or bland essential communication. I call this Writing" (Letter, 05.06.1937). Marge was delighted and hastened to express her thanks: "To say thank you for your letter is not enough. It is worth writing a book for your appreciation alone. I never felt quite sure if the infuriating pains I put myself to in order to say exactly what I mean (rather than 'almost') were really worth while. But I do feel they are now since you notice and like the results" (Letter, 08.06.1937).

The friendship with Swinnerton continued for the next four years; he was the first in a series of older male correspondents who belonged to various branches of the cultural establishment—authors, clergymen, university teachers. In seeking out and enjoying contact with such men, Marge appeared not only to be replacing her father with more expert advisers, but also compensating for her own lack of higher education by claiming a form of intellectual equality with those who had enjoyed it. Marge sent Swinnerton her books and he remained an admiring reader, although they never seem to have met again. His approval and constructive criticism continued to mean a great deal to her.

Marge produced her own rough sketch for the blurb of the new novel, the central portion of which read: "It has been evident for some time that Miss Allingham has been creeping into that province sacred to the straight novelist. In this her last book she has fulfilled that promise." The critics seemed to get the message; they echoed Swinnerton's praise in a most satisfying manner, which reached its climax in the words of the *Evening Standard's* reviewer, "I place Margery Allingham among the first six present-day novelists" (Hoskins 1938); high—if exaggerated—praise indeed.

Although the period between the completion of *Dancers* and its publication was dogged by money worries—only a month after sending the manuscript to Heinemann Marge had written in her diary, "Oh dear God, give me a bit of luck soon" (24.02.1937)—by late summer she could bask in the general aura of success which the Carters and their friends felt was theirs. "Success," as one of them remembered, "was very much in the air," and it seemed as if, after years of hard work and privation things were opening up for young professionals—"She and they were all 'doing well' and becoming names" (N. M. Gee, letter, 12.01.1984). One outward sign of this was the request Marge received at the end of the year from the editor of *Time and Tide* to write occasional book reviews, a task which she accepted, for, as she wrote to Swinnerton, "I thought (and think) it is an honour and because it was pointed out to me that it was time I read something else besides a few favourite authors." It was probably Pip who did the pointing out, since, if Marge's diary is to be believed, it was his idea that she should take on the reviewing job. Nor was he so wrong for, as Marge admitted to Swinnerton, "I was brought up on Dumas and Shakespeare (a rum mixture but very stimulating) and they have ceased to be authors so much as gospellers" (Letter, 13.07.1938). *Time and Tide* had been founded in 1920 by Lady Rhondda (Margaret Thomas), who later in the decade became editor. Originally the magazine had been left wing and determinedly femininist (Lejeune 1984, 65–66), and was, at the time Marge became associated with it, at the height of its influence, offering a platform to a number of distinguished writers and critics. She was to write regular reviews of new novels for *Time and Tide* from February 1938 to August 1944.

Towards the end of August 1937, Marge began to struggle with a new novel, but found it unexpectedly difficult to concentrate on work; she described herself as being "in a funny mental state. Getting to dislike myself as a responsibility" (Diary, 26.08.1937), and became irritated with her "pottering instead of working" (27.08.1937). However she got down to the book by September, and the absence of diary entries for the next three months seems to indicate that she was writing busily. Then on November 12 she notes: "Having great difficulty with Shrouds. Am in one of those moods when I wonder if it's worth writing or if I ought to take up washing as a profession. Sometimes I feel it may be all right and at other times that it's just dead and bloody" (Diary, 12.11.1937). Marge's problems were partly due to the dissatisfaction she was feeling with Malcolm Johnson's reactions to her work; she thought that Johnson, and to some extent Mary Leonard, who, having left Doubleday's, was now Marge's American agent, were both trying to force her work into the wrong mold. She wrote to Winifred Nerney, Mary Leonard's successor at Doubleday's London office, that the new novel, *The Fashion in Shrouds*, was "very good indeed *of its type* and left alone it will find a public but if they muck it about it will be an inferior Police at the Funeral" (Letter, 07.11.1937). Further interruptions were caused by having to take time off from the novel to write more stories for *Strand*. Nevertheless, by early March 1938, 60,000 words had been written, and from then on it seemed plain sailing. The ten last chapters were written in just under a month, forcing from Marge such comments as, "Feel resentful in my heart. Want to live," "Ploughing fiercely on," or "In the last lap. Feel I'm conking out. Slugging on." Finally on April 5 she dictated for twelve solid hours to Grog, and the finished manuscript was sent to Heinemann four days later. The sustained effort was not in vain: *The Fashion in Shrouds* was a great success with the critics and produced the oft-quoted remark by the *Observer*'s reviewer: "To Albert Campion has fallen the honour of being the first detective to figure in a story which is also, even when judged by the fixed stars of criticism, a distinguished novel" ("Torquemada" 1938).

In May 1934, Marge had written in her diary "Meiggs . . . can't come to the match but proposes to visit us in September" (23.05.1934). This was Russell Meiggs, who brought to her something of the world of disinterested intellectual investigation. Throughout the thirties, Marge had gradually assimilated perspectives on the world, of which she had previously been unaware. Increased contact with young professional men and women confronted her with the material goals which success could imply; acquaintanceship with the established world of letters through Frank Swinnerton had increased the attraction of a literary reputation; as far as was possible, she was reading more widely than before, and her reviewing activity in the final years of the decade made her more aware of developments in the novel. However, systematic intellectual investigation on the basis of accumulated knowledge was totally unknown to her. She had once thought a university education desirable, and at times still felt her lack of an academic higher education intensely. Meiggs, two years older than Marge, had been head of Pip's house at Christ's Hospital before going on to Keble College, Oxford. When Marge first met him—Pip had invited him to Chappel to play cricket—

he was a fellow of his college, a good-looking young man with a thick shock of hair, an engaging manner, and a knack of making himself attractive to intelligent women: "You . . . go through life in a rather affable charming fashion, promising people (women I mean) much more than you are prepared to give them. I don't think you realize you're doing it . . . but you have a diabolical knack of guessing what they want and presenting yourself as the embodiment of that one particular need" (Letter, October 1938). What Marge needed, what she longed for, was intellectual companionship, a person with whom she could discuss ideas which were forming in her head upon subjects she could not share with anyone close to her, and particularly not with Pip.

From December 1936 to mid-1939, Meiggs and Marge corresponded more often and more regularly than they actually met. Marge's letters are among the most intimate she was ever to write, even though almost all of them are concerned with religious matters. The period following her father's death had seen her beginning to order and formulate her thoughts on subjects, such as the existence of God and human beings' relation to Him, which she could not possibly share with the cynical, extrovert Pip or with any other of her immediate friends. Meiggs was just the person Marge needed at the time. Not only did she find him "the least academic person that I ever met" (Letter, 01.01.1938), a patient, understanding, and helpful listener, but his intensity and his very physical presence attracted her. Marge was still comparatively inexperienced emotionally; since her youthful romance with Reggie Goode at the age of twenty-one, she had spent over a decade virtually chained to her work, with little opportunity to expand her knowledge of people except as entertaining interruptions at weekend parties. During Easter weekend 1938, Meiggs was a house guest at D'Arcy; Marge noted: "Long walk to the sea, was just a tiny bit bored (I'm balmy). Turns out to be more usual than I thought. Interesting facade. Very young. Highly relieved" (Diary, 16.04.1938). Marge's relief was that she had discovered Meiggs's normality—though a man with an acute intelligence, he was just another man. A later letter makes it clear that the Easter visit was the first Meiggs had made to D'Arcy under normal circumstances rather than for a party or a cricket match. She goes on to suggest that there was a time in their relationship when her feelings had been involved:

> An infatuation which springs up at first sight and is nurtured at three or four year or tri-yearly party meetings in an atmosphere of moonlight and alcohol and which dies happily and comfortably . . . at the first ordinary normal encounter as at Easter

. . . is one of those dear little corpses which should be allowed to lie . . . along with the other delightful and silly little emotional experiences of life. (Letter, 12.08.1938)

Soon after this, war broke out, and the correspondence between the two became less regular, until it came more or less to an end with Meiggs's marriage in 1941, and Marge's critical portrayal of him in *Traitor's Purse*. The existing letters are important, not for their revelation of a minor emotional affair in Marge's life, but for the lengthy expression of her own idiosyncratic religious beliefs.

In spite of being put forward in letters which sometimes run to more than twenty pages, Marge's ideas are by no means lucid, nor are they always consistent. She was clearly conscious of their imperfections and insisted: "Although I know very little, I do know *all* I know first hand. I have had to try out the few virtues I possess to see if they were virtues and not affectations" (Letter, 01.01.1938). Furthermore, as she admitted, "In common with most of my generation I would blush to call myself deeply religious" (1941, 15). What emerges, after these reservations are made is a theory of the existence of God and of human nature in relation to God, which is based in part on Marge's conviction, "that Christianity . . . is essentially an *intellectual* idea. . . . It is so simple yet so dependent on reason" (Draft of letter to F. W. Crofts, November 1937). Marge started from an assurance of the existence of God, but God as "it" rather than "He"—a force rather than a person. This led to her conviction that God is "a moving pattern of causes and effects, warnings and fulfilments, rewards and encouragements, all working together" (Letter, December 1937). Essential to her conception is the idea of God and human beings being part of the same pattern. She insisted that she came to this belief as the result of reviewing her own experience of life, and trying to account for coincidences, warnings, and rewards. She described the realization that they could all be accounted for by her pattern theory as having come to her as a shock of recognition, "If you haven't had this experience it is quite indescribable" (Letter, 01.01.1938). This conception of an underlying structure beneath the apparently chaotic surface of life is a very literary form of belief, characteristic of someone whose writing is concerned with the concealment and revelation of structural relationships.

Her theory led her to reject the idea of a personal soul and she found comfort in a belief that human beings are composed of millions of mortal elements, which, after death, can recombine and even reproduce themselves. In all this there is a strange combination of naiveté and quasi-mystical insight; Marge herself felt that she was not expressing anything unorthodox and was hurt when Meiggs suggested that she was: "I have always felt that that was the one thing I was not" (Letter, 01.01.1938). Realizing that in attempting to put down her religious philosophy on paper, she had probably only succeeded in making it all sound far too complicated, she wrote: "What it all boils down to is this: If you are a 'good child' you will find sooner or later that there is a design in your life" (Letter, 01.01.1938). Marge's ideas on these matters never substantially changed in later years; the beliefs of the woman of thirty-four had—like everything else in her life—been worked out painstakingly and Meiggs was used as a sort of corrective sounding board. It is striking that none of these ideas enter into her fiction explicitly until the early fifties, where they are partially embodied in the figure of Canon Avril in *The Tiger in the Smoke*. For the time being, they were for private consumption and in this role were to sustain her through the difficult war years.

By the spring of 1938, most of Marge's financial worries had disappeared: she was being paid well for her *Strand* stories, money was flowing from America, and the prospects for a continuation of the status quo were good. This did not keep her from jokingly complaining to Meiggs that, "running an outfit like this by means of the pen and brush is comparable with juggling with 500lb weights—it requires prayerful concentration at times." She also touched on the competitive pulls of her career and her household with the remark: "It's this trying to build up a sincere reputation and yet keep the circus going . . . I do want to do the two if I can" (Letter, 07.03.1938).

The business of keeping "the circus going" was, however, soon to be taken out of her hands, or rather the time was approaching when there would be no circus left. Only a week later, Dr. Madden came to call, and in the course of the evening talked about war. Rumours and speculations were rife in Tolleshunt D'Arcy, as everywhere else in Britain, throughout the year. In the middle of summer, Marge, Pip, Grog, Cooee, and some of the locals were chatting together when someone mentioned the Czechoslovakian crisis: "Out in the yard that evening my own immediate reaction to the sudden thought of war was much the same, I suppose, as most of the others'. . . . War simply meant death to me" (1941, 20–21). Nevertheless, the traditional August cricket party took place with the usual Saturday night fancy-dress party. The motto this year was "Spy Night at the Embassy," and Alan Gregory had decorated the house with life-size cardboard figures of flunkeys armed with machine guns and other ominous weapons in keeping with the times. On the Monday there was cricket against Chappel, with lunch on the stone-flagged terrace next to the conservatory. Three months later Marge wrote to William McFee in Connecticut: "Under present arrangements, within two hours of a breakdown in negotiations, this house will automatically become a temporary sanatorium for doubtful looking refugees, the main A.R.P. post for eight miles and a temporary decontamination station. . . . Life makes fiction rather milk-and-watery" (10.11.1938).

6

The Sanctity of Sudden Death

In an age when all the deepest emotions can be successfully laughed out of existence by any decently educated person, the sanctity and importance of sudden death was a comforting and salutary thing, a last little rock, as it were, in the shifty sands of one's own standards and desires.

Margery Allingham

The five major Allingham novels of the thirties are all variations on the structural pattern of the classic detective story: a murder is committed and only a limited number of people, in four of the five books basically one household, can be suspected of being the murderer. True to Marge's established psychology of murder, the killer is always a person who stands outside or apart from the group in his fixed belief that he is equally outside the constraints of accepted law and morality. There, however, the similarity ends. Within the strict limitations of the detective story formula, Marge exploited the potentialities of variation to the utmost. In one novel the murderer is dead before the narrative begins, yet two further violent deaths occur. In two other books, Campion has to offer himself as bait in order to force the murderer to reveal himself, while in another novel the murderer is also Campion's client. In yet another work Campion (and the reader) is mistaken as to the identity of the villain until two pages before the end. There is also a novel in which Campion already knows the identity of the murderer halfway through the book, sharing with the reader the attempt to assemble the necessary evidence for an arrest. Throughout the decade, Marge systematically probed the resources of the detective story in her effort to relate the form to her experience of the contemporary world. As she wrote to Frank Swinnerton: "I do like the detective story formula. It's a definite shape to fill and I can get the proportions right if I have its rigid lines to go on. I get a little sick of murder but I think it's worth it" (Letter, 13.07.1938).

The term "serious" or "straight" detective story has been used so often in previous chapters, that I feel bound to attempt to define this loose term before dealing with the books to which it applies. In the first place it is used to set Margery Allingham's major novels of the thirties apart from the preceeding thrillers. Further, the "straight" detective story indicates an attempt to adher to traditional formulae and patterns. "Serious," on the other hand, signals a change of mood both in the story and in the protagonist, Albert Campion, as investigator. Gone is the idealized rural setting; gone, too, the master criminal and the struggle between the amateur forces of good and organized crime; gone, last of all, the fairy-tale adventurer with the Wodehousean appearance and patter. The detective story formula implies an individualized conflict between opposing skills and intelligences. In place of an inventive free-for-all, as in, say, *Look to the Lady*, Marge willingly accepted the tried formula ("the box") of the established detective story; *Police at the Funeral* and *Death of a Ghost* were consciously "an attempt at the straight murder mystery, the tale cut to fit the box" (1963, 11).

In the adventure thrillers, plot and action took clear precedence over characterization; the serious detective novels reversed the priorities. The consistency of the reviewers' recognition of this is noteworthy; *Police at the Funeral* was praised for the author's "genius for characterization," to which one critic added the explanation that the author was "interested in her characters as human beings, not as mere adjuncts to some murders" (Anon. 1931). Similarly, several reviewers of *Death of a Ghost* agreed with James Agate's assessment of Allingham as having "a very considerable gift for characterization" (Agate, 1934). It is significant that Marge herself endorsed this approach to her books; for her, character rather than plot was the key to fiction—and that is the basic development in her writing between 1929 and 1931. As she remarked during a talk she gave at a Foyle's Literary Luncheon in 1938: "I've never had a plot yet that didn't arise out of a character. . . . Without a character a story doesn't exist as far as I'm concerned. It doesn't seem to mean anything" (1938a, n.p.). The emphasis on characterization at this stage in Marge's career was an integral part of the turn to serious detective fiction. In an unpublished and undated article, "On the Writing of Dialogue in Detective and Mystery Fiction," she commented: "It is a fact that most readers of mystery stories read for plot but are held by and afterwards remember a tale for the characters in it." In other words, her much-praised gift for characterization was a valuable asset which was developed with a certain pragmatism.

The first ideas for a title suggest how seriously Marge took *Police at the Funeral*. Her notes include such suggestions as "Murder in the House," to which is appended the comment "gruesome?", or "Here's Mystery" (which was the title for some time), to which was added the query "Cheap?" She was clearly concerned to set this book apart from the adventure thrillers without in any way suggesting that it could be less exciting or less rewarding to read. With this perhaps in mind, she lets Campion consider how "active adventure, however strenuous, was apt to be less harrowing than taking part in this slow nemesis" (1931a, 136).

The novel's chief setting is the gloomy old house of Socrates Close in Cambridge, the home of the widow and three middle-aged children of Doctor John Faraday, late Master of the fictitious Ignatius College. The house itself is a very real presence throughout the novel, contrasting solid Victorian affluence and moral worth to the horrors of modern day murder; it becomes a symbol of the fear and helplessness which violent crime induces in respectable, law-abiding society. When the shocks and excitements are at their height, Campion receives "a fleeting impression of the house as some sick, many-petticoated creature crouching frightened in the unrelenting darkness" (129).

Although the mechanics of the crime are extremely ingenious—suicide appears to be murder and murder suicide—it is, as Marge clearly intended, memorable for its characters. A particularly well-drawn figure is Great-Aunt Caroline Faraday, who, like most of the characters, is brought alive more by her speech than by authorial description—a feature of Marge's fiction which she was to develop throughout the decade. Old Mrs. Faraday is fixed in the reader's mind by such remarks as, "I am past the age when it is proper for one to preserve the decencies by deceiving oneself" (67), or by her instructions to Campion: "You will attempt to find out who is responsible for these outrages, although I am not insulting you by suggesting that you behave like a policeman" (68). It is part of Marge's narrative strategy to present Mrs. Faraday as a highly intelligent woman who belongs to a former age and to whom events such as murder, police investigation, and journalistic curiosity are not only anathema, but belong in roughly the same category as smoking in the drawing room, indulging in early morning tea, or a lack of manners.

From the moment that Mrs. Faraday's son, William, is introduced into the story, it is quite clear he is to play an important role; he is a complete "personality" from his first entry: "Mr. William Faraday was a shortish, tubby individual . . . of about fifty-five, with a pink face, bright greedy little blue eyes, yellowish-white hair, and a moustache worn very much in the military fashion, without quite achieving the effect so obviously intended. His hands were pudgy, and his feet, in their square-toed glacé shoes, somehow enhanced the smug personality of their owner" (45). As in the case of his mother, William's dialogue contributes to the definition of his character and position in the novel: choleric, bombastic, socially impotent, and largely irrelevant. This is well illustrated in the scene when the unsavoury Cousin George invades the house: "Coming here, behaving like a—like a drunken anarchist in a house of sorrow. . . . If it hadn't been for Mother I'd have taken a dog-whip to the fellow, old as I am. Yes, I shall go for the police. I'd like to see that fellow taken out of here in handcuffs. . . . Yes, well, I've made up my mind. I'm going" (205). Two touches—the slight pause, indicative of the speaker's uncertainty, before the characterization of George as an anarchist, and the repetition of the formula "Yes, I . . . ," inviting contradiction and thus offering an escape from action—suffice to convey an analytical portrait of the man.

William shares with Campion a number of significant moments, taking on (as in *Dancers in Mourning*) the role of companion-confidant. As an element of Marge's discourse, he supplies the informational frame within which the plot unrolls. William comments on the discovery of the body of his cousin, Andrew Seeley, who, though apparently murdered, committed suicide after having left various death traps around the house for his relatives, "Extraordinarily typical of Andrew . . . that he couldn't even leave this world without making a lot of bother for us all" (46). The full irony of this remark can only be appreciated once the reader is in possession of the solution to the mystery, a point which is made explicit when William says to Campion at the conclusion, "I was right all along. . . . D'you remember what I said to you the first time I saw you?" (246). A remark which compels the reader to return to the earlier page, thus completing the frame.

On numerous occasions in *Police at the Funeral*, Campion's representative normality is insisted upon; at one point he is told, "I was afraid you were going to be one of those clever people one reads about who know everything from the beginning" (110), and it is Campion himself who points out that "deduction is only adding two and two together" (105). In fact all the necessary clues are available to the reader by the end of the ninth of twenty-five chapters, in the form of continual references to the personality of Andrew Seeley. Even though characterizations of the dead man as a beast or devil may not necessarily lead the reader straight to the solution, Campion's examination of Seeley's room leaves little in doubt. It contains a collection of signs which point to Seeley's mental derangement: pornographic books, a library of books on sexual psychology, deliberate attempts to give the impression that he is kept in poverty, perverse statues, and, as a final hint both to Campion and the reader, a photograph of Campion's uncle with a forged dedication.

Inspector Oates's final verdict on the case, "They seemed such nice people" (252) indicates a line of continuity from the earlier novels: the contrast between outer appearance and the omnipresence of evil. This continuity may have led the *Sunday Times* reviewer to call *Police at the Funeral* "one of the most satisfying thrillers of the year"—satisfying because "the writing is good" (Straus 1931). Marge was pleased to be reviewed in one of the "better" papers, and reported that as a result "Heinemann have decided that I am to try a novel." She also revealed that what she had attempted in *Police at the Funeral,* and what she was continuing to experiment with in the new book, *Death of a Ghost,* was "realistic writing, reserving only the murder plot as a sort of balancing pole until I get really steady" (Letter to W. McFee, 31.01.1932). Sudden death also functions as a way of refocussing attention on human nature and society; as Marcus Featherstone says to Campion, "It makes you see life from an entirely different angle somehow, doesn't it?" (76).

Towards the end of January 1932, Marge read the opening fifteen hundred words of her new novel, *Death of a Ghost,* to her father, who found it "very promising" (HJA Diary, 22.01.1932). Two days later, she wrote to Mary Leonard:

> Unfortunately I am not getting on very fast. . . . At the moment we have three old friends, a strange dog and a three month old baby in the house, Mother in the offing, more relatives over the way, and a host of callers . . . to say nothing of my regular ten thousand words a week. However, the tale promises well and should turn out—unless something untoward happens—to be a yarn of the Police at the Funeral type, but with more attractive characters and a more colourful and romantic atmosphere. (Letter, 23.01.1932)

We should remind ourselves that throughout the following year, 1933, Marge was working on *Death of a Ghost* parallel to *Sweet Danger* (published March 1933). Nevertheless, in a letter to her father, probably written in early December 1933, she said that the "novel should be with Evans in a day or so" and mentioned that she was feeling anxious about it, "but I feel obstinately pleased with it as a job of work. If they don't like it they're barmy. That's my private opinion." She need not have worried; at the beginning of January 1934, Malcolm Johnson acknowledged receipt of the novel with the words: "When Watt sent me the manuscript, they added in a postscript that Heinemann's were delighted with the book, and I hasten to associate myself with that opinion. I think it is by far the best book you have done" (Letter, 02.01.1934). Marge herself read through the corrected manuscript a few days later and noted, "A queer, progressive tale with an accumulative effect" (Diary, 23.01.1934).

Death of a Ghost is dedicated "to H. J. Allingham by his industrious apprentice"—a public acknowledgment of the debt Marge felt she owed her father and, perhaps, a private gesture to herself that this was to be the book which would mark the final establishment of her independence. Be that as it may, the essential focus of the novel is private from the outset. On the opening page we read: "The assassination of another by any person of reasonable caution must, in a civilized world, tend to be a private affair" (1934, 11). This remark contains two important, though obvious, assumptions: that the murderer is man of "reasonable caution," and that the world in which he lives really is civilized. Marge leaves readers to draw their own conclusions about the latter proposition, but the main focus of the novel is on the personality of the murderer. The foundation conflict is not that of the insane assassin versus civilized society, but a very private one: the intelligent investigator against the ingenious murderer, whose strategy is "an essay in the second degree of subtlety" (108). That which distinguishes *Death of a Ghost* from Marge's other novels of the period is that just over halfway through the novel the murderer's identity is known to Campion and revealed to the reader: "Mr. Campion knew that Max Fustian had killed Mrs. Potter as soon as he saw him that evening" (145).

Death of a Ghost revolves around the paintings of the late John Lafcadio, who designed to keep his talent before the public eye after his decease by ordering in his will that beginning five years after his death twelve sealed pictures should be exhibited annually and sold by his agent. Unfortunately, the agent died before the first show, so that Max Fustian, the new owner of the Salmon Gallery, has taken charge of the Lafcadio heritage. The murders that take place result from Fustian's instigation of the forgery of two pictures by a talented young artist (the first victim) using a former model of the famous painter's (the second victim). Fustian—in an early list of characters drawn up by Pip in one of Marge's notebooks he appears under the highly suspicious name of Maximilian Fuerstheimer—is convinced of his safety, his importance, and his power. The premature revelation of the murderer's identity means that the reader has to be assisted to arrive at and endorse the same conclusion as Campion, and then still be able to share in the suspense leading up to the final arrest. The key to the success of this endeavour lies in the presentation of Max Fustian.

For the experienced reader of Allingham's fiction, Fustian is a suspicious character from his very first appearance: "Max Fustian surged into the house, not crudely or noisily, but irresistibly, and with the same conscious power with which a successful actor-manager makes his appearance in the first act of a new play. They heard his voice, deep, drawling, impossibly affected, from the doorway" (28). The verb "surge," the adverb "irresistibly," the phrase "conscious power," and the comparison to the "successful actor-manager"—he who is both performer and director—all combine to characterize Max as the potential megalomaniac familiar from earlier novels. These informational hints are amplified by two scenes which present the reader with clear indications of Max's role in the novel. The first comes after the murder of young Thomas Dacre, the painter; suspicion appears to have fallen upon his former girl friend, Lafcadio's granddaughter Linda. Max immediately steps forward and announces "I'm going to confess to a murder" (75), which he proceeds to do at great length and with a number of inaccuracies and inconsistencies. Inspector Oates rejects his confession as a mere chivalrous gesture to shield the girl. Shortly after, Campion visits Fustian at his gallery and is invited to watch his strategy for selling a bogus Jan Steen to a politician who fancies himself as an authority on Flemish art. The picture is examined exhaustively and the question of the painting's authenticity is discussed at great length. Just as the politician has made up his own mind that the painting is probably genuine, Fustian hurriedly offers his definitive opinion that the painting is almost certainly not a Steen. The politician, seeing his own judgment queried, dismisses the objection and asks for the picture to be reserved for him.

At the end of the gallery incident we read: "Mr. Campion . . . was aware that the root of the uncomfortable impression chipping at his mind . . . was something that had happened during the last few minutes" (100); and there, with just a tantalizing suggestion, the matter is left. In the next chapter, in conversation with Campion and Fustian, Belle Lafcadio (the painter's widow) recalls the man who actually painted the bogus Steen. At this point Marge's gift for orchestration comes into play. This is basically nothing more than the way in which passages are so juxtaposed as to lead the reader, almost unawares, either to an inevitable conclusion or to the next climactic moment of the narrative. Max's reaction to Belle Lafcadio's recognition of the painting and to her subsequent scolding is to remark to Campion, "The memory of the old! . . . The coincidence, too! Extraordinary, wasn't it? Quite an instructive afternoon" (108). Once more two words stand out: "coincidence" and "instructive," which in turn find their correspondence in Campion's later musings, which send "an unaccustomed thrill down his spine": "What he had noticed subconsciously at the Salmon Gallery was an unmistakable family likeness between Max's story to the politician and his confession to Inspector Oates" (108). The chapter ends with Max in a taxi "thinking of Mrs. Potter"—a revelation from which Campion, but not the reader, is excluded. So that when the following chapter opens with the statement, "On the morning of the Thursday on which she died Mrs. Potter rose a trifle earlier than was her wont" (110), the reader's discovery of the murderer's identity is even more premature than Campion's, who takes another thirty-five pages to reach the same conclusion. From then on it is simply a question of how Campion will be able to prove his case. As in the later novel, *The Fashion in Shrouds,* the murderer's guilt can only be proved by Campion offering himself as a living bait. Fustian is finally arrested, but cannot be brought to trial since, after his sudden degeneration into insanity, he dies in the prison infirmary.

Once again an Allingham novel is marked by the author's acknowledgment of the reader's presence. In one remarkable scene, Marge invites the reader to share with her the pleasure of the orchestration of detail: Campion, on the brink of delivering himself into Fustian's hands, attends the Cellini Society's cocktail party, where he is to meet Max. Before the latter's arrival, Campion observes "Old Brigadier-General Fyvie . . . bellowing his latest *mot*" (221). If the reader has been paying attention this name is not unfamiliar. The novel began: "There are, fortunately, very few people who can say that they have actually attended a murder" (11); two paragraphs later we are offered the spectacle of two guests invited to the showing of the Lafcadio picture who pass on the path to the studio. One, the Bishop of Mould, is arriving; the other, Sir Walter Fyvie, is leaving and thus missing the murder—a disappointment for a man "who would have genuinely appreciated so odd a distinction." Fyvie's presence at the second gathering, therefore, acts as a discreet reminder to the reader of the possibility of a new catastrophe.

It is surely moments such as these that must have led the critics to their almost unanimous evaluation of *Death of a Ghost* as "a novel of which it cannot be said that the main interest is a criminal one" (Bentley 1934, 19); "a clever novel even without the trail of crime that it describes" (Anon. 1934a, 4); "taken either as an uncommonly good detective story, or as a human comedy, this novel is very well worth reading" (Anon. 1934b, 150). Marge was pleased with the reviews and by the fact that the book was selling. What clearly delighted her was the general acceptance of *Death of a Ghost* as a novel. On March 22, 1934 she noted in her diary, "Wonderful notice from Agate in Express." James Agate's review highlighted just those qualities in Marge's writing which I have been at pains to emphasize: her exploitation of language and her sense of the reader. He writes, "Miss Allingham is that very rare bird among writers of detective thrillers, a writer who by her sense of words tickles the reader's palate, while at the same time engaging his reasoning faculties and at least once in the book making his blood run cold" (Agate 1934, 4).

Marge's awareness of the social implications of murder is essential to the concept of the modern mystery, the convenient label for the three novels which followed *Death of a Ghost*. In her introduction to the omnibus volume *The Mysterious Mr. Campion*, she countered the criticism that the interest in the mystery was evidence for an increased fascination with crime, violence, and decadence: "I wonder if it is nothing of the sort, but rather a sign of a popular instinct for order and form in a period of sudden and chaotic change . . . there is, also, something deeply healthy in the implication that to deprive a human being of his life is not only the most dreadful thing one can do to him but also that it matters to the rest of us" (1963, 7). The emphasis is not on the institutions of law and order but on the individual members of society; this explains why, for example, John Widdowson, the murderer in *Flowers for the Judge*, is not arrested by the police and committed for trial, but is "executed" by his cousin. It is also the reason for the way in which the two following novels (*Dancers in Mourning* and *The Fashion in Shrouds*) end before the apprehension of the murderer, allowing Marge to focus attention upon the emotional involvement of the entire fictional community, rather than upon the mechanics of organized justice. In this context it is all the more interesting to note that the only trial scene that does occur (in *Flowers*) is used more from reasons of narrational strategy than from a desire to make the majesty of the law an integral element of the plot or story.

Marge began work on *Flowers for the Judge* on January 17, 1935, and had completed the first 30,000 words by early April when she read it to her father, who found it very good. For the next few months she was able to concentrate entirely on her writing, even if the worry about money was not yet banned. She wrote to Mary Leonard, "Cooee is working wonders with the staff and although it means I have to collect a bit more cash I don't have to think of very much else" (Letter, March 1935). She was, however, reckoning without the interference of Malcolm Johnson, who seemed to want to create a particular image of the Allingham books for Doubleday's. Johnson saw the first seven chapters or so in April and was also sent a synopsis for the remainder of the book. Early in the autumn of 1935, Mary Leonard passed on to Marge a list of proposed alterations. Under Johnson's prompting she pointed to the success of William Powell's screen creation of the character of the Thin Man, and suggested that "Campion has just as much right to his place in the movies." This infuriated Marge, who replied at length:

> This story I've sent you is a novel not a thriller and if he brings it out in the Crime Club with a horror cover and a catchpenny blurb he will not do well with it because it is as silly as bringing out a marmalade in a tin and calling it boot polish. You and he have both read this book with The Thin Man in mind because Mr Campion is sometimes funny. It is not a bit like The Thin Man and so you think if you take out one foreign ingredient you will make it like it. This is lunatic. (Draft letter in a notebook, late 1935)

The main action of *Flowers* concerns events at the respected publishing firm of Barnabas Ltd. One of the partners, Paul Brande, disappears and is later found murdered in the firm's strong room. His death was caused by carbon monoxide poisoning resulting from the deliberate introduction into the locked room of exhaust fumes from the car of the junior partner, Mike Wedgewood. Mike, who is a close friend of Gina, the dead man's sadly neglected wife, is arrested and sent to trial. The senior partner, John Widdowson, engages another cousin, Sir Alexander Barnabas, for the defence, and also employs Campion—a friend of Mike Wedgewood's—to get to the bottom of the mystery. Campion once again finds an ally and confidant, this time in Ritchie Barnabas, Mike's older and somewhat ineffectual cousin. The trial is brought to a sudden end when John Widdowson is found dead, killed apparently accidentally in a similar manner to Paul Brande. The mystery is at an end, but Ritchie Barnabas has disappeared.

The theme of mysterious disappearance not only lends the plot a sense of continuity, it is also the essence of the frame tale within which the novel develops. *Flowers* opens with an account of the unsolved mystery of Tom Barnabas, Ritchie's elder brother, who apparently vanished into the fourth dimension in 1911. The story of his disappearance became something of a legend giving rise to a number of variants: "All the stories have their own circumstantial evidence. Only the main fact and an uncomfortable impression are common to all" (1936a, 1). This is a reflection upon the contrast between fictional narrative and the colportage of gossip and rumour in daily life: the fictional narrative is unique in its composition and multifarious in the interpretations made of it, whereas the gossip tale is already multifarious in its compositon since the only continuity lies in the prenarrational raw material. The frame effect of the disappearence motif is created by the concluding narrative of the novel. Traditionally the detective story containing a trial scene ends with the verdict and a brief tying together of loose ends; *Flowers for the Judge* has two post-trial chapters in which Campion and Mike Wedgewood go to the continent on the trail of Tom Barnabas, who, after "disappearing," left England to become a circus proprietor. They catch up with the circus in Avignon, where Campion learns the truth about the 1911 disappearance and also discovers Ritchie, who has been metamorphosed into the clown, Moulin-Mou. Marge exploits the grotesqueries of the final scene to present the solution to John Widdowson's opportune death. At the circus, Campion watches the antics of the clown, who, at the climax of his act, throws buns to the audience one of which lands in Campion's lap. He takes it with him to meet Mike and Gina, who has just joined them:

> "Horrible," said Mike, staring at the unattractive object with suspicion. "Who gave you that?" Mr. Campion looked at them solemnly.
> "The King's Executioner," he said so gravely that they did not question him. (306)

In *Flowers*, Marge returns to a London which is a very different city to the London of *Death of a Ghost*. At times it is even reminiscent of the London of Dickens—the fog motif of the early chapters is employed in just the same way as in *Bleak House:* "The fog, which enveloped the city and now crept into every corner, hung about the air like smoke, giving the single swinging bulb a dusty halo" (24). At other times Marge finds her own epithets for the city as in the words of the old London policeman who has retired to Norwich: "London's got the fascination of a girl you never quite get to know" (293). It is also a London which is peopled with a host of carefully, even lovingly, drawn minor characters—a feature which Nicholas Blake commented on in his review of the book (Blake 1936, 364). There is, for example, the senior secretary of the the firm, Miss Curley: "her black velvet dress was of that variety of ill-cut, over-decorated and disgracefully expensive garments which are made in millions for the undiscerning" (4); or the charwoman, Mrs. Austin, who receives the news of Paul Brande's death: "The full arc of Mrs. Austin's knitted bosom swelled. Her long face with its festoon of chins grew blank and she emitted a long thin sound midway between a scream and a whistle" (32).

In spite of the critical acclaim for the characterization, what makes *Flowers* interesting as a novel are the narrative strategies which Marge employed. In incorporating portions of a formal trial, she is clearly aware of the narrative potential offered by courtroom procedure. The trial with its speeches for prosecution and defence, the testimony of various witnesses, and the revisionary function of cross-examination, presented her with a further chance to exploit the shifting perspectives she had already experimented with in *Sweet Danger*. In the two trial scenes in the novel (chapters 16 and 19), the dominant perspective is that of Miss Curley, since she is not emotionally involved with characters as people, and is thus the person with the clearest vision: "She had wedded herself to the firm of Barnabas Limited. . . . Thirty years later she loved the business as a son and a master" (5). The organization of chapter 16, however, allows for a series of disconnected interpolations of the verbatim report of the Attorney-General's speech, and a brief shift to Gina Brande just after he has begun: "To Gina the Attorney-General was just a voice repeating facts she already knew. . . . To her the one reality was Mike himself, sitting directly in front of her" (235). The contrast between words becoming meaningless through constant repetition, and the acutely felt physical presence of the prisoner is in itself a further reflection on the process of narrative in the detective story. The repetition of salient facts as an aid or reminder to the reader is commonplace in the genre. Marge, however, hints at the threat of linguistic redundancy inherent in such a device.

When the trial continues in chapter 19, Miss Curley wonders "rather helplessly if the truth could be any more apparent after five days' talk" (268)—a clear continuation of Gina's earlier reflections. Generically the detective novel is always a collection of individual stories; in this chapter, a whole series of tales are told. The choice of witness-storytellers is significant: Roberta Jeeves, the author of the detective novel, published by Barnabas, in which an identical murder to that of Paul Brande was described in detail; and Peter Rigget, the clerk who not only attempted to suppress his discovery of the body, but who also tampered with the evidence. The deliberate focussing on the fictional model for the crime suggests why Marge chose a publisher as the murderer: someone, whose profession it is to arrange for the production and distribution of fiction becomes the person who in real life acts out a lie, and attempts to hide it by inventing stories which will incriminate somebody else. In one sense, *Flowers* is deeply concerned with the notion of fiction as lying. Peter Rigget, on the other hand, is diametrically opposed to the cousins of Barnabas Limited, since he comes from a lower-middle-class family, is an unattractive character both physically and morally, and yet he is linked to John Widdowson (the killer) in that he attempts to confuse the carefully arranged fiction of Paul's murder by his own clumsy artifices. When Sir Alexander Barnabas, as defence counsel, cross-examines Rigget, we are presented with a complex symbolic action representing the attempt of the reader/critic to unravel the complications of devised narration. It is at this point that one is reminded of Campion's first impression of Cousin Alexander's rhetoric: "Mr. Campion . . . felt he was listening to the truth in dramatized form" (160).

Flowers for the Judge is a book consciously contemporary with its times (in contrast to the two straight detective stories, which both had an air of nostalgic recollection about them). As Gina explains to Campion at the beginning of the story: "We—well, we're post-war people" (15). Nothing makes this clearer than an incident during the initial meeting between Gina, Mike, and Campion, when Mike holds out his bare, cupped hand to take Gina's cigarette-end and throw it in the fire: "He did not speak, but nodded to her, his whole body expressing urgency and unconscious supplication. It was a ridiculous incident, so trivial yet curiously disquieting. Bewildered and half amused, the girl dropped the burning fragment into the hand and Campion glanced away involuntarily so that he might not see the man's satisfaction at the pain as he carried the stub over to the fire" (19). It is a measure of the new sophistication of Marge's modern mysteries that the unspoken emotional intensity of the relationship between a young man and the unappreciated beautiful wife of his own cousin can be conveyed to the reader. This is achieved both through the action and through Campion's reaction to it, so that even through the double filter of fictional character and narrative voice the message remains clear.

Flowers was published in February 1936 to a chorus of friendly reviews which praised the characterization, the humour, and above all the writing. While the *Nottingham Guardian* dubbed it "a distinguished piece of work" (27.02.1936), James Agate went into rhapsodies: "So far as I am concerned Miss Allingham's mysteries are never the reason why I read her books. I should be perfectly willing to read this one backwards . . . entirely because of the writing" (Agate 1936, 8).

One result of the critical success was that Marge was invited to the Ivy Restaurant in London by Frank Swinnerton, the author of over twenty works of fiction and criticism. I have referred elsewhere to Marge's friendship with him; it is, however, worth noting that it was *Flowers* which brought them together, a book which Swinnerton praised not so much for the overall ingenuity of plot and felicity of expression, as for the carefully observed details—what he called Marge's "reliance upon your own sense of what the world is like" (Letter, 15.03.1936). Consciously or not, Swinnerton had hit on the very thing that Marge had been attempting: a greater realism and greater contemporary relevance. She replied: "It is a very comfortable thing to find that you approve the touches I was so afraid I might be making entirely for my own pleasure" (Letter, 16.03.1936).

Marge spent New Year's Eve 1936 writing to Meiggs, "a long rambling tale of the Tolleshunt D'Arcy circus." Apart from purely local and domestic goings on she refers to the abdication of Edward VIII, which had been announced less than three weeks earlier. The reactions of the D'Arcy household are revealing; Edward's decision "all but broke down the life long amity of the brotherhood." Pip and Alan Gregory had the first major disagreement of their lives; Grog "took the sentimental and impractical view," whereas Pip reacted with extreme conservatism: in a note he wrote at the time he referred to "the disgrace inflicted upon us by King Edward VIII." Marge herself was surprised "to find the 'sanctity of the job one's sworn to do' so overwhelmingly important." On the other hand, she revealed a stubborn individualism and antiestablishment attitude in her account of a Heinemann's party she had unwillingly attended. Among those present were F. Tennyson Jesse ("a wizened little lady . . . who looked as though she were having a nervous breakdown"), Somerset Maugham ("who looked much more as if it were belly trouble he had than a predilection to vice"), and H. G. Wells, who was accompanied by "a covey of young girls . . . and did not look as if he were too pleased about it." The letter ended with a description of the wife of one of the Carters' friends, who, although herself an Oxford graduate, had been prevented by her husband from practising her chosen profession: "I gather she was one of those girls who . . . decided to 'sacrifice' herself, her brains and her training to a business which seems to be undertaken successfully by the silliest little bloody with the mind of a housemaid." (Letter to Meiggs, 31.12.1936).

The three topics I have picked out from the letter are significant in so much as they all found their reflection in the two novels which followed *Flowers*. Campion is hampered by inborn conservative attitudes (particularly with respect to marriage), yet at the same time Marge reveals a sympathetic understanding of neglected wives, or of the wasted potential of intelligent and sensitive married women who are expected to be simply wives and mothers. This in turn is part of a general suspicion of established opinions and thoughtless conformity.

Dancers in Mourning seems to have developed out of two related compositional ideas for a detective story: the detective suspects the wrong man until just before the end of the book; the detective is engaged to investigate a murder and then falls in love with the wife of the man who, according to all the evidence, must have been the murderer. *Dancers* is a novel about the way in which the interference of emotion leads to the misreading of signs. It is set in a community of theatrical people, of whom someone says: "Theatrical people aren't like ordinary people. . . . They're *theatrical*. Things mean more to them than they would to you or me, little things do. . . . Being in the theatre is like living in a tiny little village." (1937, 18). The reader has to be prepared for the encapsulated exaggerations of fiction within fiction; for characters who will be consciously artificial; for a closed world replete with meaningful details—in other words for the characteristic world of detective fiction. Given these conditions, clues play a peculiarly significant part in the story, for there will be clues that because of their very ambiguity will lead to false interpretations. Yet, since they are ambiguous, the reader can at any time choose the correct alternative reading, and thus move ahead of the mistaken investigator, Campion, towards the inevitable conclusion.

In the opening sentence of the novel, William Faraday of *Police at the Funeral* reappears, signaling an invitation to recognize the transformations that have taken place within the traditional formula. It is Faraday, as Campion's friend, who draws him into the investigation of a series of petty attacks on Jimmy Sutane, famous dancing star of the musical theater. Sutane invites Campion to his country home, White Walls, for the weekend. It is here that Chloe Pye, an ageing soubrette attempting a comeback in Sutane's show, is killed. Although apparently an accident—she falls from a bridge under the wheels of Sutane's car—her death finally proves to have been murder. Campion meanwhile has fallen in love at first sight with Sutane's wife, Linda, and decides that he must back out of the case rather than abuse his host's hospitality. With the second murder, that of Benny Konrad (Sutane's understudy), who is the victim of a bomb attack which kills two other people and injures twelve, Campion's difficulties increase. He is convinced that all the signs point to Sutane as the murderer. Up until this time, hampered in his assistance of the police by his emotions, he at last offers them certain suggestions as to where and how further clues might be discovered. When the results of the police investigation are communicated to Campion, he is still convinced that his theory is correct. A fortuitous piece of evidence enables him to see the error in his thinking, and to recognize the real killer. However, the fascination of *Dancers* lies not in the bare bones of the plot structure, but in the deft manipulation of the narrative discourse to both mislead and direct the reader.

The second paragraph of the second chapter, in which Campion arrives at White Walls to meet the Sutane menage, reads, "Yet the whole story was there, so clear to read if only he had been looking for it" (22). This statement heralds the offering of clues, some of which are accepted and understood, others overlooked, yet others misread both by Campion and the reader. Shortly before lunch the company is listening to the composer, Squire Mercer, improvising on the piano; Chloe Pye comes in, sits down on the music bench, and after a while says to Mercer, "I'll play you one of your own songs that you've forgotten" (33). The song is "Water Lily Girl," and Chloe plays "the verse as well as the chorus." Neither Campion nor the reader are in a position to recognize this as a clue at this early stage in the novel, since the secret lies in the words that Chloe sings. However, to have given the text of the song in chapter 2 would have been to make things too easy for the reader. By withholding the information a pattern of misunderstanding is initiated.

After Chloe's death, William Faraday and Campion spend the night at Mercer's house; again clues are offered. Campion comes to see that "Mercer did not think at all in the accepted sense of the word," and that what connections he made between ideas was part of "a dark procession taking place in some subsconscious part of the brain" (81). Uncle William puts it a little more crudely when he suggests that Mercer's success with "those footlin' songs of his" has "put the feller out of gear" (82). For Campion this is simply synonymous with Mercer's self-centeredness. Once more it is only later that the full import of both men's observations is made clear; Inspector Yeo characterizes the still-anonymous murderer: "the man who did this job wasn't the imaginative type. He's straightforward and ingenious" (208). Mercer, however, is "out of gear" in very much the same way as Marge's earlier villains and murderers were: he is a complete egotist. On another occasion he almost gives himself away to the reader by concentrating on his new tune which he wants to call "Pavane for a Dead Dancer" with reference to Chloe's death. In reply to William's shocked objection he says, "All this other affair will be forgotten long before we can get a song out" (235). The reader may well share William's moral outrage, but he does not immediately recognize Mercer's dangerous self-absorption.

Another decisive clue concerns Uncle William's reliability as a witness. During the investigation of Chloe Pye's death, William swears that he and Mercer were both in the music room: "I didn't see the woman after dinner. I'm no witness. I was in the little music-room behind the dining-room, listening to Mercer. I don't mind his strumming when there's no words" (84). When Campion questions him further, William insists that he was there until Linda brought the news of the accident. Thus, in the reader's mind and in Campion's, both men are excluded from the list of potential suspects. A corrective to this misreading is offered some fifty pages later: Campion goes to the small music room in search of Uncle William, "who was still napping, the empty decanter at his side" (133). The significance of William's nap does not immediately hit Campion; only when he has at last discovered the truth is there a reminder of this brief scene. William Faraday's incorruptibilty seems to be an immoveable obstacle to the theory of Mercer's guilt; this realization is followed by the passage: "Campion moved slowly across the terrace and stood looking into the house through the wide French window. . . . In the deep armchair, his chubby feet crossed, his hands folded on his paunch, the empty decanter at his side and his crimson face immobile in the sleep of the happily drugged, lay Uncle William human" (282–83). Throughout the novel clues are given, repeated, and in the repetition made to reveal their meaning. As a result the reader is made aware that had he only paid attention, he would have been able to arrive at the correct conclusion.

At the close of the novel, Campion approaches Sutane for what he feels will be a final interview leading to the latter's confession and arrest. The conversation begins to the accompaniment of Mercer at the piano—"his new tune, 'Pavane for a Dead Dancer,' had grown from a motif into a completed thing" (274)—and is thus narrationally related to the opening scene at White Walls in chapter 2. Campion begins by announcing that the police have discovered Chloe's marriage certificate; he and the reader believe that this will prove that Sutane was her husband; only Sutane knows this to be untrue. Marge then embarks upon a daring experiment by having the two men antiphonally narrate the story of the anonymous figure of "Chloe's husband," in the third person. The reader is clearly invited to share Campion's belief that "he" refers to Sutane, and is excluded from Sutane's knowledge that the reference is to Mercer. This dialogic strategy forces Campion to reflect: "It was a mad interview, a conversation in a dream, with nothing solid or static in the world, only a sense of inexorable disaster coming nearer and nearer every second" (278).

Disaster, or rather relief from disaster, is heralded by that same tune that acted as overture to the first murder. Campion, listening to Mercer playing "Water Lily Girl," suddenly recalls the text and realizes its significance—that Chloe was asking for a rendezvous ("I'll be waiting by the lake, Water-Lily Girl")—and remembers that "Sutane had not been there. Sutane had been . . . rehearsing." The narrative then picks up the name Mercer as the matching subject of a list of statements which could be made about the murderer. Once the grammar of the narrative has been corrected, the truth seems not only inevitable but comprehensible: "Who then was the little god of this circle? Not Sutane, who was the worker, the man who recognized his responsibilities and was secretly appalled by them, but Mercer, who was cozened, flattered and protected until his opinion of his own importance lost all touch with reality" (282).

Dancers was Marge's most successful novel to date, earning her critical laurels as "a first-class writer" (Dolland 1937) and "one of the cleverest of today's mystery novelists" (Irvin 1937). Frank Swinnerton's praise was fulsome, but he had one criticism to level at the book: "I wanted Campion to be a little less piano. . . . I didn't much care for his infatuation with Linda . . . you must remember that the real value of Campion in the centre is that he is a focal point" (Letter, 05.06.1937). Swinnerton was, I think, totally mistaken about Campion's involvement with Linda Sutane. When he first sees Linda and is emotionally bowled over by her, his reaction is defined in the words "he gave up his customary position as an observer" (35). Marge was thus enabled to exploit his new position as an insider and participant—a role that she was to expand and consolidate in *Shrouds*. Linda Sutane, furthermore, is initially described as "young and gentle and, above all, *genuine*" (35; my italics); this last quality sets her off against the artificialities of the theatrical people around her. She acts throughout the novel as the representative and standard of normality.

In reply to Swinnerton's comments about Campion, Marge wrote: "I see what you mean. . . . I've been trying to get him on the scenes again for several books now with less and less success. I fancy I've been treating him with that amicable contempt one (rather horridly) often accords a really nice old friend. . . . I'll try to look *at* him again. Also Amanda . . . shall return to keep a critical eye on him" (Letter, 08.06.1937). It is a measure of Marge's respect for the older writer that she carried out these promises in *The Fashion in Shrouds*, virtually to the letter. By the end of the book, Amanda and Campion, who have been at centre-stage throughout, are—after a tactical pretence of being engaged—actually on the brink of seriously considering marriage.

At one point in the novel, Amanda is characterized as having, in common with Marge, "a passionate and friendly interest in all the many and exciting surfaces of life" (1938f, 159). It is just this sort of interest that makes *Shrouds* the most consciously realistic of the Allingham novels of the thirties. This is what she had in mind when she wrote a dedication (later rejected) to William McFee: "I want you to accept the dedication of this book and to try, if you will, to read it because I think you will like it. After all real blood is not only to be spilt. It has certain other functions first; and I have tried in this story to make sure that the people in it . . . have their fair share of the living stuff . . ." (unpublished typescript).

Although the book is partly set in the milieu of haute-couture, the "fashion" of the title indicates a more general theme. The epigraph to the novel draws attention to the two parents of fashion, "snobbism and a conscious striving for effect" (4). Snobbery is provided by the mon-eyed, luxury-loving group of characters who combine to finance and run the leisure paradise of Caesar's Court. The remainder of the epigraph refers equally to the story and to the discourse of the novel, both of which are marked by complex contrivance. Fashion also implies change, which may lead to the state where, as one character remarks, "anything can happen" (65)—a very convenient prerequisite for a mystery story. On another level fashion is appropriate to a book, which, as B. A. Pike noticed, "has an obsessively feminine quality that sets it apart" (Pike 1977, 117).

In *The Fashion in Shrouds,* Marge repeats the murderer-as-egoist theme; Ferdie Paul, impressario and director, "who looked like Byron" (24), and who speaks patronizingly of death: "Forget it. You'll upset yourself" (32), is introduced into the novel, not only as the man behind the grandiose scheme of Caesar's Court, but also as the man who "made Georgia Wells" (22). As a latter day Svengali, Paul allows nothing to distract his star from her theatrical destiny. Her first (secret) husband, who wished her to leave the stage lest it damage his own career, was driven to suicide; her second, who also intended to force her to leave the stage, is murdered with an injection of insulin. As in *Flowers,* Campion is forced into presenting himself as a sacrificial lamb in order to prove Paul's guilt. However, at the heart of the novel is not so much the villain as his protégé, Georgia Wells, with her career v. husband syndrome. She, together with Campion's sister, Val Ferris, and Campion's pseudo-fiancee, Amanda Fitton, the engineer, provide the main thematic interest of the novel.

Val and Georgia are presented in the stereotypical situation of two women in love with the same man, Alan Dell, a brilliant aeroplane designer, who is initially infatuated with Georgia. Val comments to Campion: "I envy those women who just love normally and nobly with their bodies. . . . Female women love so abjectly that a reasonable hard-working mind becomes a responsibility. It's a cruelty that shouldn't have to be endured. I tell you I'd rather die than have to face it that he was neither better nor even more intelligent than I am!" (64) The contrast between "female women" and "a hard-working mind" reveals something of Marge's own problems in her relationship with Meiggs, which she generalizes into the basic problem of the tension between the professional independence of the creative woman and conformist male expectations concerning her role in matters of social and personal relationships. Nevertheless, the final sentence, with its suggestion of the inability to acknowledge openly that a woman could be morally or intellectually superior to the man she loves, hints at Marge's innate conservatism, which still thought in essentially traditional categories: the husband must be cast as a superior being, and if in reality he is not, then it's a minor, or at times major catastrophe. In her own life, Marge seems to have partially resolved the problem by adhering to a strict compartmentalization. As a professional woman, she insisted on the absolute autonomy of her position; as a wife, she was willing to play a conformist role. There was, for Marge, a very true sense in which her fiction was a personal vehicle of escape. In *Shrouds* she is at pains to focus on the essential—as opposed to conventional—differences between men and women. Val explains to Campion that whereas men tend to think things out and take "the conventional view and the intelligent path," women's "feeling is twice as strong as our heads" (132). Rather, however, than leading to total resignation, this observation introduces Val's retort to her brother, "You may have the mental discipline, but we're the realists" (133). In *The Fashion in Shrouds*, men are poseurs, bombasts, idealists, even, occasionally, infatuated lovers; never are they as realistic about the circumambient world, or their position in it, as are the women.

The key to the mysteries of the novel is contained in a quotation from Laurence Sterne: "Providence, having the advantage of knowing both the strengths and the weaknesses of men, has a facility for unostentatious organization" (219). On the level of the murder investigation this explains what Campion refers to as the "curious hand-of-fate quality" which the structure of events has had (269). Only one man has access both to canals of information about the strengths and weaknesses of his victims, and to the machinery for "unostentatious organization": Ferdie Paul. If, on the other hand, one contrasts "unostentatious organization" with the "conscious striving for effect" of the epigraph, one is immediately aware of the sets of antitheses—fashion and the unfashionable; male and female; order and crime—between which the novel vibrates. Finally, the motif of strength and weakness is an essential part of Marge's analysis of femininity. At the end of chapter 17, as Val and Georgia are discussing the topic of love, the narrating voice comments: "They were two fine ladies of a fine modern world, in which their status had been raised until they stood as equals with their former protectors. . . . Their freedom was limitless . . . yet, since they had not relinquished their femininity, within them, touching the very core and fountain of their strength, was the dreadful primitive weakness of the female of any species" (210).

In seeing "falling in love," and the expected social consequences, as the essential weakness of the sophisticated career woman, Marge was by no means being as traditional as one might suppose. Far more, she put her finger on the essential male-oriented nature of the society of her times: women may have gained enough freedom to pursue a career, theoretically they may even have achieved a measure of equality *in certain professions*, but men presumed that in the process they would have "relinquished their femininity"; that is, become masculine women without physical attraction, or, more significantly, without the traditional surface willingness to be submissive. The only alternatives for the professional woman in love were to revert to conformity and accept the subordinate role of the "beloved," or, by remaining single, to confirm male prejudices of her lack of attraction or her essential immorality. This is clearly behind Val's response in the brief exchange which follows:

> "Love really can rot any woman up," Georgia observed contentedly. "Isn't it funny?"
>
> "Dear God, isn't it dangerous!" said Val. (210)

When Alan Dell later proposes marriage to Val, he does so as a conventional male: "I don't want a mistress or a companion. I want a wife" (262)—in other words, Val must give up her career and submit to him in all things. Within the context of the fiction which Val has served—the successful independence of the professional woman—her acceptance of this offer would appear to be totally inconsistent. The inconsistency even seems to extend beyond the novel to Marge herself; her own life was, surely, an example of a contrary position: she was married and yet she continued to write and strive for success. Pip, however, had not only never made such demands as Alan Dell, but he had never been in a position to do so, since, until the end of the thirties, he remained financially dependent on the income Marge made from her writings. Nevertheless, it is consistent with Marge's inherent conservatism, and with her awareness of the expectations of her equally conformist readers, that in her fiction she could envisage the sacrifice of professional independence to the demands of a masculine vision of domestic bliss.

Ultimately, Marge seems to opt for a relationship based neither on passion nor on renunciation, but on something more homely—as in her own case. Commenting on the sufferings engendered by Val's thwarted passion, Amanda uses the phrase "cake-love" for the sort of love experienced by the other woman; when Campion queries the expression she replies:

> "Cake-love as opposed to the bread-and-butter kind."
> "Oh, I see. You're plumping for bread and butter, are you, my young hopeful?"
> "I'm full of bread and butter," said Amanda with content. (107)

This clearly recalls Marge's description, in a letter of the same period to Meiggs, of her relationship with Pip, that their love was "bread and butter stuff" (see chapter 5). In her treatment of the theme of femininity and the relations between the sexes, she attempted in *Shrouds* to present a view of contemporary society based both on the vicarious knowledge of the written word and hearsay, and on her reflections upon her own experience. "I wanted to write a full-scale novel of contemporary manners of a formal classic kind I had never tried before and, because time was so short, I decided to combine this with the . . . detective book already half assembled" (1965a, 11).

With *The Fashion in Shrouds*, Marge once again put forward her claim to be regarded as a serious novelist, and the critics unanimously recognized her. Apart from "Torquemada's" well-known comment quoted in the last chapter, there were the notices in the *Daily Sketch*—"To graft a novel to a thriller is no easy matter, but Miss Allingham has succeeded" (30.06.1938); the *Daily Telegraph*—"Her whole narrative is threaded with artful conceits" (12.07.1938); the *Evening News*—"a first-class combination of two usually quite different kinds of novel" (12.07.1938); and finally the accolade of the anonymous reviewer in the respected *Times Literary Supplement*: "a novel which may be thoroughly recommended even to those who normally eschew detective fiction" (09.07.1938). By the close of the thirties, Margery Allingham and the detective story had gained serious literary recognition.

7

Living a Thriller

*I've got a hunch that the thriller as we know it is on its last legs.
We're living a thriller over here now.*

Margery Allingham

During the thirties Margery Allingham lived an unconventional life for a woman; virtually isolated behind the walls of D'Arcy House, she worked in order to support her small and predominantly male household. With the coming of war, she emerged from behind those walls, mixed with the village folk, abandoned her former atypical position, and began to play a number of traditionally female roles: caring for other women and their children, comforting her neighbours, and visiting the sick and elderly. Marge's emergence into the outside world was by no means a renunciation of her nonconformity. For most of the war years, she not only actively supervised the village's preparations for defence in the face of air and land attacks, but she also continued to write, producing three novels, a nonfictional account of the coming of war to the countryside, and reviews of more than two hundred and fifty books.

Since their move to D'Arcy in 1935, the Carters had not played any well-defined role in village life; the village itself had been little more than a rural backdrop to work or leisurely amusement. This changed quite abruptly with the Munich crisis and the mobilization of the Air Raid Precautions (ARP) forces on September 25, 1938. Two days later, Pip and Marge—at the behest of the ARP Officer in nearby Maldon—found themselves distributing gas masks to the villagers. Suddenly Marge found that she and Pip were fulfilling the role expected of them as residents of the Old Doctor's house; the former vicar of Tolleshunt D'Arcy, Rev. Bobby Graves wrote to her that he and his young wife were delighted "to see you and Philip taking your proper place at the head of village affairs" (Letter, 28.09.1938).

Early in October the announcement arrived that eighteen thousand evacuees from the East End of London were due to arrive in the area. The local butcher, Mr. Doe, had been appointed Billeting Officer and a committee was formed; Marge "for one began to enjoy it all enormously" (1941, 48). At a more serious moment, she saw the underlying problem of the billeting scheme and pointed out, in a letter to *The Times*, that the extremely negative reaction of country communities to the government's evacuation plans was caused by the threat of "a sudden invasion . . . by almost twice their own number." She went on to suggest that such an inundation "might easily be quite as detrimental to the morale as any bombardment" (1938c). However, the awaited hordes did not arrive and the village returned to its established pattern of life. But not for long. In November lectures were held in the village school on how to deal with poison gas attacks and incendiary bombs. At first Marge was able to see the irony of warlike lectures in a schoolroom decorated with German prints of biblical scenes, until she realized "that they were talking about a corrosive poison to be sprayed over one civilized people by what was presumed to be another." Her reaction was characteristic of her mood over the following twelve months: "I wondered if we were all insane" (1941, 55).

Marge had already begun a new novel in June 1938, originally titled "Bring Out Your Rubber-Tyred Hearses." For the first time in ten years Albert Campion was not one of the characters; his role as investigator was played by a dour Scots policeman, Inspector Bridie, whose accent was modelled on that of the Orkney Scottish ex-army instructor who gave the poison gas lectures at D'Arcy. *Black Plumes*—as the book was eventually entitled—was completed by the end of the year and published in January 1939. It was not particularly successful; the *New Statesman*'s reviewer accused Marge of "trying to write a novel on top of a detective story" (Anon. 1941), and Marge herself referred to the novel as "'Harrods' stuff done to keep the house together" (Letter to F. Swinnerton, 24.02.1941).

After the preliminary alarms of BBC news and the newspapers, in mid-February came the dull shock of Nazi Germany's invasion of Czechoslovakia. A month later Pip had become Head Warden for the district, responsible for giving warning of enemy air attack or any other incident of war. In addition, he and his deputy, Grog, "distributed strange equipment . . . filled in hundredweights of forms, arranged lectures and exercises" as well as passing out gas masks for adults and children (1941, 64). Marge, no new novel on the immediate horizon, continued to write her book reviews for *Time and Tide*. She also wrote a short story ("The Dog Day") for the *Daily Mail*'s summer series "Seaside

Hotel" (Alec Waugh and C. S. Forester were among the other contributors), and another for the *Strand* ("The Meaning of the Act").

With the outbreak of war only a month away, the annual cricket
party took place from July 31 to August 3, 1939. Significantly the
weather was disappointing and even the cricket between D'Arcy and
Chappel was not up to standard. Most of the familiar figures of former
years came, many of the men now already in uniform. As though tempting fate, the fancy dress party on the Saturday night was given the
motto "Eve of Waterloo Ball," which Marge discovered "was suddenly
not funny any more." She was later to write: "The whole celebration
was playing second fiddle for the first time in memory, and under the
skin everybody felt another sort of party was due to come off at any
moment and there was still rather a lot of preparation to be made for
that" (1941, 67). The fears of most of the guests that weekend were
exacerbated by Leslie Cresswell who, Cassandralike, summarized their
inevitable involvement in the approaching war with the words: "When
this is over you'll be old" (1941, 68).

Three weeks later Parliament passed the Emergency Powers (Defence) Act, which enabled the government "to act as it liked without
reference to parliament" in the interests of the nation's security (Calder
1969, 36); at the same time military reservists were called up. A day
later, August 25, the Anglo-Polish treaty of mutual alliance was signed,
which made Hitler call off his planned attack of Poland, at least for the
time being (Taylor 1965, 550). However, on September 1, German
troops finally marched into Poland, and war became frighteningly imminent. At D'Arcy House Pip and Grog commandeered the dining room
for their wardens' post, to be manned night and day on four-hour shifts.
Pip put up Dr. Salter's huge wall map of Europe in 1804, and com-
menced redrawing the frontiers in pencil. A general atmosphere of
dogged preparedness dominated. "We seemed to me to be going to war
as a duty, a people elderly in soul going in stolidly to kill or be killed
because we felt it was the only wise course to take" (1941, 80). At 11.15
on Sunday, September 3, 1939, Chamberlain spoke on the radio, "a
tired, old man telling of the bitter blow to *his* hopes of peace" (Mowat
1955, 649). The Second World War had begun.

After listening to the news, Marge went out into the garden—ever since
childhood she had taken refuge in gardens in times of stress—"waiting
for a comforting thought" (1941, 82). It came to her that her generation
had reached full maturity with a growing feeling of personal dissatisfaction, without a clearly defined faith, and without any hobby. For Marge,
however, comfort and a hobby were on their way in the form of eight

bus loads of evacuated young mothers, some of them expectant, and their small children. "I was frankly delighted to have something to do. I had taken a look at my own work and decided it was beyond me, probably for ever" (1941, 81). The billeting committee sprang into action and for the next three months Marge's life was dominated by the daily problems of D'Arcy's new inhabitants.

In her work of supervising accommodation, mediating conflicts between host families and their often unwilling guests, arranging for the establishment of a temporary maternity home, and offering marriage guidance to young wives anxious about their husbands or to impatient husbands wanting their wives to return home, Marge found unexpected assistance from a newcomer to the village, Jane Degras. Her husband, who wrote under the pen name of Mark Benney, had achieved some notoriety for his autobiographical account of a life of petty crime and imprisonment. Marge had reviewed his novel *The Scapegoat Dances* in May 1938 and admired his powers of observation if not his moral position. Jane was an intellectual and a socialist, and as such was suspicious of Marge and her almost feudal position in the village community. For Marge, however, the experience of this friendship was new and invigorating: "We got to like each other for what was good in each other: we were both honest women. . . . I liked her because she was so gloriously sincere, so vehement, so indignant, so vulnerable . . . and so intelligent" (Letter to A. D. Lindsay, 31.12.1941). Marge felt that she needed someone like Jane to give her a clearer sense of proportion at such a hectic time.

Apart from the disruption of habit caused by the evacuees, D'Arcy shared the country's anticlimactic experience of the seven-month Phoney War. The village's first air raid warning, early in the morning of the second day of the war, proved a false alarm; the massive bombing of London, which Pip had maintained would follow the outbreak of hostilities, did not take place. On the western front all remained very quiet; the only news of enemy action concerned Russia's invasions of Poland (September 17) and Finland (November 30). It was symbolic of the times that, in early October, the local builder and family friend, Albert Smith, decided to reglaze the conservatory at D'Arcy House. In reply to Marge's objection that she did not see the sense of mending anything in view of Hitler's destructive behaviour, Albert replied, "You don't want to *give way to him*" (1941, 132). The general lack of enemy activity was such that by mid-December the Wardens' Post had been moved out of the dining room and upstairs to the studio where it would not disturb normal life, and most of the evacuees had left. Only partly sad to see them go, Marge felt that the evacuation had done the village good, even if only because it had been a time of shared suffering—"like one nice long cry" she wrote to Meiggs (November 1940). Nevertheless, she reported that on the whole the village folk had been glad to see the last of their visitors: "the Londoners didn't make grateful or well-mannered guests" (Letter to McFee, February 1940).

Around this time Marge sent the first instalment of a new novel to Paul Reynolds, her American agent in New York; this was her tale of betrayal in wartime, *Traitor's Purse*. Before the end of the year, Reynolds reported that the fiction editor of *Woman's Home Companion* "was terribly enthusiastic" about it (Letter from Reynolds, 29.12.1939), and in January 1940, the *Companion* agreed to pay $10,000 for serialization, on the condition that the remainder of the story fulfilled the promise of the opening. Marge cabled Reynolds, "Magnificent, ready continue immediately." Yet the very uncertainty of the war situation was not conducive to sustained effort; as Marge wrote to McFee: "The war is more uncomfortable than terrifying at the moment but the chief strain lies in the uncertainty of everything. It's very disconcerting not to be able to plan ahead at all" (Letter, February 1940).

With Joyce Allingham already in the women's naval service (WRNS), and Mary Orr having joined up as an army (ATS) transport driver, Pip was beginning to chafe at the enforced inactivity of civilian life. However, he was already thirty-five and, in spite of increasing recruitment, registration for military service did not even reach men of 34 until July 1940. However, Pip volunteered for the Service Corps (RASC) and his appointment as a lieutenant arrived on March 6. Marge did not like to see him leave, "feel we're a three-legged stool with one leg going" (Diary, 06.03.1940). However, he was posted to nearby Colchester and for the next three months was able to spend some time at home. On Pip's departure Marge inherited much of his civil defence work including the position and the responsibilities of Chief Warden. The war, which was at last entering its active phase, began to dominate her day-to-day life, and with this came a sudden flow of determination and patriotism that seems to have been characteristic of the country as a whole: "If you have lived half your life's span without a passionate belief in anything, the bald discovery that you would honestly and in cold blood rather die when it came to it than be bossed about by a Nazi, and that freedom to follow your heart or not is . . . an actual necessity in your life, and that you are not alone in it . . . then that is something to have lived for" (1941, 153).

The months of April and May 1940 at D'Arcy were filled with action; ARP meetings, the checking of emergency food stores, and mobile unit exercises alternated for Marge with work on *Traitor's Purse*. She regarded this new book—"a cross between my old stuff and the new type" (Letter to Dwye Evans, 21.03.1940)—as a combination of the thriller's action and speed with the psychological insights and attention to style of the modern mysteries of the late thirties. Although the ARP work was very time-consuming and took her away from her writing, Marge still felt that her involvement in the outside world was "stimulating although worrying" (Diary, 17.04.1940). When the Germans marched into the Netherlands in early May, the threat of an enemy invasion on the Essex coast seemed even closer. Marge responded by putting her "precious story in a biscuit tin," which she put under the bed every night (Diary, 10.05.1940). Her reactions to the events which now followed one another with ever increasing speed and unreality— the defeat of Holland, the capitulation of Belgium, the forming of the Home Guard, Churchill's famous "blood, toil, tears and sweat" speech—were equally confused. At one moment she writes that in spite of the strange terror of the times, she also found them "ennobling . . . if the *mind* can take the pace." The very next day she writes in her diary, "A very sad worrying world; didn't feel very brave but astonishingly fatalistic" (Diary, 19–20.05.1940).

Three days later, D'Arcy House was invaded, but only by a company of Cameronian Highlanders who camped on the cricket meadow and whose officers, their batmen, and a bayoneted guard slept in the house itself: "To blunder into the back hall to find a smooth-faced fair-haired child sleeping sweetly . . . his rifle clasped in his arms like a toy, was one of those things you could have wished not to have seen until you remembered how lucky it was for you that there were children to do it" (1941, 190). The household soon adapted to the new situation, and Marge returned to her thriller wondering whether she was not slightly ridiculous to go on writing at such a time. "Still," she answered her own doubts, "young men read thrillers when they are flying out to bomb Kiel and so maybe it was all right for middle-aged ladies to write them" (1941, 183).

Shortly after the soldiers' arrival, the false rumour came through that the Germans had finally landed in Kent; Marge recorded that her reactions were "pure astonishment and anger. Cheek. Absolute cheek" (Diary, 25.05.1940). What actually followed was the evacuation of Dunkirk (27.05.–04.06.), one result of which was that Pip was given eight hours leave prior to some mysterious action which never took place. Two days later the Cameronians left, only to be replaced almost immediately by a new group of soldiers who proceeded to barricade the entries to D'Arcy with road blocks. It was around this time that Jane and Mark Degras left the village, depriving Marge of a friendship which, because of the contrary natures of the parties involved, could have been particularly fruitful if it had only lasted longer. In the midst of these comings, goings, and alarms, Marge still managed to continue work on the final chapters of *Traitor's Purse*, although she found the situation virtually impossible: "On my part the completion of my thriller was a vital necessity. . . . My part in the family war effort was to keep the home going and pay the taxes. . . . My tale was about a man with amnesia and required a mental contortionist with uninterrupted leisure to write the blessed thing. I was putting in about seven hours a day on it" (1941, 191).

With the novel finished and Doubleday satisfied (they had agreed to publish *Traitor's Purse* in the following spring), Marge turned her attention with new energy to the war on the home front. The result was an extraordinary correspondence which began in the pages of *Time and Tide* and continued privately for several weeks. It all began with Marge's letter, which was published under the heading "The Church: A Bridge or a Barrier?" and was a plea, not for new beliefs in time of war, but for stronger guidance and leadership from the Church: "With God we shall assuredly save ourselves and mankind from chaos, but between most of us and God there is the Church. In this desperate hour let it be a bridge and not a barrier. In this hour our faith in the Primate should be as great as our faith in the Premier, our belief in the efficiency and honesty and strength of the Church as implicit as our belief in the government" (*Time and Tide*, 13.07.1940). Although these sentiments may sound old-fashioned, even naive, in our sophisticated late-twentieth-century ears, Marge's letter brought responses from a number of the magazine's readers including the poet and novelist Charles Williams, who felt that her "noble and passionate appeal deserves wide meditation" (*Time and Tide*, 20.07.1940). It seemed that Marge had touched on a subject which troubled many of her contemporaries: the church had lost its ability to inspire. As she herself put it in a letter to the magazine's deputy editor, Theodora Bosanquet: "the only time my own rather unemotional and practical faith wavers is when I am in Church or happen to hear some particularly idiotic religious broadcast" (Letter, 17.07.1940).

Marge was soon corresponding with several churchmen who reacted favourably to her criticism. Finally the post brought her a letter from William Temple, then Archbishop of York, who suggested that she read an article which he had just published, outlining his view of the church's position. It was characteristic of her fascination with intellectual discourse with educated men, to which Meiggs had introduced her, that Marge replied with a closely typed, six-page letter. She not only commented extensively on the Archbishop's views, but offered him a spiritual history of her generation. Marge characterized herself and her contemporaries as a hesitant and suspicious group, always expecting the worst. This led her to a view of the dangers of the time as being not merely the immediate physical ones posed by the war, but more particularly the spiritual danger of failing to recognize God and His power. In reply to Temple's theory of finding God through socialism, Marge proposed that Christian belief should lead to a practical and virtuous form of that doctrine. What the Archbishop thought of her ideas we shall never know—no reply of his has survived.

The Battle of Britain raged over the southeast of England from mid-July to mid-September; no sooner had it ended, than the German bombing of Essex began. During August the concentration was on Colchester, then, in the last three months of 1940 the attacks began to include the outlying villages (Benham 1945). It was inevitable that sooner or later the bombing would reach D'Arcy, and sure enough one night in October the first attack came. Marge went to bed "and decided that if they were going to kill me it was no good thinking about it" (Diary, 20.10.1940). The next night the bombing increased, and in a fright, Marge rushed upstairs to take shelter under her fourposter bed. Unfortunately she had forgotten that the space was full of hat boxes and cases; she ended up hysterical, partially deaf, angry, and finally, delighted to be unhurt. When, at the end of October, Pip was on leave at D'Arcy, his stay coincided with almost continuous bombing. Marge described it fairly lightheartedly to Winifred Nerney: "Bombs all over the bloody place, duck, and our own ack-ack (mobile) shooting sometimes be'ind and sometimes before. We finally went to bed and put our heads under the clothes and left it all to take care of itself" (Letter, 02.11.1940).

During the late summer of 1940 Marge started making notes on the coming of war to Tolleshunt D'Arcy, which were later passed over to Nerney, who in her turn showed them to Malcolm Johnson, who wrote: "I have been brooding over Margery Allingham's notes. I think she could do a most impressive non-fiction book about life in . . . an English village during wartime. . . . I see a book . . . full of the courage she expresses so well in her letters; the sort of book which would make the ordinary person here realize what the war means" (Letter to W. Nerney, 11.09.1940). Nerney responded enthusiastically, pointing out that she felt that Marge "would find it far easier to do such a book at the moment than to write a detective novel" (Letter to M. Johnson, 03.10.1940). Marge seems to have got down to work in earnest, for on October 20 she sent the first instalment of *The Oaken Heart* to Paul Reynolds. Later she told him that she felt that she had given Johnson "exactly what he asked for but that may easily not be what he wanted" (Letter to Reynolds, 15.12.1940). The book is more than just a description of the impact of the war on a typical English village—only partly for reasons of censorship is D'Arcy disguised as "Auburn" throughout. It also contains Marge's own statement of all that such a village and its inhabitants meant to her and, as far as she could see, what it could symbolize for England as a whole. She found it easy to write since no invention was needed and, as she explained to Swinnerton: "It is not about the middle and upper classes for we have hardly any. I was brought up with the cottagers . . . and so I know them fairly well, in fact I think I'm more like them mentally than anyone else I ever met" (Letter, 15.03.1941). When it was finished, Marge felt that the *Heart* was "very good and sincere" (Diary, 18.05.1941). Johnson was delighted with it, and after reading it, the housemaid Christina Carter commented, "Yes, it's all true. I wonder you bothered to put it down" (Letter to Swinnerton, 19.08.1941).

In the meantime, Pip had been posted to North Africa, to the Western Desert; Marge did not see him again for over three years. Even before Pip left, she had begun to discover that with the necessity to develop initiative and take practical action in the outside world without his aid, the war years held the promise of an increase in her personal freedom. In November she wrote to Russell Meiggs, who was now at the Ministry of Supply: "It's taken me some time to realize it and longer to admit it, but (so far) the war has been my salvation. I've had my holiday at last and it has worked; I've recovered my health and my mental equilibrium. . . . I haven't felt so enthusiastic and glad to be alive since I was sixteen or so" (Letter, November 1940). Naturally Marge missed Pip, and often recorded the fact in her diary in the years which followed. Yet there was also a sense in which she was relieved of the burden of his presence. Now that he had regular paid employment, Pip was not dependent upon her financially. Thus Marge was freed of the obligation to feel that she had to write to make sufficient money to maintain the style of country life that Pip enjoyed. What she now did, she did for herself. It is worth noting that she was able to see her own emotional state as characteristic of the country as a whole; to Reynolds she wrote that she saw "England so *young* and roaring to go," and that she found it all "really very stimulating and exciting" (Letter, 15.12.1940).

Privately Marge could identify herself more and more easily with D'Arcy; she had after all "made personal friends with practically the entire village" and as she sat in the dining room with Grog, watching over the Wardens' Post, she realized that she knew all the people who passed the open window. The extent of her identification is expressed near the close of *The Oaken Heart* in a eulogy on the village: "Auburn is a right thing and will survive all wrong things. . . . I love it as one does love one's home" (1941, 254–55). However, another part of Marge still belonged to her writing; on January 6 she finished *Traitor's Purse* and sent it off to Dwye Evans at Heinemann's, who liked it. On publication the following month the novel received some kind reviews and the almost habitual praise from Frank Swinnerton: "It is an unblemished delight . . . the writing full of play and originality. . . . It is altogether your own" (Letter, 03.03.1941).

War was rapidly changing the character of the D'Arcy household; in September 1940 it gained a new member in the shape of Mrs. E. J. Hughes, "Granny," who, at eighty-seven was still in excellent health and mentally very alert. "With dreadful Victorian complaisance" she was soon insisting that "but for the *noise* you wouldn't know there was a war on" (Letter to Swinnerton, 15.03.1941). During a particularly severe air raid, when this stoical attitude became too much for Marge, she insisted that Granny and Christina should shelter in the cavity beneath the main staircase. Half an hour later, when the worst of the raid seemed to be over, Marge returned: "Granny scrambled out to meet me. 'If you're not so frightened now, I'll go back upstairs to bed,' she said" (1941, 219). From then on Granny stayed in her bed at night while the German bombers carried out the commands of "Hilda"—as she insisted on calling Hitler.

Mrs. Hughes may have enlivened the depleted household, but still the depletion continued. Late in May 1941, Marge noted in her diary that Grog was debating whether or not to go into Colchester to join the army, "I shall miss the old basket" (Letter, 22.05.1941). By autumn he was a Pilot Officer in the RAF and when he came to D'Arcy on leave, Marge wrote to Joyce that he looked "very fine and astonishingly clear . . . the RAF has bitten him and I think he's making good" (Letter, 27.11.1941). D'Arcy House was now a household of women, none of whom could share in the essential aspects of Marge's life—her writing and her developing intellectual interests. Nevertheless, she was neither lonely nor unhappy. To Frank Swinnerton she reported: "To my astonishment I am very happy indeed. I have no reason to be except that I feel the adventure of being alive has begun again. I had rather got to a point where I was working hard in luxury *in order* to work hard in luxury, now I'm lucky if I'm just able to work hard. . . . I fancy, any way I've been rejuvenated" (Letter, 15.03.1941) These remarks reveal something of the paradoxical in Marge's make-up: the slightly ironical realism

Marge with Her Grandmother, Emily Jane Hughes, ca. 1944

with which she comments on her work situation is in marked contrast to the almost naive romanticism of her feeling of adventure. Mark Degras had also noticed this aspect of her personality, but later falsely attributed it to what he felt to be the patrician side of her nature: "Margery had a bright heraldic vision of the world, where ladies fair and lovely knights fulfilled proudly any obligations that *noblesse oblige* laid upon them." Degras also offered a vivid glimpse of Marge in the first years of the war with "flowered shirts and chiffon scarves aflying," and added his view of her as having an air of being "a freshly-dusted porcelain figurine" in spite of her bulk. (Benney 1966, 115–16).

Meanwhile Marge had offered the manuscript of *The Oaken Heart* to an old friend, Robert Lusty, who was codirector of the firm of Michael Joseph; he accepted it delightedly. The book appeared in Britain at the end of August 1941, some three weeks before U.S. publication. The reviews were very favourable; the critics agreed that not only was the book written with great understanding and insight, but that it would also last. This view has proved to have been over-optimistic; the *Heart* was reissued in 1959, but soon went out of print, remaining unobtainable until a small edition appeared in 1987. Frank Swinnerton was among those who believed in the future of the new book: "It is a book that will last long . . . because what it contains is something that could only have arisen from the rare conjunction of long and sympathetic understanding . . . of local character and your own *comic* perception of life" (Letter, 25.08.1941). Although the *Heart* sold well in Britain, in the U.S., the country for which it had been written, it was a failure. This did not perturb Marge unduly, although she found it difficult to understand. Above all she was, as she wrote to Reynolds, very grateful to him and Johnson for having encouraged her to write the book: "I am more glad I wrote it than anything I can say. If I never wrote anything else before or since I'd still be glad. You see it's the first book I've *ever* written which has 'come off' in the sense that it says exactly what I meant it to" (Letter to Reynolds, 12.10.1941).

The Oaken Heart again brought Marge into contact with the academic world, whose approval she valued so highly. This time it was the Master of Balliol, Dr. A. D. Lindsay, a former Vice-Chancellor of Oxford University and close friend of Archbishop William Temple, who, having been given the book for Christmas, wrote to her at the end of the year that "it rejoiced my heart to read it and I hope stimulated my mind" (Letter, 27.12.1941).

A major reason for the poor sales of the *Heart* in the U.S. may well have been the approaching inevitability of America's entry into the war. With the Japanese attack on Pearl Harbour and the subsequent expansion of the theatre of hostilities, Marge felt that "war may last twenty years now." However, with characteristic bravado and determination, she decided to plant a hundred apple trees at the end of the garden, "It's a bit of a gesture but my new motto is 'I stay'" (Diary. 11.12.1941).

Shortly before the publication of the *Heart* in the U.S., Marge told Reynolds that she would like to write the first part of a "straight tale" she had in mind. Reynolds gave the idea some thought and, from the point of view of an agent, suggested themes which were certain candidates for the American bestseller list: "the novel of family against family, or a generation story" (Letter, 30.09.1941). A month later, Marge wrote to him that she was about to start work on a "'family' novel" which had been in her mind for the past eight years, "based on the various versions of the same story which has been whispered to me from time to time by members of the older generation of my own family" (Letter, 21.10.1941). This family mystery concerned their origins in the illicit alliance of John Allingham and Charlotte Duncan at the beginning of the nineteenth century. Domestic legend, as recorded in a roughly drawn family tree in Marge's hand, and possibly dictated by her grandmother, transformed John Allingham into a "Mysterious W. J. Allingham of Ireland," who was married twice, the second time to his cook, who was a gypsy. Marge announced that the book "must say something reasonably profound" and "must have a thunderingly good *tale*. . . . I believe I've got both" (Letter, 21.10.1941). What is more she was determined, in spite of the war, family duties, ARP, and the village, to put "the book before everything." Marge was setting out to prove that she was a "real writer," a serious novelist.

Only a week later she was writing very much in the same vein to Robert Lusty of a project which was so far advanced that it now had a formulated title: "Now at close on thirty-eight I intend to have a shot at what I hope is the first part of my mature work. . . . I feel that everything I have ever done before has been in some measure a preparation for the phase which I hope is beginning with this book. When it is done I will send it to you, it is called DANCE OF THE YEARS" (Letter, 28.10.1941). Marge continued to work away at the new novel with complete commitment for the remainder of the year; it was to occupy her for seventeen months and would dominate her life and her thoughts throughout that time.

There was little personal news from the outside world for Marge. Pip, now a captain in the RASC, reported meeting her brother, Phil, in the Libyan desert, but the exigencies of military secrecy and the slowness of the mails—letters took months to arrive—brought her little other news from North Africa. Although in later years Pip was able to paint quite a lighthearted picture of his desert experiences, it is clear that neither were they without hardship, nor was Pip without nostalgia for home. Around the time that Marge had adopted her "I stay" motto, Pip published a poem, the title of which had the same ring of stubborn hope: "Nothing Can Change." It is one of the very few public expressions of his affection for Marge that has survived:

> The street and the forge
> The may and the maypole, the gossips,
> Dear friendly trees and walls, my house,
> The porch, the knocker, the door—open—
> And you, waiting . . .
>
> I have only to shut my eyes
> And nothing can change

(Carter 1941).

Pip's conventional sentimentality is all too obvious, as too is his talent for giving expression to the thoughts and ideals of middlebrow English conservatism, which was to stand him in good stead in his postwar journalistic career. His escape into daydreaming was parallelled in mid-December by Marge's expression of a tougher more determined reaction to the pain of separation: "Miss him very much. Finding life a bit of a sweat. Only thing to do is to shut mind and look ahead" (Diary, 16.12.1941).

Marge's one sure source of entertainment, communicated in letters to Joyce in Ceylon, was Granny who seems to have taken the events of the war very much in her stride: "She came bundling in in great excitement the other day having seen . . . a map of Europe. 'Isn't it wonderful they're on our side?' she said, bursting with delight. 'Who?' I said. 'They're right on top of us,' she said. 'If they were against us we *should* be for it.' 'Who?' I repeated. 'Why,' she said, '*the Scotch!*'" (Letter, 18.10.1941). Mrs. Hughes also found work for her old hands to do by sewing patches of brightly coloured material to any garments which she found lying about in the bathroom. Marge reported to her sister, "I've got one nightshirt with a crescent on the stomach and a sort of swastika on the seat" (Letter, 27.11.1941).

It was around this time that Marge began to lose contact with her former friend and correspondent Russell Meiggs. She had portrayed him in *Traitor's Purse* as Lee Aubrey, the autocratic, charming director of a private research institute who was so blindly convinced of his own intellectual superiority to those in charge of England's affairs that he conspired to cause financial chaos so that he could step in and take charge. Although the action was fanciful, the physical and psychological descriptions were unmistakeable. Aubrey is shown deliberately exploiting his attractiveness to women; even Amanda, Campion's fiancee, falls a prey to his charms: "She was talking to Lee Aubrey, who was leaning towards her, his big-featured face young and revealing, and belated puppyishness apparent in his attitude" (1941a, 36). At the end of the book Amanda almost echoes Marge's own criticisms of Meiggs (made in her letter to him of October 1938), which he must have recognized : "Lee has a habit of making extravagant passes at people conveying that he's hopelessly in love with them, so that they'll respond and he'll have the flattering experience of declining their affections with sweet sympathetic understanding" (207). Marge wrote to Joyce that Meiggs took the novel very personally, "It may have done him good. I hope he'll be all right." From the way she continues it is clear that in the prewar days she herself must, at least temporarily, have succumbed to Meiggs's charm: "there was no one ever quite like him as far as I was concerned" (Letter, 18.10.1941). The estrangement was emphasized when, in mid-December, Meiggs got married; Marge commented: "I wish him very well. There's a lot of good in him" (Diary, 17.12.1941).

The opening months of 1942 brought disastrous news from the Far East: on February 15 the Japanese captured Singapore, taking over eight thousand British soldiers prisoner. Fortunately Joyce had left the colony late the previous year. From the comparative safety of Tolleshunt D'Arcy, Marge was able to see the war as "a fascinating spectacle however terrible" (Letter to Reynolds, 26.02.1942). It would, however, not be long before the village became a totally restricted area, which prevented visitors from reaching Marge. She did still manage to get up to London on rare occasions, when she would meet the last of the old group of friends who was still in circulation, Leslie Cresswell. As an invalided veteran of the First War, he had not been called up. Marge found him remarkably unchanged, "still grumbling, still rude and lazy" (Letter to J. Allingham, 27.11.1941), but also a source of comfort. One aspect of Cressie surprised Marge, and revealed something of his emotional dependence on her: "It may sound unlikely but he reminds me more of my early girl friend Angela [Doubleday] than anyone I ever met. . . . We're not unlike each other temperamentally and it's very nice to have someone left out of the gang to talk to occasionally" (Letter to J. Allingham, 07.02.1942).

There was also her new friend, A. D. Lindsay, with whom she was corresponding regularly on social matters. Lindsay had taken a lead in organizing education for the armed forces in 1940 and was working on his study *The Modern Democratic State*, the first and only volume of which was published in 1943. As in her prewar letters to Meiggs, Marge used the correspondence to think aloud and work out her own views on social politics. In a sense Lindsay's temperament was well suited to Marge's intellectual simplicity and deeply felt convictions. He was a man of strong character, whose attitude to society reminded her of her father (Lindsay was twenty-five years older than Marge). He has been described as: "A powerful personality who could be ruthless with those who opposed what he believed to be right. He did not suffer gladly either the intellectually pretentious or those whose orthodoxy was conventional and not thought out. . . . He could not believe that it was possible for a man to have convictions on which he did not act" (Hill 1971, 643). Marge wrote to Lindsay that her attitude to belief had been instilled into her by her father, who discouraged her from holding views; "My only fixed stars lay in my religion . . . and all the rest was to be regarded as material to be observed" (Letter, 31.12.1941). Marge and Lindsay could ultimately never have wholeheartedly agreed about modern democratic society; Marge was too much of a conservative spirit, Lindsay too much of a radical. However, she found in him a male, authoritative extension of Jane Degras's socialist ideas, which had so shocked her three years earlier. Characteristically, she showed a remarkable willingness, if not to learn, then at least to consider and comment on unfamiliar concepts and ideas: "I may be wrong but I believe in the democratic balance and the undying fight—the capitalist management . . . and the strong trades unions and men's leaders. All the same the lack of understanding and the bitterness on the two sides is horrible" (Letter, 09.01.1942). The qualification at the end is typical Marge: she always found it easier to see the individual and the personal rather than the the theoretical or ideological.

It was in a letter to Lindsay that she first attempted to formulate the theme of *The Dance of the Years*, which was to be concerned with questions of heredity and environment. She was not yet able to state her ideas clearly although she insisted, "I know what I want to say . . . and so I am attempting it" (Letter, 14.01.1942). She had already shown the first two chapters to her aunt, Maud Hughes—a good barometer of popular taste—who "was unexpectedly keen" (Letter to Reynolds, 01.01.1942). However, Marge was not finding it an easy book to write; she hoped to have it done by November, but was most concerned to get it clear. She had certainly not chosen the ideal time to write a novel which demanded historical research and extended concentration: "It's taking time, more time than I expected, but it's not *its* fault. The interruptions of various kinds are considerable and the book marches on well between them" (Letter to Reynolds, 26.02.1942).

Among her interruptions was the duty, as Emergency Food officer, to make the necessary arrangements for the distribution of food in the case of enemy invasion. Then in March she was invited to give a talk on the BBC's Overseas Service about changes in English village life. Marge observed that the "creative germ" belonged to times of peace; wars simply "speed things up, they make things happen so fast that you can see them happening" (1942, n.p.). This same immanence of change led to a talk on "Invasion As It May Affect Tolleshunt D'Arcy," which Marge had to give in the village hall in April. Caught thus between the wide world and the needs of the village, Marge summed up her life at this point to Reynolds: "I'm living very happily. I eat my rations, smoke what the lady at the corner shop can spare and I work on the book, my various war jobs, reviewing etc. . . . My household has gone down to nothing in comparison and I live on a few pounds quite as comfortably as anyone else" (Letter, 26.02.1942).

As Rommel and his troops swept across the North African desert towards Tobruk, which they finally took on June 20, Marge, ignorant of Pip's whereabouts (apart from the fact that his address was now "No. 9 Water Tanks Company" and that when he wrote it was always cheerfully) was struggling away at her novel. She worked as hard as she could throughout the summer and managed to borrow a secretary in August to type up what she had written: "It's taking a long time but I think it's worth the trouble," she told Reynolds (Letter, 20.08,1942). By mid-September she had the first 60,000 words ready to send off to New York.

Although Reynolds was cautiously enthusiastic, he warned Marge that he did not feel that the new book was going to be a bestseller. Nevertheless, he passed on the manuscript to the Boston publishers Little, Brown, with whom preliminary negotiations had already been held. It was clear to both Marge and Reynolds that publication by Doubleday would identify the *Dance* in the public mind with her crime novels; in addition the decision was made to publish the novel under the name "Margery Allingham Carter." On November 4 Reynolds cabled, "Little Brown wildly enthusiastic . . . one thousand dollars advance now. . . . What an ignorant agent you have." Marge was delighted and promised to deliver the final manuscript early the following spring. She was "working very hard and fast now," she wrote in a letter confirming the delivery date, and added: "It is the first time I've ever

Marge during the Second World War

done anything *solely* to please myself. . . . It's a 'night on the tiles,' a 'means of getting relief,' a 'day off.' It may sell . . . but if it doesn't I feel I'll get into a great new phase of popular stuff until I can have another go" (Letter, 25.11.1942).

The Dance of the Years did not fulfil all the hopes that Marge had placed in it, nor did it sell very well. It *did*, however, usher in a "great new phase of popular stuff," which was to lead to the serious crime fiction of the fifties, such as *Tiger in the Smoke* and *Hide My Eyes*. Nor did Marge see the *Dance* merely in the context of her writing. Since her intellectual and emotional selves were indivisible from her work, the new novel, written for her own pleasure, was, as Marge put it in a later letter to Reynolds, "doing me as good in health and mental stability as an eighteen month holiday" (Letter, 10.12.1942).

Although the *Dance* was going well and life at D'Arcy was fairly peaceful, a new problem had arisen, which was to plague Marge for the next fifteen years: the Inland Revenue. As early as the end of 1941, Marge had complained to Reynolds that taxes were becoming a burden. The situation, with tax on high incomes rising, was that anyone earning irregularly and sometimes very well (Marge's U.S. income in the first half of 1941 was almost three thousand pounds) had to beg for payment to be so spaced out that the tax would not be crippling. Marge felt acutely the unfairness of such a system *for authors:* "The whole thing resolves now into a question of balance, i.e., the exactly *right* amount plus something else, and that something else is reputation . . . that's the only thing an author *can* put his work *into*" (Letter to Reynolds, 16.02.1942). In the autumn of 1942 she told Reynolds that with Pip abroad and earning, their joint income had risen, and that Pip had even been welcomed back from action in the desert by the paymaster with a tax demand for one hundred and fifty pounds. She concluded, "Over here now we only live (and apparently fight) to pay our taxes" (Letter, 28.09.1942); this tone of bitterness recurred whenever a tax crisis threatened.

The year ended well for Britain; on November 15 the church bells all over the country were rung, not to warn of invasion, but to celebrate Montgomery's victory over Rommel at El Alamein—a significant turning point in the fortunes of war. On a more personal level Marge received news of Pip's transference from the western desert. He had been appropriated by the Army's public relations department and began work as editor-in-chief of army publications in the Middle East, based, at first, in Baghdad. To know that he was out of any immediate danger, plus the news that Joyce, too, was out of harm's way in East Africa, was a great relief to Marge. It looked as though she could settle down to finish *The Dance of the Years* in peace.

Several factors combined to turn the novel into something less than the serious breakthrough that Marge had hoped for. First and foremost were the conditions under which she was writing: she continued to be First Aid commandant for the area, as well as being "the underground liaison and resistance agent in case of invasion" (Carter 1969, xv). Then the cautious, slow start had led to delays in completing the novel: "This three month delay is serious," she had written to Reynolds (10.12.1942) "but you must remember that it is an unusual situation." Little, Brown became impatient and in January 1943 began bullying Marge to finish. Finally, of course, she was writing something very different from anything she had ever done before, and was attempting to put over something of her philosophy of life which would make the book "as close to a moral tract as [Marge] could force her ironic talent" (Mann 1981, 203). The novel was finished on March 2 and sent off to Reynolds a month later. She sent Dr. Lindsay a copy of the manuscript; he replied enthusiastically but with reservations, "I am not entirely convinced about the middle" (Letter, 25.05.1943). Reynolds, too, blended praise with a warning, "Whether Americans want to read a satire of Victorian life . . . is a mattter I don't know" (Letter, 14.05.1943). Marge replied by openly admitting that she was, as far as serious novels were concerned, a beginner, but at the same time calculating the benefits for her future writing: "All I can tell you at the time of writing is that I did what I wanted to do as well as I could at the time. . . . It has been a new experience for me and until I came to do it I did not realize what a very different technique I should need. I have learnt a great deal about novel writing though through doing it" (Letter to Reynolds, 19.06.1943).

In October, *The Dance of the Years* was published simultaneously in Britain and the United States (in America the title was changed to *The Galantrys*—the family name of the protagonists). In the middle of the month Reynolds warned Marge, "The New York Times reviewed the book this morning . . . it is a very unfavourable review to put it mildly" (Letter, 13.10.1943). He was not exaggerating; the reviewer, having characterized Marge's style as elegant and highly mannered, uses this description as a way of leading into his main attack that the novel "is always artificial, always studied," that the characters never came to life, that Marge was a persistent moralizer, and last and most most damning of all: "In spite of much clever writing," the book "is dull and unconvincing and toward the end . . . is downright silly" (Prescott 1943). Other reviewers were not so damning, although the weaknesses of the second half (written under pressure) were noticed. Marge, however, took encouragement from the reactions of the home press; at the beginning of November she wrote Reynolds that the majority of British reviews had "been very good indeed and it is selling well" (Letter, 02.11.1943). Both Alan Pryce-Jones in the *Observer* and Edward Shanks in the *Daily Dispatch* were complimentary, whereas a fellow novelist, Howard Spring, was probably nearer the truth when he suggested that *Dance* was "more like a sketch for six novels than one shaped work" (Spring 1943).

Marge's bid for acknowledgment as a straight novelist seemed to have failed and yet, surprisingly enough, she at no time expressed the disappointment she must have felt. Her resilience may well have had something to do with an ongoing preoccupation with the phenomenon of change in literary fashions. Two years previously she had written that one effect of the immediacy of action in wartime might well be a return to a greater reliance on imagination in preference to realism, in order that fiction might "provide an example" to the so-called real world (1941b). This led Marge to consider anew her own specialization; she felt that the continued imminence of sudden death would put paid to the attraction of the thriller. She visualized that its place would be taken by "a much more domestic yarn" (Letter to Reynolds, 26.01.1942). Such a change contained the germ of her willingness to remain with the genre: an abandonment of sensationalism and a focus on social living would be more likely to allow her to pursue serious themes. Thus it is not so surprising that even before Marge had finished the *Dance* she wrote to Dr. Lindsay: "Now I feel like an adventure or two with Mr. Campion and Mr. Lugg. The trouble I seem to have is that I must put down all I think to escape from it, and a too constant devotion to one vein leaves me with a whole mass of fermenting ideas, which have to be let out and aired" (Letter, 02.03.1943). This view of her writing as a way of distancing herself from her own thoughts, reveals why it was so necessary for Marge to write *The Dance of the Years*: it had been a way of removing a whole barrier of ideas from her mind, thus freeing her creative energies for that which she could best do. The act of writing was to continue to have this therapeutic character for Marge until the end of her career. Virtually every thought, every reflection upon a pressing problem, was committed to paper, and in novel after novel she not only explored new facets of her experience of life, but, in doing so, purged her mind of emotional and mental preoccupations.

On September 8, 1943, Italy capitulated in the face of massive allied advances; the war seemed to be entering its final phase, but this did not indicate an end to difficulties. Marge wrote to Reynolds: "I am certain that this thing is going to end fairly suddenly and a long hard reconstruction period set in" (Letter, 03.12.1943). The immediate reality of war had retreated from D'Arcy giving Marge time to review her financial position, which was such as to make a commercial success desirable. "I must make some money" she told Reynolds (Letter, 13.09.1943) some four months after she had begun planning a new "thriller," *Coroner's Pidgin* (U.S. title: *Pearls before Swine*): "It should be a fast moving yarn about smart people on leave, packed with plenty of 'situation,' which is what editors usually mean when they say 'action'" (Letter to Reynolds, 20.06.1943). This new book took Marge a year to write; it was not that easy to get back to crime fiction after her serious engagement with the *Dance,* and she was plagued, as always, with a sense of her own inadequacy. Some time previously she had confided to Leslie Cresswell, "I've never contemplated a book without feeling that I'd mysteriously lost my gift and would never write again" (Letter, February 1940).

Before the new book was completed, Pip, now a lieutenant-colonel and the founding editor of the British army's magazine *Soldier,* had returned from the Middle East. He established his London headquarters in the top floor flat at 91 Great Russell Street, which he and Marge had rented in the autumn of 1940 from Doubleday's, whose London office was on the ground floor. *Coroner's Pidgin* was finished at the end of July and duly sent off to Reynolds who was enthusiastic. It had been written to appease Campion fans (Letter to Reynolds, 11.11.1944), but more particularly it represented Marge's attempt to give a preliminary anaylsis of what the postwar world was going to be like, and how men and women trained to wartime thinking and action would adapt to peacetime conditions.

With Pip's safe return, the war was to all intents and purposes over for Marge. It had (as her companion throughout the troubled years, Christina Carter, testified) "sort of brought her out a bit" (Interview, 12.10.1983), and in doing so given her intimate contact with the villagers and people around her. She had written of this to Frank Swinnerton: "I like the country folk and I feel more at home with them *mentally* than anyone else" (Letter, 30.08.1941). Thus when, in November 1944, she was invited to Oxford to lecture to servicemen on leave about "The English Countryman," she accepted with alacrity. She also certainly saw in the visit an opportunity to meet Dr. Lindsay after three years of correspondence. The meeting, according to Meiggs, was a failure: face to face Marge and Lindsay were aware only of a vast gap between their personalities, their education, and their respective situations in society. Marge was tongue-tied (Interview with R. Meiggs, 28.03.1984). As to the lecture, it was, to judge from Marge's copious notes, a rambling affair filled with anecdotes and minor details. Wisely enough she began by pointing out that she was a writer and not a talker, and later that, whereas the average countryman was inarticulate, she was incoherent. The experience strengthened her instinctive unwillingness to speak in public.

It is paradigmatic of Marge's life that as the war was drawing to a close in May 1945, one of her novels was being published while the next was already forming in her mind. Even before the publication of *Coroner's Pidgin* in the United States, at the beginning of May, she had written to Reynolds that she would like "to get a new story done this summer" (Letter, 27.04.1945). Meanwhile Pip was happily "back at drawing and newspapers at the War Office" (Letter to Reynolds, 23.05.1945). VE-Day came and went, Churchill resigned, and a Labour Government was voted into office. Marge had always had reservations about socialism; before the war she had described it to Meiggs as "Christianity with the human perception taken out" (Letter, 01.04.1937). It seemed to her a singularly inappropriate doctrine for the country: "How hopeless it is to try to go red in Tolleshunt D'Arcy. D'Arcy doesn't want to be any gentleman's brother—thank you" (Letter to L. Cresswell, February 1940).

Tom Driberg, who was the successful Labour candidate in Marge's constituency of Maldon, recorded in his autobiography that, whereas Dorothy Sayers lent furniture for Labour's committee rooms, "though personally friendly," Marge "thought it wiser to leave everything to Churchill and not 'disturb the people'" (Driberg 1977, 183). For her the postwar years were to begin, not with visionary hopes for a better world, but simply at home among her own people and with a new manuscript waiting to be completed: "My life and household is slowly returning to something like normal and I see I shall soon have no excuse for being slow with copy" (Letter to Reynolds, 22.11.1945).

8

Communicable Form

I have been trained to remark since I was seven and I must always be watching and noting and putting things into communicable form. It has become a second nature and is inescapable.

Margery Allingham

Marge's writing of the war years acknowledges the spirit of the times in so far as it seems to exist between the parentheses indicated by a scientist's statement in *Traitor's Purse:* "This is refined warfare" (1941a, 89), and the realization expressed by a character in *Coroner's Pidgin* that "we're not quite the gay don't-cares we used to be" (1945, 30). Marge's "serious" novel, *The Dance of the Years,* written between these brackets, looks both backwards and forwards, with an emphasis on the latter, as indicated by the original dedication to Marge's grandmother, "who always promised me 'a nice day tomorrow.'" The two thrillers are linked by central characters who act from irrational convictions of their own unique importance as agents in the service of higher ideals. Lee Aubrey's inflated opinion of his own capabilities leads him to attempt to subvert his nation's finances in order to create the chaos which only he can master; Theo Bush, in *Coroner's Pidgin,* masters the theft of the nation's art treasures so that they will be preserved for delivery to the conquering German connoisseurs.

The true interest of both books lies, however, in the initial ideas which control them. In *Traitor's Purse* Marge was absorbed with working out the problem of an investigator, Campion, who suffers from amnesia while faced with the urgent necessity of locating and preventing a crime from being committed. Thus there is a sense in which the novel is a *writer's* tour-de-force, in which the reader can only participate on the author's terms. In *Coroner's Pidgin,* the events of the mystery plot are played out against a background of serious questions of general concern at the time of publication: what would British society after the war be like? what would change involve for those whose success was a direct product of the carefree conditions of their world in the 1930s? After *The Dance of the Years*, the new thrust of Marge's fiction was to be towards the investigation of personal problems shared by the society of her readers.

Much of the success of *Traitor's Purse* depends upon the simple fact that for much of the novel the reader is in possession of more knowledge about Campion than Campion himself, and is thus fascinated by every step in his gradual retrieval of memory. It is, however, unfortunate that Marge believed it essential to her purpose to preserve Campion's isolation from assistance in his dilemma. His motive for refusing to confide in his closest ally, Amanda Fitton, is particularly suspect; early in the novel she withdraws her eight-year promise to marry Campion because of the stronger, more sensual attraction of Lee Aubrey. The reader is expected to accept Campion's reaction as honourable: "He could hardly tell her now. To reveal his helplessness at this juncture would be both to plead weakness and to appeal to her pity, and to appeal to pity is very loathsome to love" (32).

Campion's sentiments are in strong contrast to the changes in social mores and conventions of which Marge at that time was only partially aware. *Traitor's Purse*, written virtually parallel to *The Oaken Heart*, shares with that book a bright-eyed, conservative patriotism which was soon to disappear from her writing. Speaking of Campion, Marge emphasizes the biographical link between writer and fictional character:

> He belonged to a post-war generation, that particular generation which was too young for one war and most prematurely too old for the next. It was the generation which had picked up the pieces after the holocaust indulged in by its elders, only to see its brave new world wearily smashed again by younger brothers. His was the age which had never known illusion. . . . Yet now . . . something new had appeared on his emotional horizon. It had been something which so far he had entirely lacked and which had been born to him miraculously late in his life. . . . It was a faith, a spiritual and romantic faith . . . a deep and lovely passion for his home, his soil, his blessed England, his principles, his breed, his Amanda and Amanda's future children. That was the force that was driving him. (115–16).

Given this type of patriotic faith, treason becomes the ultimate crime, the final sin, which Campion, a somewhat handicapped knight, has to combat. *Traitor's Purse* is a book imbued with the unreflected optimism of early wartime. It suffices that Campion can contribute to the thwarting of Aubrey's plans; the limited perspective of wartime obscures any future dimension greater than global victory over the enemy.

The very nature of the problem which fascinated Marge from the start—Campion's amnesia—dictates that the pattern of antithesis suggested by the thematic story of the triumph of right over twisted wrong, and elaborated in the further antitheses, crime-justice, right-wrong, patriotism-betrayal, should find its echo in the more general contrast of ignorance and knowledge. Campion is presented as someone whose very lack of memory taunts him with the notion of the narrow borderline between that which he lacks and that which he knows to exist: "The curtain between this misery of ignorance and a very clear vision indeed was tantalizingly thin" (41). Marge also reveals a nice sense of irony, which springs from the situation of the detective robbed of his share of common knowledge. When Campion silently leaves Aubrey's house at night to keep a rendezvous with the local police superintendent, the latter greets him with the words: "It's as well to be careful. We don't want to give a lot of fancy explanations. Once you start that game, it's my experience that you have to go on remembering what you've said for years afterwards" (61).

The essence of Campion's situation is contained, much later in the novel, in a narrational comment: "In his blindness he had discovered his objective. In his miserable ignorance he could not identify it" (167). On this level *Traitor's Purse* is a surprisingly sophisticated crime novel. The classic detective is a man whose near monopoly of knowledge enables him to combine facts into a perfect solution of a problem; thus a detective whose only knowledge is gained instinctively, and who, even in possession of the facts is unable to see them for what they are, is potentially a figure of fun. Perception *and* exploitation of this irony without any lessening of tension in the narrative is a rare achievement. Marge was fully aware of what she had attempted: "My own opinion of *Traitor's Purse* is that it was a bit sophisticated for a very wide public" (Letter to Reynolds, 24.06.1941). Later, however, she complained to Frank Swinnerton that a war-crushed Heinemann had given insufficient effort to the promotion of the book: "I'm afraid it's to be dismissed as a rubbishy thriller" (Letter, 15.03.1941). Nevertheless, the reviewers were not only kind but, in some cases, extremely enthusiastic. In the *Daily Telegraph*, George Bishop called the novel "one of the best tales she has written" (Bishop 1941); and the anonymous reviewer of the *Christian Science Monitor* went even further in suggesting that it "may really and genuinely mark an epoch in the development of the detective story" (Anon. 1941a).

To write anything about *The Dance of the Years* is a strange and difficult undertaking: the novel has been out of print for over forty years, nor is there any likelihood of it ever being reissued. Nevertheless it would be inexcusable to omit the book, which was such a conscious bid for recognition as a serious novelist. Marge's book reviews for *Time and Tide* reveal that she had a clear notion of what she believed were the necessary elements of a successful novel: living, realistic characters, who would reveal the author's interest in people; a compelling story; and the willingness to say "exactly what one has in mind" (1938b,d,e).

Marge approached the writing of *Dance* convinced she had both a good story and something to say. As far as the story is concerned, it is worth noting what she wrote in a review at this time: "The very long, 'tell-us-a-story' narrative embracing whole lifetimes and great patches of physical adventure takes a lot of beating as pure entertainment. When it is soundly built and truthfully coloured it is almost irresistible" (1941c). *The Dance of the Years* sets out to do just this; it tells the life story of James Galantry, born early in the nineteenth century, and even attempts a prophetic look at future generations up to the opening of the Second World War. The bare bones of the story are promising material and lay ready to hand in that which Marge had discovered about the history of her own family. James is the son of an ageing country squire, William Galantry, by his second wife, the gypsy Schulie. He thus corresponds in fact to the William Allingham (1803–74) who was the illegitimate son of John Allingham and Charlotte Duncan. James marries Lizzie Timson, whose full name is Elizabeth Jane (1943, 174), the Christian names of the Miss Jackson (1822–72) whom William Allingham married in 1839. Much of their married life is spent "in Penton Place, off the Walworth Road" (1943, 147), which was in fact the home of Marge's great-grandfather. Numerous other examples could be quoted to prove the autobiographical authenticity of the details of Marge's story. It is not, however, the Allingham family saga which was at the heart of the new novel. While she was still working on chapter 4, Marge wrote to Dr. Lindsay: "Its theme is an idea which has been growing in me for years. I cannot believe that the things people mean when they talk of 'heredity,' 'environment,' and 'reincarnation' are not rather childish conceptions of a very big but also very obvious truth" (Letter, 14.01.1942). It is this truth which is behind the title of the novel and which might be summed up as the principle of continuity. For Marge, times changed, people were born, lived, and died—but nothing was ever really lost. In a letter to her sister-in-law, Betty Carter, on the occasion of the death of Betty's and Pip's mother in April 1941 Marge had written: "I have always found it very difficult to believe in a Heaven . . . in which one met old friends at some sort of perpetual garden party, *but* I can conceive (just) a continuation in which I should be quite as much a stranger, *and as well looked after,* as I was when I arrived in this world." As a sentiment expressed in a letter of condolence this idea is comforting; as the explicit thematic motif of a full-length novel it tends to become mawkish and embarrassing. Early in the book the idea is expressed simply as "the Round Dance of God" (19), which is later transformed into the "Dance of the Years." As such it is a conception which conveniently and somewhat too neatly takes care of the unexpected in life: "After all it is how the dancers tread their individual measures which makes their performance what it is; the path being, as it were, but their place on the platform for the time being" (101).

The metaphor of the dance acts structurally to unite discrepant elements throughout the book. Love, sex, marriage, and birth are all explained in terms of the pattern of the dance, which does not end with death. At the end of the novel as James Galantry dreams of his great-grandson in 1941, he tells the younger man, "There is no dying. . . . There is no escaping. *Somebody is doing all this*" (310). The somebody, the force, behind the all-embracing dance is not, as the reader might imagine, simply God, but God plus the Earth as the mother of humanity: "God is your Father, but I am your mother, and I love you too" (311). This brief summary of the fundamental idea behind *Dance* reveals a basic conceptual weakness of the novel: the *idea* is too intrusive and too naively mystical to be able to carry the weight of the narrative. The insistence on articulating the "message" reveals the inability of the fictional narrative to exploit the metaphor intelligibly.

The anonymous reviewer of the *New Yorker* put his finger on the structural weakness of the book when he wrote of the second half: "She has tried to make a three-generation novel out of what should have been strictly a portrait of a man and a class" (Anon. 1943). The first half of the book takes James Galantry from conception to marriage and contains the expression of those themes which Marge was to elaborate in her return to crime fiction at the end of the war: change and the necessity to adapt to new circumstances. In *Dance,* change refers to the upheaval of the industrial revolution, the transition from the eighteenth to the nineteenth century: "Change as inescapable, as relentless and as painful as the change from youth to middle age" (15). As a writer, Marge's response to the phenomenon is not quite the same as her reaction as amateur philosopher. While she attempts to fortify her characters and readers by reference to her conception of the eternal dance of the years ("This history . . . is the story of James and the permutations of James," 222), as a writer she cannot ignore the weapon of language, and the consolation of communication: "James taught William one other thing.

It was that discovery of his about the liberation which lies in expression. It was not easy for James to pass this on for he had never learned how to set himself free, but William grasped the theory. He had not the gift of words, but he saw what they were for and what they could do. He made this piece of information a very useful asset" (207). On this level *Dance* is particularly concerned with various forms of expression; Shulie the gypsy "had her own methods of communication" (19); two other characters exhibit "verbal dexterity" (105); the tale which Lizzie Timson's father tells of the rape of his daughter "was passionate, incoherent and utterly convincing" (158). Unfortunately this idea is insufficiently exploited, and far too much of the novel is concerned with working up to the expression of its pseudophilosophical theme. In retrospect Marge somewhat sadly told Reynolds that she would "never write another like it and probably never one with so much thought in it" (Letter, 10.11.1943). Apparently unwittingly she had put her finger on the source of the novel's weakness: the author's thoughts are all too apparent, the realm of narration and the realm of ideas never completely cohere.

Superficially, in *Coroner's Pidgin* Marge was returning to the thriller "as opposed to a 'tec tale" (Letter to Reynolds, 15.06.1945). Nevertheless, the themes of *The Dance of the Years* and the experience of writing it were still very much with her. In the form of an investigation of the passing of the old order, and an anticipation of the new, the new novel continued the fictional reflection upon the continuity of experience. To this end there are continual reminders of the curious atmosphere of the last months of the war—the sense of living both at war and in peacetime. The measure of the change is supplied by regular references, both implicit and explicit, to Marge's earlier novels.

Coroner's Pidgin does not, as has been suggested, make a statement about war (Pike 1977, 324), but about change. This note is sounded at the outset when we are told of Campion that: "He had changed a little in the last three years; the sun had bleached his fair hair to whiteness, lending him a physical distinction he had never before possessed. There were new lines in his over-thin face and with their appearance some of his own misleading vacancy of expression had vanished" (1945, 6). The lightheartedness of the thirties is replaced by outward signs of maturity and age, signifying an unfamiliar distinction and seriousness. Here is a new Campion for a new age.

At the center of the book is Johnny Carados, in peacetime already a dominant figure, and in war one of the new breed of heroes: the dashing, daredevil RAF pilot. With clearly established roles in both

worlds, Carados is a transitional figure. In the thirties he was surrounded by a subservient group of admiring friends, for whom, by the
mid-forties, his word has become law, his hero status unquestioned
("Johnny's *sans reproche*" 149). For Marge, memory lent a nostalgic romance to the circle of friends she and Pip had built up by the late
thirties. Such "gangs" seemed to her to be a typical phenomenon of the
period, and thus Carados's entourage gains representative status: "Together they had formed one of the most closely knit of all the little gangs
which had characterised the social life of pre-war London" (14). To
some extent, *Coroner's Pidgin* examines the ability of such social phenomena to survive not only the public rigours of war, but also the
internal divisiveness of intrigue. The plot is initiated by the discovery
of the body of a dead woman in Carados's bedroom; at first it is assumed
that this is a move to disrupt his plans to marry the young widow of
one of his RAF friends, which in turn threatened to disrupt the established Carados circle. Campion is drawn into the investigation against
his will, and is thus present at a first gathering of the group: "They
were all there . . . all infinitely more competent to deal with any situation for being once again together" (51). Unfortunately the harmony
of togetherness is broken almost immediately by Ricky Silva, the circle's
aesthete, who is a reminder of Benny Konrad in *Dancers,* and more
particularly of Rex in *Shrouds*—part sensitive aesthete, part suspect for
displaying somewhat stereotypical homosexual mannerisms. Having
been forced into "the battledress of a private of the British Army" (51),
Ricky translates the effects of war into communicable form, "This war's
made people awfully reckless and—*coarse*" (56). It is Campion who is
made to realise that "the life of a man like Ricky Silva as a conscript
private . . . did not bear consideration" (55). It is notable that the other
character who is granted a similar perception of the coarsening effects
of war is Campion's servant Lugg: "You've got slightly common out at
the war. . . . Where's yer feeling?" (154). The universality of the experience is deftly suggested by confining its articulation to two such anti-
thetical characters: the slightly pansy young man with artistic taste, and
the comedy figure of the elderly ex-convict.

Shortly after the scene mentioned above, the theme of the tawdri-
ness of memories is introduced, by the delivery to Johnny Carados of a
small parcel. It contains "a battered, artificial rose" and "a string of
unconvincing pearls" (57), which function, within the plot as signs
pointing to the link between Carados and the dead woman. Seen in
conjunction with the information that the household "had a lot of this
sort of thing for the musical comedy party in 'thirty-eight'" (58), the rose
and pearls are a potent symbol of the inability of the frail pleasures of

the late thirties to survive intact into the postwar period.

The numerous references which Marge makes in *Coroner's Pidgin* to her earlier books are more than just playful intertextual quotations. They function, too, as signifiers of change. For example, Carados's long time girlfriend-companion, Eve Snow—"the most lovable comedienne in the world" (26)—is another successful stage performer from the milieu of Jimmy Sutane in *Dancers*. She, however, is given a greater hardness and adaptability, as, if nothing else, her hit number in the show of the moment indicates, "Momma's Utility Baby Gets a Riveter's Lullaby" (99). This is austerity age glamour with a vengeance. A similar reminder of continuity and change comes when, early in the investigation, Campion is brought face to face with his old companion of past adventures, Stanislaus Oates, now chief of the C.I.D., who comments: "I've never believed you've ever quite recovered from that business at the beginning of the war. You were working for a week in a state of amnesia" (47). The reference to *Traitor's Purse* is used to cast doubts on Campion's veracity, and on his competence. Yet, the book goes on to prove that, although called upon to solve a very different puzzle, Campion has lost none of his ability to act with efficiency and perspicacity. The experience of the war has hardened him and accustomed him to the problems which war has created—the very problems which he felt so inadequate to deal with in the earlier novel.

Occasionally the reference to an earlier book seems very minor in appearance, as when Campion tells Susan Shering about the museum of wine which Carados helped found before the war. He remarks that the museum, of which Theo Bush, the eventual villain of the piece, was curator, was in a "little house in Jockey's Fields, near Barnabas the publishers" (72). The reminder of *Flowers for the Judge* acts as an indirect pointer to Bush as the criminal, similar in megalomaniac character and motivation to John Widdowson of the earlier novel. At the same time there is a suggestion that the refinement and elegance of the past has become museumlike and irrelevant to the world of the present. Similarly, the unlikely revelation that among the treasures of the museum lost in enemy action was the Gyrth Chalice (117) from *Look to the Lady*, is tantamount to stating that not only have the sacred objects of yesterday become meaningless, but also that the whole world of the early adventures is irrecoverably past. The effect is similar to that of Oates's mentioning "a dreadful little man called Knapp—Thos Knapp" (163), who made an unforgettable cameo appearance in *Mystery Mile* as a minor member of the underworld. Oates reports that after Knapp spent time in prison early in the war, he "is now in Italy pulling his weight"

(163)—war achieves that which years of peacetime correction has not, namely respectability. Marge was to explode this myth seven years later in *The Tiger in the Smoke.*

One last quotation should be mentioned; much of the conversation and some of the action of *Coroner's Pidgin* takes place at a restaurant, the Minoan, in Frith Street, which is Campion's "introduction to the era of elegant make-do" (67), so characteristic of the immediate postwar period. This restaurant is run by two temperamental men, Stavros and Pirri, who are less flamboyant versions of the Hakapopoulos brothers in *Shrouds.* Whereas the latter were flagrant condoners of murder and breakers of the law, the former are characterized by little more than their vicarious experience of lawlessness as they attempt to build up a profitable business in the hopelessly austere world of transition: "At last people are willing to spend and I—I have nothing to sell" (215). The reminder of the early novel is, however, remarkably well chosen. In contrast to the Hakapopoulos's restaurant in Lord Scroup St., Soho, which was notable for its "mysterious blackness," "cold darkness," and "muffled quiet" (1938f, 237), the Minoan has "glossy white walls," "green-tinted table linen," and an air of "temporary tastefulness" (67). The contrast and distance between the worlds of 1938 and 1945 could hardly have been put more eloquently.

Much of *Coroner's Pidgin* is devoted to the conception—so characteristic of human existence in the closing months of the war—of a simultaneous existence in the two totally different worlds of war and peace. The image, first enunciated by Carados ("I'm living in two worlds, Campion. . . . Two utterly different worlds," 32), becomes a sort of leitmotif with variations, shared by some ("There are so many different worlds. . . . We each have to live in two or three," 69) and felt deeply by Campion: "A world in which everyone was young and everyone might die tomorrow was not the same world as the one mirrored in Stavros's new white paint. Johnny Carados belonged to both. It appeared to Mr. Campion that that fact might well account for quite a lot" (70–71). Whereas for Carados the peacetime world of the past has lost its flavour—"how small peace-time affectations seem these days" (127)—Eve Snow (a tougher, more rational woman than many of the prewar figures) rejects the insistence on the double world image on grounds of its suggestion of privilege for the male combatants: "If you tell me you're 'at war' I—I'll hit you, Albert. Good God, aren't we all at war" (107). The insistence on this motif is part of Marge's overt discussion of the contrast between different periods of her and her contemporaries' lives. It is part, too, of the insistence on the parameters of transition. On the one hand, for those involved in the active waging of war, "ordinary peace-time considerations and institutions come to look a bit remote" (103); on the other, the peacetime that is approaching is clearly going to be very different from the peacetime of memory.

The fact that it is Carados who introduces the "two worlds" theme, and shares his feelings about it with Campion is exploited within the narrative to create an echo of the strategy Marge employed in *Dancers*. Campion's knowledge and understanding of Carados's confusion, of his insistence that wartime morality and allegiances are different to those of peacetime, allows him to entertain—and at the same time reject—the police suspicion that only Carados could be behind the criminal activities of the story. Oates, the professional criminal hunter, underlines Campion's dilemma when he says: "That's why you'll never make a policeman. . . . You don't see it as I do; you see a man, I see a menace" (172). Yet when it comes to the inquest on one of the true menaces, Dolly Chivers (Carados's secretary and Theo Bush's wife, whose attempt to manufacture evidence against Carados was thwarted by Campion's swift action), police evidence deliberately distorts the facts: "Mr. Campion had heard a great deal of police evidence in his career, but he was impressed by the Inspector. The statement of fact, just sufficient for credence and not enough to make any sort of picture, was masterly" (248). The studied avoidance of true-to-the-facts realism in Inspector Holly's narrative, which erases both Campion and Carados from the scene of crime averted, is another sign of a change in the times. Yet at the same time Marge is insisting on the omnipotence of narrative, of language itself.

The novel comes to a close on a note carried over from *The Dance of the Years*: the theme of the interdependence of all living phenomena. Campion's unwilling suspicions and fears are negated when Carados, whom he (and the reader) had been led to believe dead—the victim of a heroic act of self-destruction in atonement for his crimes—returns. He is late for the inquest, having been on a special secret mission behind enemy lines. Campion asks him, "This other business was nothing to do with it?" to which Carados replies, "Nothing is *nothing* to do with anything" (253). This is an expression of Marge's philosophy of the grand pattern of existence in a nutshell—and, of course, an essential principle of all crime fiction.

The naive patriotism of the early war years, the stoic fortitude of *The Oaken Heart*, and the determined crusade against evil of *Traitor's Purse* could only have become the clear-headed rational awareness of change and the complete integration of belief and fiction in *Coroner's Pidgin* by way of the almost introspective self-reassurance of *Dance of the Years*.

9

Starting up Again

I have got used to seeing my husband only at weekends—in some ways more unsettling than not seeing him for three years!—and the routine of life is starting up again.

Margery Allingham

For Marge, "starting up again" was like the setting in motion of a well-oiled machine, a form of changing gear after climbing a steep hill. Apart from the three years' separation from Pip, her life had not experienced any sudden caesura. Rather, there had been a momentary change of direction followed by the continued routine of writing, punctuated by war work and participation in village life. Nor was there any abatement to her activity in the decade that followed the war: she wrote and published three novels, four novellas, fourteen short stories, a play, and more than thirty review articles. Yet this same postwar decade saw changes which were more thorough, more final, and more universal than Marge herself had foreseen. With the rest of the population she experienced the impact of peace under a Labour government, suffered under the new austerity, and shared in the slow return to affluence of the New Elizabethan age under the Conservatives. Her professional life was marked by profitable success both in the United States and in Britain. Together with Pip, who flourished in his own journalistic career throughout the decade, she enjoyed a spasmodic social life at D'Arcy that was no longer the happy-go-lucky gathering of a gang of close, old friends, but a more sophisticated "entertaining," often with celebrities and always with show. Yet beneath the surface veneer of fame and success lurked the specter of ill health, the irrational and nerve-wracking torment of the Inland Revenue, and the discovery that wartime physical separation from Pip was to be succeeded by a peacetime emotional separation as he developed his own career, his own interests, and his own affairs.

Historians of the late forties paint a picture of a gloomy halfway house era, in which people remained unsure of what the future might hold, convinced only that the England they had known would not return. On the one hand "the country lay in a crepuscular zone with the shadows of night as firm upon the landscape as the heartening hints of the rising sun" (Marwick 1982, 22); on the other, "England needed her sense of continuity as she needed air" (Hopkins 1963, 104). Marge saw little of the promise of sunshine and was nostalgic for the past. Although aware of the irreversibility of change, she resented the pervasive gloom produced by the clumsy efforts of Labour to deal with the problems of peacetime: "This extraordinary country does seem to have got itself into a fine old muddle at the moment. It may be just another of our celebrated 'bloodless revolutions' but even so it is not comfortable. At no time during the war was living so difficult here—bombs notwithstanding! This government seems to have destroyed the value of work" (Letter to Reynolds, 26.04.1946).

It is characteristic of a certain continuity in Marge's thought that her criticism of the government should be based on their destruction of "the value of work"; one is reminded of her complaint in the thirties that Pip and Grog had not learnt the value of work done for its own sake. Marge's socialism—if that is the right label—was of the romantic rural variety, hopelessly out of date and removed from the realities of an industrial urban society. Yet she held her beliefs passionately and saw in the muddle and confusion of the Labour government "the death knell of socialism here for the next fifty years" (Letter to Reynolds, 04.07.1946). By the end of 1946—after a summer which had been washed out by incessant rain—she could see no improvement in the situation and reported to Reynolds: "Things are really bad here this winter. No one is well fed which is to say that most people are reminded that they are poor at least three times a day and that's bad for anyone's temper. . . . To make matters worse the workers have more money than they've ever handled (which still foxes them) and all they can buy with it is a seat at a football match or a flutter on the dogs" (Letter, 23.11.1946).

However gloomy the overall situation appeared, Marge found consolation in having Pip home again. He had spent the last eighteen months of the war editing the extremely successful army magazine *Soldier*, which he had founded together with Colonel Sean Fielding in 1944. After establishing the magazine in Brussels, the editorial office followed in the wake of the allied armies, finally settling in Hamburg, where Pip completed his army service as a lieutenant-colonel (Anon. 1954). In March 1946 he was demobbed, and went almost immediately to the *Daily Express* as features editor, although Marge commented on him retaining the image of "the returned soldiery" well into the autumn (Letter to Reynolds, 30.09.1946). After a brief stint editing a small illustrated magazine, *Town and Country Review,* for Beaverbrook, Pip was offered and accepted the assistant editorship of the glossy society weekly *The Tatler,* now being edited by his army associate Sean Fielding. Pip now spent the weekdays at the flat in Great Russell Street, returning to D'Arcy at weekends. For a time Marge tried to spend as much time with him as possible, but she found herself unable to work at her writing in London. As a result, the Carters settled into a pattern of working apart and relaxing together, which was to last for the next eleven years until Pip left the *Tatler* in 1957. Fortunately this turned out to be an amicable and highly convenient arrangement. Pip rapidly developed the taste for elegant and expensive living which had been noticeable in his years as a would-be country squire. Now, however, he had professional entrance into a world which would otherwise have been closed to him, and which he found highly congenial. This meant that he was being enabled to cultivate a lifestyle that would increase the distance from Marge; for, although she enjoyed city life in small doses, it was not a world in which she felt at ease.

For the first time in the Carters' married life Pip was earning regularly and well, and Marge's income, though somewhat sporadic, was higher than in prewar days. Unfortunately, as Marge pointed out to Reynolds, increased income unavoidably meant increased taxation: "The fact of the double tax, coupled with the effect of my own and my husband's incomes being lumped together inescapably for super-tax purposes, means that I stand to get something like 3d or 4d out of every pound I make on your side. It does not encourage one to work" (Letter, 26.02.1946). Because of this, Marge was sceptical about writing short stories for the American weekly supplement *This Week,* which, because of its huge circulation, would have been very profitable. She was convinced that she would never see more than about a fifth of the money for a type of story which she did not even particularly wish to write. However, she did acknowledge that she was only able to meet the Inland Revenue's demands with the aid of the sort of money which she could earn in the United States. At the end of 1946, she told her English agent, W. P. Watt, that the taxation problem was forcing her to face up to an impossible decision: "In view of the present taxation on married people I am forced to do one of two things. One of these is to devote

Pip in the Late 1940s

part of my time making extra money in the U.S. in order to pay supertax due on my earnings. The other is to give up writing altogether and do my own housework and cooking as our government expects a married woman to do" (Letter, 12.11.1946).

For the first twelve years of her married life Marge had consistently played the unconventional role of wife as breadwinner. Her attack on the otherwise progressive Labour government's acceptance of the traditional role for married women reflects the instinctive militancy with which she rejected a conformity which forced the individual into preconceived moulds. While seeing that one of the factors which augmented the taxation problem was the maintenance of separate establishments—D'Arcy House and the flat in Great Russell Street—Marge never for a moment considered moving to London, nor would she consider the alternative of forcing Pip to return to the country: "I can hardly expect him to give up his career, can I?" she asked her friend Louise Callender of Heinemann's (Letter, November 1946). This is not so much the expression of a certain pigheadedness on Marge's part as her absolute refusal to submit to an authority whose dictates she considered irrational. During the war Marge would either have had to give up D'Arcy House or get behind with the payment of her taxes and had chosen the latter course. When, in August 1945, the American *Good Housekeeping* had paid $8500 for "Wanted: Someone Innocent," the short novel she had written immediately after completing *Coroner's Pidgin,* she used the money to pay her tax arrears. Now that Pip was earning a good regular salary, they were jointly subject to supertax, so that the only solution was to write another serial for the American market. Marge spent the last part of 1946 doing just this, although she was also hard at work on the new Campion novel. She finished the novella "The Last Act" in January 1947, but unfortunately it was rejected by both *Good Housekeeping* and *Colliers.* The search for a lucrative sequel to her first serial success haunted Marge's work for the next three years.

More Work for the Undertaker, which took Marge almost three years to finish, was an attempt to return to the form of past successes; it is certainly her most nostalgic postwar book. In her letters she announced that it would be a novel comparable to *Police at the Funeral, Dancers in Mourning,* and *Flowers for the Judge,* by which she meant that it would be "a really good mystery," "a Detective Story Proper," and "a decent detective story of the solider type" (Letters to Reynolds. 30.09.1946 & 10.03.1947; L. Callender, November 1946). Late in 1946, Marge hoped that the new book, which had been begun in June 1945, would be ready for publication early in 1947, but the drive to finish "The Last Act" continually forced her to defer her completion date. Throughout 1947 she worked slowly but steadily on the *Undertaker*; Marge had learned her lesson with *The Dance of the Years,* and for the remainder of her life refused to be hurried: "I am working well if slowly . . . but I am satisfied with the story and feel it's one of the best solid detective stories I've done" (Letter to Reynolds, 23.06.1947). This certainty about the book grew on her, so that in September she felt able to write to her editor at Doubleday's, Isabelle Taylor, "I think it's going to be the best I've done" (Letter, 29.09.1947).

Meanwhile, Marge had agreed to do a weekly book review article for the revamped *Daily Sketch,* the *Daily Graphic,* for twenty guineas a time. The articles would commence in April and she would be given the books to review six days in advance. The extra money was useful, but a further demand upon her already limited time was the price she would have to pay for it. Yet Marge regarded reviewing as good practice for her more serious creative work: "The reviewing takes a bit of time but I think it's good for me. I know I *have* to get the stuff in because the printer is waiting and that gets me into the habit of working steadily" (Letter to Reynolds, 24.05.1947). This was a habit she had cultivated ever since the days when she used to write for her Aunt Maud's magazines, but Marge seems to have needed the discipline and craftsmanship which such writing demanded. The regular weekly appearance of her *Daily Graphic* reviews even seemed to build up her faith in herself as a writer: "The mere sight of my work in print every week and the knowledge that I *must* turn something in every Monday gives me a sort of confident approach to the other work. I never feel I really *can* write, you know. I'm always mildly surprised when I get something published" (Letter to Reynolds, 06.09.1947). Unfortunately after twenty-seven articles (on about three times as many books) and just under six hundred pounds, the job came to an end at the beginning of October. Marge, as she put it, had been "crowded out by the latest paper cut" in a further year of shortages and austerity (Letter to Reynolds, 13.10.1947). Apart from three articles which she wrote for the *Tatler* when Elizabeth Bowen, the regular book reviewer, was on holiday, this was the end of Marge's ten-year activity as a professional book critic.

In spite of all these interruptions, the first 27,000 words of the *Undertaker* were sent off to Reynolds in August. Marge continued to work intently on the book, reporting in October that it was going like a house on fire. The fire was probably cooled by the severe cold of the first three months of 1948; the elements brought "what was to prove the most bitter and sustained assault the British Isles had known for half a century" (Hopkins 1963, 75). Furthermore, there were frequent power cuts during the winter due to a shortage of coal resulting from continued labour disputes in the recently nationalized mines. Marge saw this as a further sign of the bungling which resulted from a government which she believed to be composed of amateurs, who hadn't "the training to lead the country" (Letter to Reynolds, 06.09.1947). In the same letter, she wrote to Reynolds of the feeling of having "suddenly woken up to find ourselves broke and on the verge of starvation," and, after a visit to London, she commented that "morale is just plain bad" (Letter, 13.10.1947). A few months earlier she had observed that "the whole place is in very much lower gear so to speak" (Letter to Reynolds, 26.07.1948). The representative nature of Marge's reactions is borne out by Harry Hopkins's comment on the same period: "there was, for some, the sense of a once great nation running down" (Hopkins 1963, 76). It is this air of lost momentum that tends to pervade *More Work for the Undertaker*, and lends the book its particular period relevance.

With the loss of the *Graphic* job, Marge was at last free to devote herself wholeheartedly to the new book; she was happy to be back with the crime novel once again, "I know more what I'm doing and I enjoy it, so it's not such an effort" (Letter to Reynolds, 30.04.1947). Since the end of the war, there had always been other demands on Marge's time, so that now, as she wrote to Reynolds, she could at last get round to her true career: "The time has come I feel to make an effort to sail back into detective fiction. I shall do it. I'm only slow" (Letter, 06.01.1948). The novel was completed on May 13, and after having it typed, Marge sent the finished work to Dwye Evans at Heinemann's. He was enthusiastic and particularly pleased that Marge had not made the mistake with Campion "of allowing him to remain for ever at the same age" (Letter, 14.06.1948).

This was to became the hallmark of Marge's protagonist, who, as she wrote to Eunice Frost of Penguin Books, "has passed from youth to middle age with me and as he has matured so have I—or the other way round" (Undated letter). In the *Undertaker* Marge felt that for the first time she had "recaptured the prewar gaiety of Albert" (Letter to I. Taylor, 19.07.1948). In addition, both the leading characters and the setting took Marge back beyond the immediate prewar days to her own childhood. Joyce Allingham has suggested that the female Palinodes are partial portraits of the Misses Georgina and Rose Luard of Sarum House, Cambridge, where Marge boarded while she was a pupil at the Perse School. Miss Jessica Palinode, whose makeshift cooking follows the advice contained in *How to Live on One-and-Six*, which was supposed to have been published in 1917—the year the Allinghams moved to

Bayswater—is modelled, to some extent, on an old lady who retired to Tolleshunt D'Arcy: "Many an odd-job gardener gave up in despair as she stood over him and demanded that he did round such unlikely treasures as stinging nettles and dandelions." Apron Street, the geographical center of the novel was, perhaps, based on Hereford Road off Westbourne Grove, Bayswater, and Jas Bowles's "Family Interments" might well have been organized from Prince's Mews, all of which Marge knew well as a child. Although the novel pays formal acknowledgment to a changed world, the charm and enjoyment of the *Undertaker* most certainly lies in these memories of the London of a past age, and the mournful celebration of its passing.

In September 1947 Paul Reynolds had begun urging Marge to visit the United States: "I think it is possible that in the next ten years you will have to look to America as your primary market from a commercial point of view" (Letter, 03.09.1947). Marge, while accepting in principle, kept putting off the trip; then in October 1948, she suggested that she and Pip might manage to travel in the following February. This plan found the support of Doubleday's, who pointed out that she would thus be in the U.S. for the publication of the *Undertaker*. In the meantime, the American magazine *Town and Country* had offered Marge $250 to write an article about herself and her theories on mystery writing. The result was "Mystery and Myself," which appeared in August 1949. Marge began by emphasising her writerly vocation—"I was designed to be a writer and . . . my life and times decreed what sort I should become" (1949, 42); she went on to insist on Pip's share in her books by pointing out that their history was "a tale of earnest cooperation entirely devoted to nothing more serious than the mystery" (94). Marge underlined, too, the disciplining importance of the form: "Let authors write novels to do themselves good, to express their own egos and release their own fears, but when it is solely of their readers that they are thinking—then, say I, let them taste the sweets of rigid discipline and write mysteries" (94). Marge even risked a prognosis concerning the future of the Campion novels, based on Pip's new career in London: "Campion is feeling the benefit. . . . He is more sophisticated than he was; he is more informed about the age in which he lives; he is still capable of being tremendously amused. So are we" (94).

Paul Reynolds, who engineered and organized the trip to America, had now represented Marge for over twelve years. He told me how, in the spring of 1937, he had written to Marge inviting her to lunch in London, she went and according to him: "After lunch I said to her that I had asked her to lunch with me hoping that she would want to let me represent her. She said that she had come to lunch hoping that I would handle her work" (Letter, November 1983). Reynolds was the son of Paul Revere Reynolds, a famous literary agent who had represented Scott Fitzgerald (among others) in the twenties. He was highly recommended to Marge by William McFee, and soon a firm friendship grew up between the two. This was characteristic of Marge's business dealings; she could never work with publishers or agents with whom she could not at the same time be good friends. For her it was impossible to compartmentalize human relationships—you either were a friend, and then everything was open to you, or you were an outsider undeserving of confidences. Reynolds's services went beyond the placing and selling of Marge's writing; throughout the war and afterwards, until food rationing ended in Britain in the mid-fifties, he arranged for regular food parcels (which were paid for out of Marge's American account) to be sent to D'Arcy. In addition, he and his wife were always ready to fulfil Marge's requests for all sorts of items from soap powder to nylon stockings. Throughout their relationship Marge trusted Reynolds implicitly—"If I may say so you are the first person I have done business with, with whom I've had complete confidence all the time" (Letter, 16.01.1948). Reynolds for his part recalled, "I cannot remember any business case where Margery failed to take my advice." Somewhat wistfully he writes: "If Margery liked you, you could do no wrong. I thought of myself as an austere cold person, but Margery would call me 'Ducky' and I think liked me" (Letter, November 1983).

Pip and Marge arrived in New York on February 28, 1949, checking in at the New Weston on Madison Avenue at 50th Street. Reynolds had prepared a full programme of engagements for the week: there were lunches with the fiction editors of the four best-paying and most highly regarded popular magazines (*The American, Saturday Evening Post, Good Housekeeping,* and *Colliers*), as well as with Fred Dannay (one half of "Ellery Queen") and Angus Cameron, editor-in-chief at Little, Brown, who had published *The Dance of the Years.* Other engagements were arranged by Doubleday's, who had organized a separate programme. At the end of the first week the Carters spent Saturday and Sunday with Reynolds, his wife Ruth, and their three daughters at their home at Chappaqua, some twenty-five miles north of New York City.

For Marge one of the main incentives for taking the trip had been the chance to find out more about the American market and to learn about the wishes of American magazine editors by meeting them personally. When *Colliers* had rejected the *Undertaker* for serialization, she had scribbled on their letter to Reynolds, "Why? We can only find out by *seeing* him," and later when Ellery Queen commented on the British-ness of a short story, she wrote to Reynolds, "All this makes me more convinced than ever that it is time I rubbed up my small knowledge of your country" (Letter, 22.11.1948). That is what Marge was now doing in a sort of crash course in familiarization with America. After lunch with Kenneth Littauer of *Colliers,* she sent a note to Reynolds: "I want you to debit all these extremely useful lunches to me. I do insist on this. Please lump them all together in a good round sum and enter them under 'Expenses in re. Publicity.' They have been most valuable to me and have provided the sort of conversations I came over to here to have. I can't tell you how grateful I am to you for fixing them" (Letter, 08.03.1949).

Although Marge does not seem to have been over impressed by New York—the first day of her visit was marred by a "foul, wet snowstorm" (Letter from Isabelle Taylor, 15.02.1950)—and although the flights in the recently commissioned Comet jet had an adverse effect on her susceptible sinuses, the immediate experience of American publishers and editors was invaluable. The fourteen days in the United States were to have an almost incalculably positive effect upon her financial position as well as an important influence on her writing. America would always be in her mind when considering possible future readers of her fiction. Marge found the trip informatory and enlightening; "it has," she wrote Reynolds after her return, "put a whole lot of things in perspective" (Letter, 28.03.1949). Later in the year she returned to the experience: "The American trip was a brilliant idea of yours. It left me a bit dazed for a while, but now that has worn off I am feeling the benefit of the eye-opener! I know now what is wanted. Whether I can supply it or not is another matter but I don't see why I shouldn't" (Letter to Reynolds, 15.08.1949).

The following year, 1950, was one of the most successful in Marge's writing career on both sides of the Atlantic. She became the third crime writer (after Agatha Christie and Ngaio Marsh) to have ten of her books published simultaneously by Penguin Books, and the *Saturday Evening Post* bought "Dark Invitation" (published as "The Patient at Peacocks Hall"). Allen Lane, the founder of Penguin, was later to become a good friend and someone Marge admired greatly as a discriminating publisher. She signed the 1952 reprint of the *Undertaker,* "This copy is for Sir Allen Lane (the best publisher in the world)." What she did not realize at the time was the size of the edition that was being put on the market. Between 1950 and 1953 Penguin sold close on one million copies of Marge's ten books, which together with those they had previously published made a grand total of a million and a half since the early war years. On the strength of her Penguin success the local paper interviewed Marge; the appearance of this interview had an unexpected result which Marge reported to Reynolds: "Christina has never taken my writing seriously but now she puts out the typewriter and has started giving me plots" (Letter, 22.10.1950).

Since the late summer of 1949, Marge had been working on the novella "Dark Invitation," the first part of which had been sent to Reynolds in December. At first he hoped that he could interest *Good Housekeeping* in the tale, and wrote to Marge that he would try to get $10,000 for it. He then showed it to Erd Brandt of the *Post*, who liked it but asked for revisions, which Marge (the ever-willing author) immediately set about making. She sent the final version to Reynolds in mid-February 1950 with an accompanying note: "I *like* this story, and since it is written in that easy fashion (like a letter), I found no difficulty at all in working on it. It has improved it I think. Anyway it ought to go *somewhere*" (Letter, 14.02.1950). On February 21 Marge received a terse cable from Reynolds: "Post buys Dark Invitation, Paul." In her diary she wrote, "So relieved was nearly sick! Hurray." (Diary, 22.02.1950). The price was $12,000, the largest single sum Marge had ever earned.

To mark her successes Marge transformed a custom going back to Dr. Salter's days at D'Arcy, the July flower show and party, into a public celebration. The first Saturday in July was traditionally flower show day; in 1950 there were twelve close friends to lunch, sixty for tea, and a dinner for forty-five. The menu (which remained virtually unchanged over the years) owed much, in those times of scarcity, to Marge's new prosperity, Reynolds's assistance, and Pip's contacts in London: fresh salmon for lunch, and smoked salmon, chicken, ham, strawberries and cream for dinner. A month later the accustomed cricket match against an eleven from Chappel was the occasion for another gathering of friends for the weekend. Marge presided as the proud and bountiful hostess, enjoying the excitement of being able to entertain so many of her friends once again: "I am sure it is wise to do everything in one big 'go,' or rather, a series of them, but it is a bit exhausting and the house looks as if a herd of buffalo had passed this way. However, I am fit, overwhelmed with new material and full of ideas" (Letter to Reynolds, 11.08.1950). The attempt to recreate something of the old prewar spirit was a risk, but a risk which seems to have been worth taking. Alan Gregory, back at D'Arcy among the guests, was well aware of this and in his letter of thanks to Marge wrote: "I wondered at one point, didn't you, when all those new bokels [Allingham word for country people] arrived and not many of the old ones, whether it was going to be the same; but it seems that as long as there are one or two of the old characters there who have grown up in the tradition . . . the others seem to fit in all right. I'm sure they all went away suitably impressed and delighted" (Letter, 11.08.1950).

Such a summer glow of contentment and assurance was bound to contain at least a hint of shadow and worry. This took shape in concern for the future of Marge's ageing mother. A year after Herbert Allingham's death in 1936, she had found a home and shelter as Rev. Marcus Laurence's housekeeper at the damp vicarage on Foulness Island off the Essex coast, north of Southend. Now, after thirteen years of glorified domestic service, Em, at seventy, was longing for a change. A year earlier she had suggested to Marge "that the time has come to make a change," and that she felt in need of a rest, she had after all reached "the three score years and ten." Em planned to move back to Thorpe Bay, Southend, where she and Herbert Allingham had lived before his death, and asked whether Marge would be willing to pay the first year's rent. For the next nine years she was to pursue a somewhat nomadic existence, moving from one hotel or guest house to another, taking occasional breaks with her cousin, Grace Russell, at Pope's Hall, then staying in a nursing home until she finally came to D'Arcy in 1959. Marge arranged a deed of covenant to cover her mother's main expenses since financial assistance was, Marge felt, a thorny matter, Em being, as she wrote to her mother's solicitor, "a person very jealous of her amour propre" (Letter, 17.01.1951). There was a strong similarity in temperament between Marge and her mother; they were both strong-minded characters who needed to have the final word in any argument. Thus it is likely that behind Marge's willingness to support Em financially there was always a subconscious desire to ensure that she could live comfortably away from D'Arcy, and from Marge.

A much more serious problem was brewing up around Marge's relations with her British publisher, Heinemann. There seem to have been some disagreements in the spring of 1950 about the terms of the contract governing Marge's work; she was interested in the possibility of having her next book—whatever it might be—published by another firm (thinking no doubt of the pleasurable relations she had had with Robert Lusty at Michael Joseph's), but Dwye Evans insisted that she still owed Heinemann one more book. The argument went backwards and forwards until at the beginning of July, Marge reported to Reynolds: "I have won my release from Heinemann. . . . I thought I would. . . . I have left it that I am free to make a new contract but that I admit I owe Heinemann one more book to be delivered at some future and unspecified date." (Letter, 07.07.1950). She did not raise the question of the

Emily Allingham, Marge's Mother, in the 1940s

identity of the new publisher, she just mentioned that she was going to leave any decision to her English agent, Watt, and assured Reynolds that she would "work much better for the uncertainty." A week later, Lusty wrote a very persuasive letter to Marge, suggesting that her interests would be best served by moving to Joseph: "I think we might be able to help you find the position in contemporary literature which is yours. If I am right, it would be a fatal thing for you to become merely a best-selling writer of high-class detective fiction. You are not a Dorothy Sayers, you are not an Agatha Christie, or any one of those people, but you are Margery Allingham, with a position and a reputation entirely your own" (Letter, 14.07.1950). This must have sounded very enticing to Marge, but she wrote a noncommittal letter in reply, and left the matter open. It was to be another eighteen months before she finally accepted Watt's suggestion and moved to Chatto and Windus, the only real alternative to Joseph that she could see, and who "have never done a detective tale before but would like to try a really first class one" (Letter to Reynolds, 11.10.1951). Marge's main concern was to find a publisher who really cared about her work, and who was willing to put every effort into promoting her writing and her sales. That Chatto also had "a good highbrow name" was all to the good.

On January 11, 1951 Marge went up to London in response to a phone call from Pip; after meeting various friends, she went on to the cinema to see Jacques Tati's "Jour de Fête." All this hardly seems to warrant the entry in her diary that evening: "Most extraordinary day of my life." Nor do the following phrases throw much light on the matter: "Freedom. Something happened to my neck." The next day she returned to D'Arcy with Pip and her Aunt Maud; in her diary she wrote "Heard all about everything. Am to have house." The apparent puzzle of such cryptic remarks teases the biographer until he can find some clue which might offer an explanation. There is, naturally, the danger of accepting the first plausible suggestion that offers itself. I trust that I have not been guilty of doing this. Four years after the visit to London, Marge was seriously ill; when she recovered, she made a number of notes on her own case history. One of these runs: "Overwork and emotional difficulties (1951–52) NOTE: Husband having a liaison with another married woman. 'Burst' in the neck followed by an emotional moment and then great well-being plus fear." Other material in Marge's papers at D'Arcy suggests that some time in 1951 she discovered that Pip had been having an affair with a woman—probably an actress—called Diane, whose husband finally went to D'Arcy to ask Marge to intervene and put an end to the business. Evidence would seem to suggest that far from coming to an end, the affair continued, for on the first three anniversaries of Pip's death in 1969, announcements signed "D" appeared in the In Memoriam columns of the *Times*.

After twenty-three years of marriage and close cooperation, the revelation of Pip's affair caught Marge unawares. The severe emotional shock was combined with a health condition from which she had suffered since the early twenties. Somewhere around 1920, Marge began to have serious problems with overweight and corpulence; this together with sudden fluctuations in her mood—from over-excitement to sudden depression—seem to have been behind her rejection of a career on the stage. According to Marge's notes these symptoms—"lethargy and lack of confidence and fears interspersed with bursts of ferocious energy and confidence"—became noticeable again shortly before the war. In 1940 or 1941, she consulted a new doctor, who prescribed a large thyroid dosage which was continued "over the next four years with remarkable results." Unfortunately this doctor died shortly after the end of the war, and thus the successful treatment was interrupted. Pip's return to England, disrupting Marge's peaceful routine of the war years, did not improve her condition, so that when the emotional shock of his infidelity hit her, she had no physical reserves to counteract it. The burst in the neck was Marge's metaphor for a sudden renewed onset of thyroid trouble. Marge's secretary, Gloria Greci, who began work at D'Arcy House in 1950, has given a description of her general condition at this time: "She was very volatile in her temperament. . . . I mean sort of up and down and so on . . . there were times when she used to get depressed; but she also used to get very high. And one didn't know whether it was something that had happened, or had particularly pleased her, but she would be really sort of childlike in her enthusiasm" (Interview, 13.10.1983).

At this distance in time it is impossible, simply on the basis of the evidence of Marge's diaries and the off-chance remarks of her contemporaries to reconstruct what exactly happened in those early weeks of 1951. It is clear that she did discover an affair of Pip's, and that this emotional shock did set off a quirky thyroid reaction. It is also true that over the months to follow relations with Pip were exceedingly fragile. He, too, seems to have been extremely upset, though more by Marge's behaviour than his own; he even went as far as to ascribe her reactions to mental imbalance. Pip's open misrepresentations of Marge's condition to his friend at the *Tatler*, Sean Fielding, led in turn to misunderstandings between Marge and Fielding, which increased the estrangement between husband and wife ("Pip seems to misrepresent people to each other," Diary 10.02.1951). Pip was, however, not as malicious as Marge imagined, he was just insensitive to her condition. He even went to the length of phoning Dr. Madden to ask whether Marge's trouble could be mental, resulting from her time of life (Diary 15.02.1951).

One of the immediate results of the situation with Pip was that Marge saw to it that the deeds of D'Arcy House were put in her name. She felt that it was impossible to trust Pip, and that she should do what she could to maintain her own position independent of him. However, such old and tried companions as Marge and Pip (one has to remember that his philandering propensities were not new to Marge) soon found a new *modus vivendi*. Although Marge was clearly aware that Pip was incorrigible, she never openly fought for her own rights as his wife, but rather chose more subtle means to insist on her position at his side and his at hers. The absence of the necessity to live close to each other through the crisis seems to have helped; Marge noted in April, "Pip and I all right. Get on very well alone" (Diary, 21.04.1951). Yet the sadness of the event was—at least for the time being—overwhelming. Marge noted the restraint between them and registered the impression that "he'd be O.K. or even better without me," although she was still realistic enough to add, "apart from material things" (Diary, 19.05.1951). On Marge's forty-seventh birthday Pip gave her "two very pretty old paste brooches." She acknowledged that he was trying to patch up the breach between them, even though she herself felt that it was asking too much of her that she should simply forgive and forget (Diary, 20.05.1951).

These upheavals early in the year, unsettling and saddening as they were, did not interfere with Marge's writing as much as they might have done in the case of a less disciplined person. Left largely alone at D'Arcy, she soon regained a serenity born of her attachment to the country and the continuity of country life. She wrote in her diary of the simple consolation of the daily routine of spring, of her conversations with Sam Taylor, the gardener, and his old father, who worked as his assistant: "Lovely, lovely weather. . . . Went round front meadow with Sam and his father, arranged for fencing and shed repairs. . . . Good day and work. . . . Beautiful weather. . . . Packed up curtains to be dyed . . . garden lovely. Cherry blossom just coming out. Old Taylor reports two nightingales in top meadow" (Diary, 24–26.04.1951).

The contours of the disturbances in Marge's private life lost their sharp clarity when the focus was on her writing. It is difficult to believe that throughout the most critical personal crisis of her married life she was writing a book which, in its overall conception, was far more ambitious than anything she had previously attempted: *The Tiger in the Smoke*. In a letter to Reynolds she hinted at the strategies she employed to escape from the hindrances and interruptions around her: "You will think I am crazy but I have found that the only way for me to get a good long tale done is to stay put and do it. I've not left the village since Xmas. I have all sorts of goings on which have held me up, but they have had to come to *me* and I have my little attic with the ladder which I draw up after me" (Letter, 21.05.1951). The small work room Marge refers to is off the large landing studio on the first floor at D'Arcy House; approached from the back stairs, its door is a good three feet above floor level, so that the only access is indeed a small portable flight of steps which Marge could draw up to discourage invasion of her calm. Here it was that much of the *Tiger* was written. The new novel had been on the stocks since August 1949, and had even been promised as a new Campion to Heinemann for May 1950. Marge was typically reticent about this work in progress, although she admitted to Reynolds that she was "getting rather excited" about it. She went on to acknowledge the tip that she had gained from her meeting with the *Saturday Evening Post*'s fiction editor, Erd Brandt, during the New York trip: "It was his lecture on the value of the 'man to be caught at all costs' theme which put me on to the tale" (Letter, 04.06.1951). Otherwise she only revealed that the new novel was "a London story, full of fog and fierceness" (Letter to Reynolds, 06.11.1950).

Work on the *Tiger* acted as the perfect antidote to Marge's troubles with Pip; as she confessed to Reynolds, "it is the first time I ever remember finding the story more interesting than outside distractions" (Letter 21.05.1951). She worked much faster on this novel than she had on the *Undertaker*; by early June the first nine chapters had been written, and the final ten were completed in a burst of activity over the next three months. By the end of September the manuscript was finished, and Grog was called in once again to type the fair copy. For Marge the *Tiger* was as serious a book as *The Dance of the Years* had been, since it said something she very much wanted to say (Letter to Reynolds, 06.11.1951). The manuscript went to Watt together with a letter that makes it clear that the decision in favour of Chatto and Windus as her new publisher had been more or less taken. Marge did not regret the change: "I like everything about Chatto that I have seen. They are treating the thing as a book, which is a nice change and I have high hopes of it and them" (Letter to Watt, 31.12.1951).

While she was still working on the *Tiger* Marge received a singular honour from the editors of *Ellery Queen's Mystery Magazine*. In August 1951 she heard from "Queen": "I am delighted to advise you that our International Poll of authors, critics, editors, publishers, and readers has voted you one of the ten best active mystery writers" (Letter, 23.08.1951). Marge was unable to attend the award ceremony in New York in September, so she received the trophy by post: a flintlock pistol mounted on an oak plaque with an inscribed brass plate. She was certainly pleased and, in her own private way, proud of the award. She was, however, much more concerned about the fate of the *Tiger*, which, shortly after the excitement of Queen's letter, was rejected by the *Saturday Evening Post*, for which, to some extent, it had been written. This rejection prompted a letter to Reynolds in which she elaborated an idea that was to be repeated on several occasions during the following years:

> All my life I have written two kinds of stories—one for the one kind of reader and one for the other; I enjoy doing either—and I have got more skilled at both kinds. While the Campion books have grown slowly more adult, the other stories have graduated . . . through *Answers* to the *Strand*, and from there via *Good Housekeeping* to the *S.E.P.* . . . . Think of me as *two* good writers of different types and you'll forgive me and get the true angle. (Letter, 12.11.1951)

It did not look as though the *Tiger* was going to succeed in its bid for serialization in Britain either; Watt had tried to get a clear answer from the editors of a woman's magazine, but there was nothing but delay. Finally Pip won back a place in Marge's affections by approaching the editors of the British weekly *John Bull* and selling the serial rights of the *Tiger* to them for fifteen hundred guineas. Marge reported to Reynolds: "I am in rather a delicate position because W. P. Watt hasn't *heard* about it yet. Pip is the culprit. . . . He got rather irritated by the set out over the *Woman's Journal* which kept me running around for a long time and so he pinched the only copy and got the whole thing through in a couple of days or so" (Letter, 21.11.1951). When Marge finally informed Watt of the sale of the serial rights of the *Tiger,* she pointed at that the price had been negotiated by Pip "who obtained the offer in the first place and the 'guinea touch' betrays his 'Tatlery' hand in it" (Letter, 25.11.1951). Thus the year which had started on so uncertain and unhappy a note approached its close with Pip and Marge partially reunited as partners in crime again.

The British reception of the *Tiger* was mixed; a number of critics praised the quality of the writing and narrative technique; others invoked Dickens and R. L. Stevenson as Marge's artistic forebears. On the other hand there were some carping voices patronizing Marge's attempt to write a "superior thriller." In the *Times Literary Supplement* she was accused of having tried too hard, while the *New Statesman*, invoking Edgar Wallace as the master of the genre, criticized Marge for lacking his "masculine cut and thrust" (Partridge 1952). The American reviewers were, on the whole, kinder; in the *New York Times* the book was described as "wittier and wiser than many of the straight novels that clutter the bookstalls" (Du Bois 1952), and Dorothy Quick referred to the *Tiger* as "one of the most important books of the season" (Quick 1952).

In February 1952 King George VI died; with his passing Marge's generation lost a last symbolic link to the almost forgotten fragile tranquility of the late thirties. In March another more mundane token of the wartime years disappeared when identity cards were abolished in Britain. Change was in the air, but it was still a change that, for the time being, appeared manageable, protected by the guarantee of a Conservative government and Churchill's presence at 10 Downing Street. Nevertheless, the fifties promised to be more exciting, and certainly more colourful than the drab late forties. As one chronicler of the decade has written: "It was a time when life was real, life was earnest, for most people. . . . But it was a time when hope outweighed despair or cynicism. It was a time when it was pleasant to be young enough to feel concerned, mildly rebellious and naively optimistic that solutions could be found" (Lewis 1978, 7). Marge may not have been young any more, but she was young enough in spirit to be able to share many of these feelings. Change, however, is ruthless towards the old; at D'Arcy Marge's grandmother, Emily Jane Hughes, died on September 25, 1952, ten days short of her hundredth birthday. For the final years of her life she was no longer the stubborn, spirited old lady of the early war years, Marge's symbol of continuity and hope, but something of "a cross between one of the larger apes and a babe of three," but still "as strong as a horse" (Letter to Ruth Reynolds, 27.05.1949). As Marge's aunt, Amy Allingham, somewhat tritely but quite accurately wrote to her: "She was a truly wonderful and interesting old lady," adding, "You made her very happy and it's something to remember" (Letter, 07.10.1952).

In unconscious anticipation of other elderly relations who might soon call upon her for support, aware of the need to preserve the rural beauty of the village, and prompted by a second sight which simply told her she might need a refuge of her own, Marge bought the now-derelict Forge for two hundred pounds in the latter part of 1953. She and Pip redesigned it as a two-storeyed cottage, with a little gable and an ornamental clock. Marge justified her purchase to a suspicious Inland Revenue: "The only thing I possess is this house, and I keep it because it is valuable to me as an office and a place of business entertainment, and because it is the only thing I have on which to borrow money. The derelict smithy dominates the village and the house, and if it became a cheap cafe, as seemed likely, the value of the house would be affected" (Letter, 22.04.1954). The apparent speciousness of Marge's argument is indicative of the extraordinary situation which had developed between her and the tax authorities, who plagued her life throughout the fifties. Since the war, Marge had been using one year's earnings to pay the previous year's tax until she was convinced that she would never be able to "make enough money to pay my tax owing without incurring a further debt too large *ever* to pay" (Letter to Reynolds, 20.02.1950). With her grandmother's death, the moment had arrived which Marge's solicitor, Arthur Underwood, had foreseen two years earlier: "You and Pip will certainly have a big decision to make which as I see it is whether your grand establishment shall be in the country with a foot in London or your grand establishment as literary lights in London and a foot in the country of a weekend cottage" (Letter, 21.06.1950).

Marge knew that Pip would never consent to a mere "foot in London," and she could not possibly become a city "literary light." The solution was eventually found in the newly purchased Forge, which was to become her temporary home away from home. It was typical of Marge that, once she had recovered from the immediate impact of the shock, she generalized the problem until it became an issue, leading to the formulation of a matter of principle: "At the moment marriage is penalized to a very dangerous extent since a man and a wife's earnings are lumped together" (Letter to Reynolds, 23.03.1953). Once she had got so far, Marge was speedily able to utilize the matter as a theme for her fiction. Out of the sordid and often undiginified wrangles with the Inland Revenue grew Marge's most charming, though also most diffuse book, *The Beckoning Lady*. Although it had been almost completely mapped out by the beginning of 1953, little progress was made on the novel that year. At first she thought that in it she might have material for a serial, but she was also convinced that this book was certainly not going to be a sequel to the *Tiger*: "I can't promise another TIGER, I had worked out something rather different and I feel it would be madness to scrap the six months preparations I have done on it on the off chance of imitating myself" (Letter to Reynolds, 07.01.1954).

During the summer of 1953 she dropped the new novel entirely in order to finish another novella, "Safer than Love," which was serialized in the *Woman's Journal* and then published in a double volume, *No Love Lost* by Doubleday and the Heinemann subsidiary, World's Work, in 1954. Marge made quite clear to Harold Raymond of Chatto's that whereas the Campion novels did not pander to popular taste ("which is why they go on selling"), the novellas were "bread and butter tales I do so that I don't have to worry too much if my Campion books are serialized or not" (Letter, 09.03.1954).

Having secured temporary financial peace, Marge began to work on the new novel with "speed and excitement." She was enjoying her writing again, and felt that it was going to be a happy book with "the sort of atmosphere we get at Tolleshunt D'Arcy when we get visitors from the U.S." The title, she told Isabelle Taylor, had been chosen for its "slightly witchy flavour" (Letter to 19.01.1954). As with all the books that Marge truly believed in, and which she felt were expressive of something that emanatated from deep within herself, she found it "very exhilarating to go 'all out' on what one wants to write" (Letter to Reynolds, 01.02.1954). The novel was finished at immense speed within the next eight weeks and continued to keep up Marge's spirits: "I am so happy doing it," she wrote, "that I don't care if no one else likes it. It's one for the gang of us" (Letter to I. Taylor, 09.02.1954). Grog was once again pressed into service to type the final manuscript over the Easter weekend. After a mammoth session he wrote to Marge: "Well, we can *still* do it—if we have to! Quite an effort.... I think it will be a good story ... a general jolly happy picture of the country as it can be on those few perfect days which we remember" (Letter, 21.04.1954).

Although very much in the spirit of Marge's prewar books, *The Beckoning Lady* belongs completely to the new world of the mid-fifties, a world which made the thirties "seem as remote as they had from the parallel position in the nineteenth century" (Hopkins 359). As the dedication ("to my Old Friends and their Merry Wives") suggests, it is, on one level, a novel about marriage. It is also a novel about the destructive and disruptive effects of modern money—both legal (taxation) and illegal (crooked financial dealings)—upon the idyll of creative country life. It is also, in the characters of Old Harry Buller and Miss Diane Varley, a loving tribute to the stubborn canniness of country folk. In many ways it is, too, Marge's affectionate, sceptical, lovingly critical portrait of Pip, in the figure of Tonker Cassands, that is at the heart of the novel. The parallels between the problems Tonker and his wife Minnie have with the Inland Revenue and those of Pip and Marge are too many to be merely coincidental. In April 1954, immediately after finishing the new novel, Marge wrote to the tax inspectors informing them that she had taken legal opinion on her situation. As a result she said that she saw only three possibilities of escaping from the hopeless spiral in which she found herself: "to become permanently bankrupt," to "desert my husband so that we can be divorced and so pay tax separately," or "to die so that you can collect my royalties as they come in over the years" (Letter, 22.04.1954). In *The Beckoning Lady*, Tonker's version of the origins of the problem is fictional, but his picture of the effects is all too true. He describes the accidental results of his financial success with the Glübalübalum, a complex musical instrument that he invented: "I got seventeen thousand quid, kept two, and in a fine burst of careless generosity gave the rest to Minnie, who was broke. . . . Like the mug she is, the poor benighted girl paid all our debts with it, including all the arrears of income tax, and so at a single stroke I sold her into bondage for the rest of her life" (1955, 103). Through the medium of Tonker Cassands' outraged outburst, Marge also put her finger on the heart of the Carters' tax problem and its dire potential solutions: she and Pip did not conform to the authorities' expectations of a married couple, and thus they, Marge and Pip, would have to change:

> Before we were married, over twenty-five years ago, Minnie and I, being astute youngsters . . . perceived that all the difficulties, partings, and troubles in married life arose directly . . . from nothing more nor less than money and housekeeping. . . . We've each got our own work to do and we don't ask any more of marriage than the tie itself. . . . We don't conform to the blueprint, so we've got to be altered. . . . And now if you please they want *me* . . . they want us to divorce (114–15).

Most of the time while Marge was working on *The Beckoning Lady*, she was in excellent health. In January 1954 she had begun a series of penicillin treatments for the sinusitis which had affected her concentration for the last decade. The new novel was due to be published in April 1955. In March, Marge had a renewed attack of sinusitis, but it cleared up quickly. She felt no premonitions that anything was particularly wrong with her; in fact, she felt fine. Then quite unexpectedly, in mid-April, she was overwhelmed by the conviction that she was about to die. This state persisted and grew more urgent during the course of the week. On Monday, April 25, the day of publication, Marge became uncontrollable, her neck swelled up and her whole manner became, in her own words, "faster and faster, wilder and wilder." The next morning she began to write farewell notes to her friends, and to make alarming telephone calls suggesting that she was on the verge of disaster. Pip lost his head completely, suggesting, as in 1951, that Marge was suffering from mental disturbance brought on by the menopause. Marge, in a final bravura gesture, opened a bottle of champagne and dosed herself with inhalants. In the evening Pip called in Dr. James Madden and a close friend, the surgeon Ronnie Reid. Marge began to turn violent and, as Reid later wrote to her, "You were no trouble whatever, you just bounced old James and me about like a couple of rubber balls" (Letter, 18.05.1955). Reid and Madden arranged for Marge to be hospitalized; Christina Carter went with her in an ambulance to London.

"The next thing she knew was waking up in a padded cell in a private clinic in Pinner, northwest of London." (Interview with Sheila Archibald, 27.03.1984). This was not the final indignity; Marge was subsequently subjected to the most barbaric of cures: electric shock treatment. This resulted in a complete—though temporary—loss of any memory of the immediate past. The use of electroconvulsive therapy, which had been introduced into England as recently as 1940, in Marge's case reveals the uncaring incompetence of the clinic personnel. This therapy was usually recommended for persons "whose livelihoods are not dependent on the use of memory and intellect" (Showalter 1985, 207). Fortunately, Marge made a rapid recovery so that the treatment could be interrupted; nevertheless, it is a sad comment on the operation of conformist stereotypes in the medical world that Pip's version of her case was accepted by the clinic doctors without further question or examination. Marge herself later put the symptoms down to an over-dose of thyroid pills, which produced a form of temporary exultation resembling a nervous breakdown. Both the clinic doctors' acceptance and Pip's lay diagnosis can only be understood by seeing them in the context of what Elaine Showalter has referred to as "the pervasive cultural association of women and madness" (1985, 4). For the next two weeks Marge slowly regained her memory, and with it came a strong feeling of outrage that Pip and her medical friends had permitted her to be treated in such a way. At the same time, she was possessed by the fear that her imaginative and creative powers might have been im-paired. Gloria Greci has recalled her return to D'Arcy: "I remember she came back and said, 'Gloria, do you think I'll ever be able to write again? Will it come out right?' . . . It took her a long time to get over what they did to her. Not only the treatment as such but the very fact that they put her up there" (Interview, 13.10.1983).

Later that year, and again during the course of a medical check up in January 1956, Dr. Raymond Greene of the Royal Northern Hospital was insistent that Marge needed surgery to remove the goitre in her throat before the condition became inoperable. In the notes that she wrote on her illness Marge concluded, "Very much better but feel I need thyroid if I am not to get nervy." She had an intense fear of surgery and was backed by Reid, who felt that she had enough medical problems to deal with, and that the real problem was a condition of the blood, hypoglycaemia (Letters to Christlieb, January 1956; Reynolds, 23.01.1956).

Once Marge was back at D'Arcy and had recovered from the effects of the electrical treatment, life slowly began to return to normal. Her sister Joyce moved to D'Arcy to take up the post of Marge's confidential secretary: "I want you," wrote Marge, "to be a buffer between me and all those people who want to get hold of me and waste my time" (Letter, 01.10.1955). Marge was now able to look back on the crisis quite calmly. "It was a most extraordinary experience," she wrote to an old friend in France, Meg Catusse, "and seems to me to have left me more well and happy than I have felt for twenty years" (Letter, 10.10.1955). In September, Pip took Marge to France for two and a half weeks to complete the period of convalescence. After visiting Mme. Catusse in Paris and spending an evening at the Folies Bergères, Marge returned home "dizzy after the holiday" (Letter to M. Catusse, 10.10.1955).

Meanwhile *The Beckoning Lady* had had the usual mixed reception accorded to any Allingham novel after 1945. Whereas the reviewers of crime fiction had dismissed it—"extraordinary madhouse of cardboard characters" (Iles 1955)—other critics, notably Elizabeth Bowen in the *Tatler*, had praised it for its specifically novelistic qualities and particularly English atmosphere: "Miss Allingham's extraordinary imagination commands the reader from beginning to end . . . it has the qualities of romantic drama, and the flavour of what is ancient and sound in England" (Bowen 1955).

In June 1954 Marge had begun thinking out "a strong story of the London Tiger type" to be called "Tether's End, W.2." Very little had actually been written by the time of her illness in the following spring, and the whole project was dropped during the aftermath of her shock treatment. She was, however, actively thinking about the book in September, when she was interviewed for the *Evening News*. She was reported as saying that she believed that any novel needed two legs to stand on: sound original ideas to begin and end with, and a story which "should arise out of the characters themselves, not from some ingenious little trick" (Hind 1955), which was clearly a criticism of the methods of many of her older contemporaries. Work on the new book was taken up again early in 1956 and continued steadily throughout the year although under somewhat bizarre circumstances.

In January 1956, she informed her accountant, Aubrey Christlieb, that "we are engaged in finishing and furnishing the Forge and setting this house up as the office." Thus began a farce produced by the Inland Revenue and performed by Marge for the next few years. Purely for tax purposes, she moved her living quarters into the Forge, crossing the road every morning to begin work at D'Arcy House where she wrote, conducted her business, and entertained those friends and acquaintances whose advice or presence could be said to further her professional career. This peculiar mode of living did not, however, prevent Marge from throwing the usual party on the first Saturday in July in order "to counteract the adverse chatter after my somewhat sensational illness" (Letter to Reynolds, 01.08.1956). Some one hundred twenty guests were served tea on the terrace, and supper was prepared for a hundred. The occasion was probably not as staid or formal as such numbers might suggest; parties at D'Arcy were "noisy, lively . . . a gorgeous old mix-up. There were young people and old people, and friends, and there were always people who would know people. It was always hilarious . . . almost like a medieval or Dickensian party" (Interview with Gloria Greci, 13.10.1983). With this gesture Marge returned full force to her old life. She was getting on well with the new novel, *Hide My Eyes*, which was to be her most lucrative production to date; she had just sold a short story to a new women's magazine, *She*; the Rank Organisation, who had taken up the option on the film rights of the *Tiger*, now had the film in production. Yet, had she but known it, Marge was now entering the final decade of her life.

10

The Proverbial Craftsman

Some writers dash the stuff off and get away with it. I can't. To get it REAL I have to chip away like the proverbial British crafts-man.

Margery Allingham

A brief remark in a letter to Reynolds about *More Work for the Undertaker* indicates the direction Marge's fiction was to take in the decade after the war: "I wanted this book to consolidate my *book* position" (Letter, 30.08.1948). The novels of this period move steadily away from the patterns of her earlier work towards a new conception of crime fiction as having as serious a purpose as the literary novel. She became increasingly irritated with people who referred to her books as thrillers or whodunits, insisting on the appellation "crime novel." Marge consciously withdrew from the example of such traditionalist crime writers as Agatha Christie, whom she greatly admired, but whose ways were not her own. In an article she wrote for the *New York Times* on the appearance of Christie's fiftieth book in May 1950, Marge defined the detective story proper as an "almost entirely cerebral" form of entertainment, which aimed "to provide a means of escape for those who do not wish to take their emotions for a ride with the novelists." (1950, 3). The combination of this totally rational puzzle element with what she referred to as the "never-never land" of the detective story was what Marge rejected for her own work after 1945. Instead, she aimed at an emotional engagement with the social reality of postwar England, and sought serious acceptance for her work as novels. It is this that accounts for the confused reaction of her critics during the latter part of her life. The reviewers of crime and detective fiction found her plots too complex, her writing too sophisticated, and her social observation distracting. On the other hand, her books were not reviewed as straight novels because of the crime ingredient, and thus failed to receive the sort of recognition Marge was seeking. Even in more recent years, academic critics with sympathies for popular forms have failed to understand the nature of Marge's aims, with the result that a representative comment can suggest that in the 1950s "her style becomes impossibly mannered and strained" (Craig & Cadogan 1981, 207). Such criticism results from the expectations of critics who continue to insist on discussing Marge's work under the limiting subgenre headings of detective story or thriller.

The three books which appeared between 1945 and 1955 illustrate the new approach to the novel whose plot centres on crimes of violence. Each one treats both a larger, generalized theme and a narrower, more specific aspect of postwar British life; each in turn moves a step further away from the solution-of-the-puzzle formula of the traditional detective story. In the *Undertaker*, Marge was concerned with the general phenomenon of the irrevocability of social change, and more specifically with the impact of innovation upon the cultivated middle-class world familiar to her since her youth. She made use of the wider issues of *The Tiger in the Smoke* to elaborate her own conceptions of good and evil, while at the same time utilizing an urgent contemporary issue: the recanalization of the human propensity for violence after its heroization as military daring during the war. Finally, in a lighter and more idyllic mood, *The Beckoning Lady* dealt with the theme of mature marriage, and, at the same time, reflected upon the social alignments of postwar Britain, which had conferred a new power upon speedily accumulated wealth.

An American friend of Marge's, the novelist Lavinia Davis—another of Doubleday's Crime Club authors—saw that the true merits of the *Undertaker* lay not merely in the convincing portrayal of social change, but in a more fundamentally writerly aspect: "the overall quality that comes up from this book, as it does from so many of your others, is style . . . the final art that hides all artifice" (Letter, 01.02.1949). The educated intellectual Palinodes are not only a fascinating portrait of the cultivated middle classes of the early twentieth century, but are also a device for introducing literary stylistic elements into the novel; as the youngest sister, Jessica, says—with reference to her money-saving cookery book: "Like all important informative books, its appeal, its true appeal, is to a desire of the emotions. I mean if you do not want most terribly to understand a certain kind of love, then you will not get the best out of Plato's Banquet" (1949a, 71). Here Marge seems to be offering a direct hint to her critics: if they do not desire to understand how the form of the crime novel can be utilized for serious purposes, they will never succeed in understanding her later works.

A palinode is an ode in which the author retracts something stated in a former poem, thus the family's name is aptly chosen for a novel which deals with the phenomenon of change, alteration, and realignments of values. At the same time it symbolizes Marge's own rejection of the simple forms she had once espoused. The Palinodes are themselves a focal point of the shift in the times: once an influential, brilliant and socially powerful family—"the whole district used to revolve round the Palinodes" (87)—they have reached near poverty. The two surviving sisters and their brother live as paying guests in the family residence, which now belongs to their father's illegitimate daughter, a former actress with a good business sense—representative of the changes in social values—who waits on them hand and foot. In an exchange with Albert Campion, Miss Jessica Palinode summarizes the position of such social relics as her family has become:

> "We Palinodes have carried one kind of squirearchy to its ridiculous conclusion, that's all. I shall forgive you anything as long as you never find us sad."
> "I think I find you frightening," he said.
> "That's very much better," said the youngest Miss Palinode (114).

With which remark the reader is brought to the connection between the social and the criminal themes of the book: whereas the awareness of intelligent anachronisms is frightening for the depth of its own self-perception, resistance to change is dangerous and, ultimately, terrifying, since it reveals a form of moral blindness. The local bank manager, Henry James—the choice of names is in itself a comment on changes in values—used his hold over his debtors to force them to become conspirators in a lucrative scheme for aiding wanted men to escape the country. The undertaker, Jas. Bowels—the reminder of undiscussed fundamental realities of human existence—comments at the end of the book on James's motives: "You'll never understand him though, if you don't understand Apron Street. It was changing, you see, and he wouldn't have it. . . . He tried to stop the clock" (225). The almost unconscious anachronism of the Palinodes may be frightening, but it has something divertingly attractive about it; about Mr. James's deliberate attempts to make a principle of anachronism there is only a chill horror.

In the *Undertaker* Marge assembles a number of reminders of her past books in the form of characters who make brief reappearances, once more suggesting both continuity and change. The purpose of this is most noticeable among the forces of law and order: since *Coroner's Pidgin* Stanislaus Oates has been head of the C.I.D., a position which "had made little outward difference to him" (9), but which imposes a barrier of rank and ritual between him and the immediate events of the crime. Superintendant Yeo, we are reminded, is now in late middle age (210), so that centre stage is taken by a newcomer to Marge's fiction, the dynamic young inspector, Charlie Luke, who "spoke without syntax or noticeable coherence but he talked with his whole body" (22). Marge makes it clear that Luke is a stylistic innovation in a world of words—symbolizing a modernity which is characterized by its acceptance of body language.

As in a number of the prewar novels, in the *Undertaker* the text frequently insists upon its own characteristic structure as a multilayered crime novel. As the familiar element of organized crime becomes apparent as the background to the more idiosyncratic confusion surrounding the mysterious murder of Ruth Palinode, Campion remarks to Luke: "It's coming, Charles. . . . It's teasing out, don't you know. As I see it, the point to keep in mind now is that there are clearly two different coloured threads, in the—er—coil. The question is, are they tied at the end? I feel they ought to be, but I don't know" (138). It is this admission of incomplete knowledge, even of temporary ignorance, that sets Campion apart from the "classic" detective of a former age. At the same time his remark is a telling summary of the basics of detective fiction: clarification and connection. For this very reason his statement is also an explanation why the puzzle aspect of the genre was so insufficient to Marge, who clearly wanted much more than the simple tying up of strands of evidence. Mr. Bowels's comment on his trade, "Sad as it may seem to you . . . a tragedy is our best advertisement" (141), would seem equally applicable to the writer of crime fiction. Marge's deliberate use of the word 'advertisement,' however, can be seen as an admission that by now she regarded the crime element in her fiction as little more than a form of bait, or even window dressing, coercing the reader into the consideration of more important matters.

For the two years from the autumn of 1949, Marge worked steadily on *The Tiger in the Smoke*. In it she brought together themes which had occupied her for some years; one of these was quite simply the setting of the major part of the tale—London. "London is a place I do find glamourous . . . it is still full of unexpected corners which seem to have been left over from history. I have often gone for long walks through London exploring and looking at the houses and making up stories about them" (1965b).

In the *Tiger* one of the "unexpected corners" is St. Petersgate Square (possibly based on Linden Gardens, Notting Hill Gate), dominated by the church of St. Peter of the Gate, modelled on St. George's Church, Bloomsbury Way. Then there is Inspector Luke's territory around the brand new Crumb Street police station, and the site of the first murder of the novel, Pump Path—"the high walls which lined it leaned together, their dark surfaces blank as cliffs" (1952, 47)—and the street market near which Tiddy Doll's gang have their basement hide-out—"ramshackle stalls roofed with flapping tarpaulin and lit with na-ked bulbs jostled each other down each side of the littered road" (76). Blatantly exploiting the potential for atmosphere and "local colour," Marge veiled this throughout in thick London fog: "The fog slopped over its low houses like a bucketful of cold soup over a row of dirty stoves" (25).

The central preoccupation of the book was first articulated in *The Oaken Heart*: "Active evil is more incomprehensible in this two-part-perfect world than active good, and so it ought to be" (1941, 193). Essential to the new novel is the figure of Jack Havoc, ex-Borstal boy with a record of savage violence, commando hero, army deserter, and multiple murderer, "a truly wicked man" (1952, 64); "a genuinely wicked man" (169), "killing recklessly and all for nothing" (166). Equally essential is the eccentrically good man of the novel, Canon Avril—"an impossible person in many ways, with an approach to life which was clear-sighted yet slightly off-centre" (29). In an unpublished "Letter to a Goddaughter," almost certainly written at about the same time as the *Tiger*, Marge commented: "Oddly most mystery story writ-ers are interested in God. Some of this is because of the Mystery and some of it is because of a certain curious naiveté absolutely essential to the successful approach of either" (1950a). It is this naiveté combined with an unquestioning and self-effacing faith in God that is characteris-tic of the Canon. Not only does Avril provide the positive balance to the thoroughgoing badness of Havoc, he was also intended as a homage to a real-life figure. An old friend of the family, Canon Luard of Layer Breton, writing to thank Marge for a signed copy of the *Tiger*, noted, "I shall specially look forward to the 'sort of portrait' which I'm sure will be an understanding one, for you and he were always such real friends" (Letter, 28.06.1952). This slight mystery is solved by another of Marge's correspondents, the journalist and writer A. M. Burrage, who had known her father early in the century, and who also received a signed copy of the novel: "I can 'see' Mr. Allingham in the Canon, since you told me it was to some extent a portrait. . . . The one thing I remember most about him was that directly I stepped into his presence I knew that he was *kind*" (Letter, 02.07.1953). Although based on a secular figure, Marge's portrayal of the Canon did not invalidate the fictional presentation of the priesthood; in fact she was congratulated on her depiction by several members of the profession. In reply to one she wrote: "Frankly, I don't think Avril was the perfect priest, he was so unlike his flock in outlook, but he was my idea of a good man who lived with God in Heaven as much as it is possible for a human animal to do so" (Letter to Rev. M. Thornton, 10.01.1957).

The juxtapositioning of the two characters Havoc and Avril was not intended to be just another presentation of the perennial struggle between good and evil. More particularly it was to be Marge's attempt to approach "the eternal problem of why Good is good and why Evil is evil" (1953, n.p.). This clearly takes the novel well beyond the conventional limits of the thriller (although the *Tiger*, with its eight violent deaths by kicking, strangling, knifing, drowning, and shooting, clearly has claims to belong, at least on the level of the plot, to that genre). The presentation of the encounter between Havoc and Avril in the shadowy church at night is both the narrational and the spiritual centre of the novel. It opens with the contrast between Havoc's "artificial wide-boy idiom" in which he questions Avril, "What's the big idea, Padre? Not Prodigal Son stuff, surely?" (194), and Avril's instinctive recognition of Havoc's fear, which he translates into the pastoral comment, "You must be so tired" (195). This initial exchange uses the contrast of linguistic registers as well as personal concerns to establish the distance between the two figures. Yet the enormity of Havoc's next line of questioning is so unexpected that the reader, though not Avril, is shocked: "Are you my father?" This emphasizes the difference in the two men's concerns; Havoc can only interpret human action in terms of conventional, material interest, whereas Avril acts instinctively according to his beliefs. After a brief interval, Havoc continues to investigate Avril's motives for coming to meet and talk with him; his question could well have been posed by the reader: "Why are you here? You're not trying to save my soul, by any chance?" (196). This question acts as a signal to open up the narrative to the sort of reflection on spiritual truths for which Avril seems to have been introduced into the novel: "The soul is one's own affair from the beginning to the end. No one else can interfere with that. . . . What is the soul? . . . I think of it as the man I am with when I am alone" (196). Since such a statement must be meaningless to Havoc—if not to the reader—Marge turns the course of the meeting to a subject where the two characters' beliefs could appear to coincide. Avril attempts to account for his presence in the church by asserting, "every small thing has conspired to bring me here," which Havoc immediately interprets in his own fashion: "That's it. The same thing happened to me. Do you know what that is, you poor old bletherer?

That's the Science of Luck. It works every time" (197). As a moralist, Marge was clearly concerned in the *Tiger* with a very practical aspect of the problem of evil: its attractiveness. Havoc's Science of Luck—"there aren't any coincidences, only opportunities" (149)—gives a superficial impression of plausibility. However, as Marge pointed out to a correspondent who queried Havoc's views: "Most young people come, at some time in their life, to the bright but erroneous thought that if the wicked seem to prosper it might be simpler if they followed evil instead of good. The basic stupidity of this notion soon becomes apparent to almost everybody but there are the few who make the fatal mistake thoroughly, and Jack Havoc was one of these" (Letter to F. Parent, 20.05.1966).

The final pages of chapter 17 manoeuvre the narrative between the exigencies of the plot and extensions of the central theological dilemma of the encounter. First, Avril translates Havoc's philosophy into his own terms: "Evil be thou my Good, that is what you have discovered. It is the only sin which cannot be forgiven because when it has finished with you you are not there to forgive" (198). Marge utilizes the didactic habits of the experienced preacher by having Avril attempt to formulate a graphic example: "Suppose you had got to Saint-Odile. . . ." This immediately bridges the gap between plot and spiritual theme, since Havoc has been searching for the location of St. Odile, where he believes a treasure to be waiting for him. From this point on, the demands of the plot are uppermost in Havoc's mind and lead straight to his attempt on Avril's life. The Canon, however, continues to focus upon the spiritual aspect of the problem; his obstinate honesty answers Havoc's attempt to obtain a promise of secrecy from him with the words: "You know as well as I do that for us who watch there can be no half turns. I can swear and you can let me go, but as soon as I am gone what will you think?" (199).

Marge presents Havoc as unwilling to kill Avril, unwilling to the point of mental anguish and tears. To his predicament the priest can only counter, "Our gods are within us. We choose our own compulsion." This is followed by Havoc's uncertain thrust with the knife and the end of the chapter. Throughout the encounter the thematic narration is always concerned with the reason for men's actions. In Havoc's—the unbeliever's—eyes, actions cannot be explained, they must simply be accepted as opportunities, whereas for Avril actions can be traced to instinctive obedience to inner dictates, the voice of God, the fulfilment of a plan he would choose to call divine. For the reader it is made so clear that Avril is right and Havoc wrong, that the course of the plot from this moment on is determined by a frightening certainty that

Havoc can only perish—as indeed he does in an impressionistically mystical manner which defies the realistic conventions of the simple detective story. Sitting on the cliff at Saint-Odile, the much vaunted treasure revealed as an antique ivory carving of no transferable value, Havoc, the police close on his trail, looks down to the pool far below: "It looked dark. A man could creep in there and sleep soft and long. It seemed to him that he had no decision to make and, now that he knew himself to be fallible, no one to question. Presently he let his feet slide gently forward. The body was never found" (224). There is a sense of immense rightness about the way in which Marge has Havoc end. He slides without any clear volition into the dark and disappears from view; he has accepted the final opportunity, which, given his new fallibility, leads to his destruction.

The Tiger in the Smoke continues exactly where the *Undertaker* left off. The text builds up a convincing link between the late forties and the war years. The young war widow, Meg Elginbrodde, is plagued by crude attempts to suggest that her husband is still alive, and the necessary police investigations commence by conjuring up memories of the immediate past: "It was as though the war years had peeped out at them suddenly" (18). The atmosphere of postwar England is sketched in by references to the Welfare State and the recent introduction of sophisticated technology into the police force: "We're wonderfully highly mechanized at Central Office these days, Campion. Teleprinters, radar, coloured lights everywhere. It's only when we get a power cut that the whole blessed police system is liable to go out of action" (62). All this harps back to the preoccupations of the previous novel: the phenomenon of change, which makes of Havoc and his methods a very different type of anachronism to the Palinodes. Havoc's mother, the old scavenger, Mrs. Cash, verbalizes the theme for the benefit of a police sergeant: "You know the sort of district this is. A lot of very good houses going down, and a very good lot of people going down too" (99). Later, Tiddy Doll, the leader of the street-band gang, attempts to assert a certain superiority over Havoc by reminding him of change: "You didn't know the fighting was over, did you, not reelly.... Things 'ave changed since the war" (136–37). As if to emphasize the importance of change for the events of the novel, Marge portrays Havoc as being "appalled" by the revelation that "there ain't no servant girls now" (151). The alterations in the fixed class hierarchy of society shock Havoc not merely because evil regards itself as the only source of subversion, but also because, for Marge, criminals (as well as detectives) tended to be conformists at heart. At the same time she would appear to have been reacting against the fixed social patterns which were the staple background of the detective story between the wars.

As a thriller, the *Tiger* moves extremely swiftly. Marge made full use of shifts in narrative perspective to maintain the tempo and suspense of the novel—"the constant change of viewpoint," she wrote to Reynolds, was "the best way of keeping the pace going I've yet discovered" (Letter, 02.09.1958). When chapter 5 opens with a flashback to a time "earlier that afternoon," the reader is immediately informed that, "from Geoffrey's point of view the whole afternoon had been a nightmare" (69), which is a very simple (almost crude) way of indicating a change in perspective. Geoffrey Levitt, Meg's fiancé, becomes the constant viewpoint from which events within the circle of the street-band gang are narrated. Since the gang is commanded with military precision by Tiddy Doll, it is particularly appropriate that it should be seen and described by the only person from the respectable world of the novel who has military experience. Later, when the focus shifts back to the house in Petersgate Square, there is a section of the text where the narrative perspective is that of the caretaker's young grandchild, Emily Talisman. She acts as helper and runner to the elderly sporting journalist, Sam Drummock, who has put himself in charge of all telephone communications to the house. As a result the viewpoint is strictly limited, depending on overheard, one-sided scraps of conversation, which Emily—and thus the reader—is left to interpret as best she can: "Emily knew it was exciting news because one of his small feet wagged in its soft red slipper. . . . It was tantalizing" (160).

One of the limitations of attempting to write a "serious" crime novel is that the unsophisticated reader of the genre must still be catered to as well as the new reader with a literary sensibility. As a result, many of the narrative devices which Marge employed in the *Tiger* were perforce made over-explicit. The various areas of the story—wartime escapades, present criminal acts, the sophisticated world of the middle class—have to be related one to another. The reader is helped to make his own connections by a series of hints or linkages. For example, one of the street-band, who was with Major Elginbrodde on a commando raid near the end of the war, received from him a souvenir in the shape of a delicately painted miniature. He comments to Geoffrey: "It used to have a frame. Solid gold, that was, set with little bits of coloured glass. A fellow in the Walworth Road gave Tom seven pounds ten for it" (90). A few pages later, Meg shows Campion's wife, Amanda, a miniature in a jewelled frame; as if this were not link enough to the earlier event, Marge adds, "a frame worth rather more than the few pounds which the dealer in the Walworth Road had given a soldier for its fellow" (107). A clumsy, but for the ordinary reader necessary, emphasis.

As in earlier novels, there are frequent reflections on the role of the reader and the relation of fiction to truth or reality. At one point, Lugg becomes the reader's representative; while driving Campion and his wife through the almost impenetrable London fog, he listens to them talking about details of the ongoing investigation. Campion recounts, step by step, the nature of the evidence in the first of Havoc's series of brutal murders. He tells Amanda, "the other thing is rather ridiculous . . . but it looked very strange written down." Lugg then articulates the frustration and irritation that such deliberate tantalizing stirs up in the reader: "Oh, for god's sake! . . . Drivin' this and listenin' to you, it's like being up to me eyes in the creek. What *'ad* the perisher wrote down?" (121). Marge is also at pains to insist that texts demand specialized readers to discover the intended meaning. On the way to the cellar hideout, at the time of the mistaken capture of Geoffrey Levitt by the street band, Tiddy Doll brutally kicked to death a former associate. When the gang finally gets hold of a newspaper, its front page is filled, not with news of this murder, but of Havoc's bloody triple killing. Doll, expecting to read about his own crime, is confused: "The news story, battling magnificently with too much jam, the laws of libel and contempt of court, was a work of art of its kind, but to the Suffolk man in the cellar it failed in the first degree and was incomprehensible" (128). This sort of awareness of the reader as a factor in the narrative, leads to deliberate manipulation of his expectations and of his attitude towards the text. From the first discovery of Geoffrey's identity, he is a source of potential embarrassment and danger to the gang. When Havoc finally arrives in the cellar hideout, his presence is exploited by Doll as a possible solution to the problem of Levitt. The resulting situation forces the reader into an anticipation of the possible outcome of this aspect of the tale. Doll arranges the site of his first man-to-man discussion of the situation with Havoc: "He seemed to be arranging for the talk to take place so close to the prisoner's bed that the gagged and helpless man must be able to overhear perfectly. . . . Geoffrey was astounded until the diabolical explanation occurred to him. Doll might entertain qualms at the prospect of removing an unwanted witness in cold blood, but Havoc would have none" (140). When, however, Havoc does notice the prisoner, Doll explains him away as a wandering drunk who the gang "shook up" a bit, and ends with the magic phrase, "and that's the gospel truth." For Geoffrey as well as Tiddy Doll the whole statement is clearly a lie, but its true function is underlined by the narrational comment which follows: "The tale was such an ordinary one that it convinced even the two who knew it to be a lie. To them it appeared to be as it were a better truth" (141).

The inclusion of interest as an important factor in the reception of the text emphasises once more the nature of fiction and the reader's relation to it. If it suits the reader to read it so, fiction may even become a better truth. For Marge, as author, the appeal to the reader's interest is crucial if the serious theme of her novel is to gain recognition and acceptance. The thriller framework now has its justification, and the theme of good and evil, together with the exemplary tale of Jack Havoc's downfall, may be seen both as a realistic study of contemporary society and as an allegorical better truth.

Paul Reynolds's reaction to *The Beckoning Lady* was characteristic of much later critical response: "I found it difficult to follow," he wrote. "There are too many characters, too many threads" (Letter, 26.07.1954). For Doubleday's, Isabelle Taylor wrote to Marge very much in the same vein: "The story is so packed with plots and subjects that you almost have enough for two or three other books" (Letter, 26.07.1954). The novel had, however, a particular significance for Marge; she had told Reynolds earlier in the year that it was "like my early tales grown up" (Letter, 16.02.1954), and to her British publishers she wrote: "This book is so much a continuation of the Campion saga that I think we really ought to stress the point" (Letter to A. Brett-James of Chatto's, 15.11.1954). This would suggest that in this new novel, it is continuity rather than change that is of importance. Further, in discussing the book, it will be necessary to differentiate between the seemingly diffuse story, and the carefully organised thematic concerns with which setting and characters are intimately connected.

Since much was made by agent, publisher, and critics of the complexity and confusion of the plot, I shall depart from the practice of previous chapters and offer a summary in order to demonstrate the basic coherence of this aspect of the novel. William Faraday, familiar from *Police at the Funeral* and *Dancers in Mourning*, spent the last years of his life as a semi-invalid in the country, where he was the guest of the painter Minnie Cassands and her husband Tonker. Four and a half years before his death he gave Minnie a large sum of money, knowing that, provided he lived for another five years, there would be no death duties payable on the deed of gift. Unbeknown to Minnie, Uncle William made a bet of 7–2 in thousands of pounds with a well-known London bookmaker that he would die before the five years were up. Thus Minnie was protected in all eventualities. Meanwhile a powerful business consortium, managed by a man whose activities are very much on the brink of legality, Sidney Simon Smith, has begun to put pressure on Minnie to sell her house and estate, the Beckoning Lady, so that—again unbeknown to her—it will have control of the whole area to develop a crooked racecourse for a shady Arab financier. Miss Pinkerton, an efficient and loyal secretary on loan to S. S. Smith, has been helping Minnie in her spare time and is thus constantly in and out of the house. It was she, who, in an idle and apparently thoughtless moment, substituted dormital for Uncle William's usual sleeping pills. Dormital is harmless unless taken together with alcohol, in which case it is fatal. William, who dearly loved his nightly tot of whisky, died. When Miss Pinkerton was substituting the pills, she was seen wasting time in the invalid's room by an unemployed tax inspector, Leonard Ohman, who had been assisting Minnie in her dealings with the Inland Revenue and driving the household mad with his prying and scheming. Ohman ran along the path to the village and waited on a footbridge to intercept Miss Pinkerton. When he stopped her on her way home, catching hold of her arm, she defended herself with the nearest object to hand (a rusty ploughshare), struck Ohman on the head, and ran off. Unfortunately, Ohman's skull was abnormally thin so that the blow was fatal. The body is finally discovered just over a week later. While the police are recovering it, Miss Pinkerton comes past and, being naturally inquisitive, sees the corpse of the man she struck in self-defence. She is shocked and overcome with remorse, which finally leads her to take her own life by swallowing an overdose of dormital followed by a large shot of gin. S. S. Smith and his associates destroy Miss Pinkerton's suicide note to the coroner to avoid unwelcome attention to their affairs, so that the premature discovery of her body is an embarrassment, resulting in their retreat in disorder from the field.

The peculiarity of *The Beckoning Lady* as a crime novel is that the two deaths are virtually accidental, and are practically incidental to the novel's main concerns. However, as has been shown, there is a perfectly coherent plot with mystery, intrigue, and two separate groupings of characters linked by the unfortunate Miss Pinkerton. She is a development of the efficient secretary of earlier novels, Miss Curly in *Flowers*, or Miss Dorset in *Black Plumes*, to mention just two. Unlike them she is not connected with the world of artistic creativity, but with the machinations of somewhat unorthodox high finance. Her true employer is "Fanny" Genappe—"the most unfortunate of the three last multimillionaires in Europe," who "had inherited not only his family's money but also their reputation for philanthropy" (1955, 21). This combination results in him spending most of his time in hermitlike seclusion, while his interests and his money are controlled by such men as Smith. Miss

Pinkerton is thus a buffer figure, allied to an impersonal and inhuman world. Without the influence of the interests of her employers she would not have committed the fatal deeds. As Campion summarises at the end of the novel:

> Smith encouraged Miss Pinkerton to help Minnie with her secretarial work . . . because he wanted to find out why Minnie wouldn't sell her house. . . . Minnie wouldn't sell the place because she did not need to. William's gift had saved her . . . if only William lived until November. . . . Miss Pinkerton knew all about this. She did all the work on both sides. She was an over-efficient person. . . . That afternoon Miss Pinkerton pottered about William's room . . . she saw a very simple method of getting rid of him. She took it. My bet is that she deceived herself into thinking that she was being merciful. (230)

When Minnie Cassands talks about her painting, she points out that she has three subjects that she always returns to: flowers, women, and children. What they have in common is that "you can't really photograph any of them without either sentimentality or brutality, and mine's an essentially realistic approach" (60). In this sense *The Beckoning Lady* also attempts to be an essentially realistic novel. There is another sort of realism in the way in which Marge makes use of so many details from her own life and surroundings. Tonker Cassands—"an idealised picture of Pip" (Letter from J. Allingham, 02.07.1986)—is the most obvious instance; he shares with Pip a bronchial laugh (99), lightning temper (107), and pride in his wife's achievements (109), as well as the habit of being a long sleeper (170) and working late into the day in pyjamas and dressing gown (185). A number of Marge's pre- and postwar friends are mentioned by name: the painter Henry Rushbury (47), her tax accountant Aubrey Christlieb (88), Paul and Ruth Reynolds, Isabelle Taylor, Lavinia Davis, and many other American acquaintances (116). It is, however, the details of the setting of the novel which most faithfully reflect the combined worlds of Chappel and D'Arcy. As Lavinia Davis wrote to Marge after reading the book, "The colour and pre-party bustle and the marvellous small details . . . have had only one bad effect on me and that is they've made me homesick for D'Arcy" (Letter, 01.01.1955). Apart from the location of the Beckoning Lady at Pontisbright (Chappel), there are descriptions of the churchyard on the hill above the village, where Marge's father is buried, the kitchen at D'Arcy House, the bar—"The Half Nelson" (81)—which Pip and Marge installed both at Chappel and at D'Arcy, and the huge refectory table in the barn (66). Above all there is the party itself, and the preparty preparations, which dominate the novel and are quite clearly based on the D'Arcy parties, which I have already had occasion to mention. The closeness of fiction to fact may be gauged from the following description of one such party during the fifties:

> It started at noon and went on well into the wee small hours. There was a glorious mix of people, writers, actors and actresses, producers, businessmen, lawyers, local neighbours—and Margery, very quickly, had everyone mingling. . . . Champagne and buffet food was going most of the day and then about 8 P.M. we were ushered into a huge old barn with enormous trestle tables set in a square, and we all sat down to a simply superb four-course meal (Letter from Audrey Cameron, 20.03.1984).

However, the mere reproduction of details from real life hardly warrants serious interest in the novel. From the outset, *The Beckoning Lady* is a book about marriage, love, and friendship. It is noticeable that, apart from Miss Pinkerton, major characters do not appear alone but in couples: Minnie and Tonker, Campion and Amanda, Luke and his new-found girlfriend, Prunella Scroop-Dory, Old Harry, and the maid of all work, Miss Diane Varley. Even the children tend to be identified in pairs: Emma Bernadine's twins, Minnie's distant relative Westy Straw and his school friend George Meredith. Such is the power of these bucolic structures that at the end of the party the inarticulate George Meredith has collected a "willowy blonde," and Westy Straw shares his point of vantage with Amanda's niece, Mary. Not for nothing is the novel dedicated to "Old Friends and their Merry Wives."

Conversation often turns to marriage or love, and the views that are expressed tend to reflect Marge's own. The theme is introduced when Campion, exploring the house, comes across a late-twenties caricature of Minnie and Tonker, in which they are portrayed as an Indian squaw and a sandy tiger: "They were dancing, or fighting, and the dust rose in clouds from under their feet" (47). The ambiguity of their actions, the amalgam of gaiety and conflict, becomes a process of self-absorbtion, which is at the heart of the ideal of marriage—lasting in spite of everything—which the novel develops. When Amanda discusses the progress of Luke's involvement with "Prune," she comments: "It's always jolly frightening when one's friends fall in that sort of love. . . . They're never the same again, are they? A fusion of metals and all that. I mean, love isn't a cement, it's a solvent. Look at Minnie and Tonker" (91). It is this conception of marriage that the novel goes on to explore; the Cassands' marriage (like the Carters') is not conventional, it does not give the impression of devoted peace or united agreement, nor does it suggest that the two of them exist to promote domestic bliss with clearly defined roles. As Tonker says: "We don't ask any more of marriage than the tie itself. We've had plenty of fights but never any real bitterness" (114). Or, as Amanda observes of the Cassands, "They adore one another, don't they? . . . Life is one long friendly fight. A permanent exhibition bout" (117). Such people tend to be cynical about romantic love, and realistic about the qualities which keep marriage going. Tonker speaks of love "with withering contempt," and comments, "What's love? How much can it stand?" To which his long-suffering wife replies, "That . . . is a thing I sometimes wonder" (181). Even Inspector Luke makes a contribution to the subject, when he quotes some Cockney wisdom to Campion: "You know what we say about marriage. We say it's like the kitchen clock. If it goes better lying on its side or even standing on its head, leave it alone" (158). This would seem to be a fair comment on Marge's own experience of marriage to Pip: it worked well given a large portion of—often one-sided—tolerance, and an acceptance of separate working worlds without suspicion and questioning. She seems to suggest that the most one can hope of a long-term relationship is the sort of positive habitude that is implied when, on the brink of a quarrel, Tonker says to his wife: "Don't cry, Minnie. If you cry you'll get a headache, and if you get a headache you'll be sick. What's the matter? Don't worry, *I'm* here. . . . We're over the first fence. We'll take the next when we come to it. Keep your heart up, old gal. All our life has been like this, hasn't it? Hasn't it, Minnie? Keep on going. We always have. Courage, old lady" (189). Marriage, particularly a marriage of long standing, is seen as essentially a process of experienced continuity; the secret recipe for success is, "keep on going."

This becomes the context within which the elaborate party takes place, a party which in itself is seen as an attempt to maintain continuity: Minnie asks Campion, "Do you remember when there were real parties, Albert?" only to remark afterwards, "All the same, these new shows are great fun. You never know who's going to arrive" (70). The vast rambling party of *The Beckoning Lady* is the next step in Marge's fictional investigation of postwar Britain: can there be continuity at all? Her answer, valid at least for rural England, is a resounding affirmative—in spite of everything. The party becomes a somewhat ephemeral symbol, standing for a turning of one's back on the disruptive reality of every day—both the demands of the taxman and the intrusion of murder. It is an intentional bulwark against the inroads of destructive change. Or, as Tonker says on the morning of the event: "There is only one must at a party. Everything must be fun. Nothing unpleasant must occur" (189). In this sense the party becomes a metaphor for the novel as sophisticated literature of escape.

That which distinguishes the narrative of *The Beckoning Lady* is Marge's instinctive sense of timing and the perfect orchestration of essential sections of the book. By this last I refer to the way in which diffuse blocks of information, or constellations of characters, are introduced and held together in a wider framework. This is most noticeable in the two chapters dealing with the party itself, chapters 15 and 16. Marge's technique here is to make use of a roaming narrative perspective kept in focus by hints and reminders of the underlying urgencies of the plot, and by the device of continually returning to a central figure as to a central theme or *sujet.*

As Tonker walks away after an initial static focus on him and Minnie as they observe the assembled company, the narrative perspective becomes mobile. Minnie is commandeered by a strange young man, sent to fetch her to the exhibition of her paintings. "Meanwhile, on the other side of the lawn Mr. Campion was standing talking with a knot of old friends" (204). This allows Marge to clarify some as yet unexplained business in the crime plot surrounding Uncle William's death. No sooner is this episode over than Campion catches sight of a grey bowler hat in the crowd, but is prevented from catching up with it by an encounter with Prune's mother, Lady Glebe. When he does at last find Solly L., Uncle William's bookmaker, another major mystery of the plot is solved—the double security of William's gift to Minnie. While this shifting viewpoint appears simply to obey the necessities of the plot, it is noticeable that all these diverse episodes and characters have one observation in common. Whether it is Tonker asking Minnie, "Gosh, have you seen Prune?" (203), or Minnie's vague young escort casually stating, "There's a girl here. I think her name is Prune" (204), or even Gilbert Whippet, chairman of the insurance company, asking Campion, "Have you seen Prune?" (205), or finally Solly L.'s observation, which brings the object of all these comments into focus: "There's some smashing girls here. Look at that one. What an eyeful, eh?" (212)—there is no doubt in the reader's mind that the unifying presence at the party is Luke's young woman, who now appears on his arm: "She had the height and figure of a model, and at the only school she had ever attended they had taught her how to walk, if little else. The rest of the miracle had been performed by Charlie Luke. . . . She was so ecstatically happy that she glowed with it as if she wore a glory" (212). In a novel whose central theme is love and marriage, Prune's appearance at the party turns that event into a festive rite, with herself as the embodiment of the joy of love. She functions doubly, both as the narrative device which unites the diversity of perspectives and as the expression of one of the text's central thematic concerns.

The chapter ends with the riotous arrival of the troupe of clowns, the Augusts, and Minnie's, "Now, of course, we're for it" (214). In the chapter which follows, Marge appears to take an enormous risk which, as it turns out, is simply narrative sleight of hand. Chapter 16 begins with a number of anticipatory hints. Miss Pinkerton's body floats further down the stream in the direction of the party: "For some time now the reeds had held the dark bundle almost stationary, and while there was no swifter current there was just a chance that it might remain where it was. But these rushes were the last of the obstacles . . ." (214). Lugg then arrives with a message for Campion which the reader cannot decode in its entirety, but which has to do with a prescription for sleeping pills, after which Tonker announces the main treat of the party: "I want you to experience with me," he tells Campion, "one of the more enjoyable spectacles of civilized lifetime. I want you to see an August talking to a spiv [a postwar British black marketeer]" (215). After thus triply arousing the reader's interest, Marge appears to retard the progress of the story by focussing attention on Minnie's step-great-grand-nephew, Westy. What in fact is happening is a complete shift in narrative perspective from the view of sophisticated grown-ups to the perceptions of an intelligent teenager. This is a very deliberate strategy, which is introduced by Westy's insights into the grown-up world: "The stupidity and obtuseness of the minds of people on the wrong side of twenty seemed to him to be more alarming than any other menace of the era into which he had been born. It was like seeing oneself sailing inevitably into a fog" (217). Thus the reader is notified that the approaching climactic events will be narrated from a viewpoint characterized by an innocent clarity unclouded by masses of irrelevant experience. The presentation of subsequent actions—the Augusts' act, the alarm of the S.S.S. man and his associates, and their panic reaction to the sudden appearance of the body—has a naive directness that sophisticated forms of narration might well have blurred into confusion. The climax is reached by way of a series of short sharp statements introduced by the sentence, "In the next five minutes all sorts of things happened" (222). George Meredith opens up the sluices, the body moves towards the garden, the imitation wherry upon which the Augusts have been clowning breaks its moorings, drawing the guests to the river bank for a better look, S. S. Smith picks up the pile of rubber masks which have been lying near his chair, and, when the waxy face of the corpse becomes visible, throws them into the water to cause a diversion. Clarity struggles with confusion and its victory is announced by the sane voice of Amanda Fitton: "Albert seven went by. There *are* only six. Get Luke quickly" (223).

The narrative strategies employed in these two chapters reveal the totality of Marge's command over her material. This suggests that the enjoyment she gained from writing the book was not only the enjoyment of writing about places, events, and people close to home, but the enjoyment of the writer secure in the knowledge that she had at last been able to exploit her novelistic talents to the full. Of course the reader remembers the characters—"the pleasant, fantastic folk she has gathered" (Anon. 1955)—the idyllic rural setting, the self-centered good humour, the air of excited festivity; but that which transforms all this into a significant novel rather than an ambitious tale of crime and detection is the writerly skill, the many-faceted thematic structure, and the sureness of touch which heralds Marge's arrival at professional maturity.

11

Running Smoothly

I've not worked as well or as long as I do now for thirty years.
It's due to having the home outfit running smoothly and not
having interruptions.

Margery Allingham

"Allinghams," Marge wrote to her British agent, "tend to perk up after
the mid-fifties and I seem to be typical of the breed" (Letter to G.
Watson, 31.03.1964). Between 1957 and 1966 she gave ample evidence
of this with three novels, a short book on the care of the aged, and
several short stories, as well as an annotated reprint of *The Oaken Heart*,
two omnibus volumes, and a handful of articles. She and Pip found a
mutually satisfactory and productive mode of living in the peaceful surroundings of D'Arcy and in the company of old friends. In late middle-
age Marge was a good-humoured, cheerful woman who appeared to
be completely in charge of her life and in full control of her professional
talents. This was, however, only part of the picture: for eighteen exhausting months she commuted regularly to London with Pip, attempting to live the sort of active social life that he adored; her battle with the
Inland Revenue continued for three and a half years, and she had to
witness the terminal illnesses of her mother and of her two aunts, Maud
and Grace, at the Forge. Marge's first concern, however, continued to
be her writing and her reputation as a novelist.

Throughout the first half of 1957 she worked steadily on *Hide My
Eyes*. Like the *Tiger* it focussed on a criminal, but this time the protagonist was smoothly spoken, self-centred, and totally amoral; Gerry
Hawker (modelled on the murderer John George Haigh) killed equally
for gain or protection. Although Marge had high hopes of the book,
both the *Saturday Evening Post* and *John Bull* rejected the manuscript.
Once again it looked as though its specifically "literary" qualities were

the stumbling block. Erd Brandt of the *Post* wrote to Reynolds, "It is quite a book, but it jumps around in viewpoint so much that it is pretty difficult to see it as a serial" (Letter, 09.09.1957).

Before starting work on any new project, Marge had been looking forward to joining Pip on a trip to Madeira, about which he had been asked to write a promotional article for the *Tatler*. The trip, however, did not take place. Shortly before the end of September Pip resigned his post, having got wind of a general editorial shake up. Although Marge regretted missing a holiday, she was not unduly upset: "Financially it is a good thing and I shall know more about the future in a week or so. It could not have happened at a better time from my point of view and I expect to be in London for most of the rest of the year" (Letter to A. Christlieb, 30.09.1957). During his ten years at the *Tatler*, Pip had contributed drawings, film and theatre reviews, and a regular social and cultural column, "London Limelight." He had made quite a reputation for himself as a social journalist and man-about-town, with the result that seven months after he left the magazine, he set up as a freelance journalist, contributing a column, also called "London Limelight," to the *Evening News*. The articles reveal Pip's energetic presence at a variety of society functions and his nodding acquaintance with most of the celebrities of London's social scene. This was the world he now revelled in, and which offered him such rewards as membership of the Thursday Club (a select dining and wining club), or election to the Lords Taverners—an all-male sporting and society club based on the Tavern at Lord's cricket ground in London.

The sudden change in Pip's professional life meant that he was no longer tied to an office routine, but he still spent weekdays at the Great Russell Street flat. Marge now began to share this life with him, leaving D'Arcy on Monday morning and returning on Fridays, exhausted. The obvious explanation is her fear that Pip would use his new-found freedom to continue and expand his affair with Diane, which she continued to combat. Very soon, however, they were forcibly reminded that they were very much man and wife. On November 12 Pip and Marge, together with Christlieb, their accountant, were interviewed in London by inspectors from the Inland Revenue's enquiry branch. The Carters were virtually accused of attempting to defraud the authorities of tax due on Marge's U.S. earnings. A stormy interview followed. Marge found the questioning so aggressive and so insulting that at one point she broke down in tears. This brought out Pip's fighting spirit. In a memorandum that he wrote about the meeting the same day he recorded: "I said very little at this interview, being nearly speechless with fury. It made me ashamed of being an Englishman to have to witness two young thugs whose sole purpose appeared to be to intimidate with unspecified menace, behaving in a way which negated the primary canons of British justice while representing themselves as acting in the name of the administration of the country" (Unpublished typescript). Pip's blimpish language reveals more about his character than about the facts of the interview. However, Marge was inwardly very satisfied with his behaviour to the inspectors; it "pleased her very much, not only because it was one in the eye for them, but also it gave her the support which . . . she so often lacked" (Interview with G. Greci, 13.10.1983).

Throughout the following year Marge continued to travel to town with Pip, accompanying him on many of his assignments for the *Evening News*, and entertaining at the Great Russell Street flat. To Ken McCormick of Doubleday's she wrote, "I don't want anything to muck up the new life Pip and I are having at 91," adding bravely, "This is more fun than we've had for years" (Letter, 09.05.1958). This was probably a piece of wishful thinking on Marge's part; in reality, although she loved London, the social whirl had never been her style, and at fifty-three it made her tired, even ill. On several occasions in the spring of 1958, Joyce had to collect her from the London flat, take her back to D'Arcy, and put her to bed.

In January, Marge's Aunt Maud, who was now well over seventy, had had a stroke in Piccadilly Circus on her way home from a film premiere—"After forty years, every film star was still her hero" (Anon. 1961, 1). It became clear to Joyce and Marge that she would have to be moved to D'Arcy, to take up residence at the Forge, which for some time Marge had planned to use as a private nursing home for the various old ladies who were dependent on her. Although in many ways the ideal solution to the problem of aged relatives, the use of the Forge as a home-cum-hospital, first for Maud, and then for Maud and Em together, was an added burden which was not without its demands on Marge's time. She described the situation a year later in a letter to McFee: "Mother and Maud are both in Joyce's little bungalow opposite here being looked after by a nurse-companion. They are very comfortable but not at all pleased I'm afraid. Phil and his wife come over to see them once a week, and Joyce and I are always in and out" (Letter, 21.04.1959).

As a result of all these diversions, interruptions, and worries, little writing was getting done. Nevertheless, Marge was about to savour the fruits of success once again. Early in May, Reynolds wrote with the news that the Readers Digest Book Club had bought an option on "Tether's End" (the provisional title of *Hide My Eyes*) for $5000. "If the

Digest exercises their option," he wrote, "the book will probably earn something like $60,000, half of which will be yours" (Letter, 01.05.1958). With the prospect of big money coming in, and now wary of the Inland Revenue, Marge decided to take the advice of both Reynolds and her old legal friend, Edward Terrell, Q.C., to turn herself and Pip into a limited company, so that their joint income could be "earned as well as taxed as one" (Letter to Reynolds, 06.05.1958). She gave her solicitor instructions to proceed with the formation of "P.& M. Youngman Carter, Ltd.," in which she would have 60% of the shares, Pip 20%, Joyce 15% and her brother Phil 5%. Nearly all the Carters' joint possessions, including D'Arcy House and the copyright of most of Marge's past and future work, were made over to the company. In addition the company was to pay Marge and Pip a yearly salary of one thousand pounds each, thus obviating the necessity for Pip's freelance work and leaving him free to devote himself to his painting and drawing.

The crowded weekdays (and nights) in London, and the claims of business, family, and friends all conspired to keep Marge from her desk, but her thoughts were seldom far from her writing. Although she detested speaking in public, in November she accepted an invitation to give one of a series of afternoon talks by authors of recently published books ("Tea with an Author") at Harrods. Marge's subject was "Crime for Our Delight." She began by suggesting that the cult of the crime novel, peculiar to the twentieth century, demanded a good measure of realism: characters and settings should be convincing, and the events "like something that might be happening next door" (1958). She went on to account for the popularity of the mystery story: "most of us are natural detectives," which she followed with a more literary explanation. Her manuscript notes are particularly tantalizing here, since it is virtually impossible to recreate what she actually said:

> The killing we harp on is not ordinary killing, not death wish. Death of an Aspect. New and main literary idea of this century. We seem to be catching up with the Greeks. Enormous amount of our stories beginning to have this second meaning or main meaning. The way one keeps murdering one aspect of a person to give birth to another. We kill one relationship, another takes its place. We lose one of our selves and find another. (1958, n.p.)

Marge saw murder as a metaphor for the instinct to suppress knowledge, facts, and ideas, and gave a psychological explanation for the fascination that crime exerts upon law-abiding readers who are willing to accept the death of a fictitious person as an allegory for the natural loss of friendship, love, or even the self. A further remark in her notes for the talk suggests that Marge believed that this was an essential aspect of the relationship between fiction and life: "True of all stories, love, adventure, travel, but *now,* we are starting to see it like this and to do it deliberately." The "we" clearly refers to writers; what they do deliberately is to insist on fiction as a process of metamorphosis and change—a form of death, of killing. She concluded with a hopeful look to the future, in which she predicted that since crime fiction was beginning "to say something," it would appeal to a wider audience than in the past.

Marge was disappointed by the reception of *Hide My Eyes,* which had been published at the end of September. "I am rather sad about the reviews over here," she wrote to Isabelle Taylor. "Despite all my pleas Chatto *would* use the word 'thriller' in the blurb with the result that the book went to the horror merchants who reported that there was no whodunit and they guessed the 'solution.' So much for trying to write a serious tale" (Letter, 30.10.1958). Both the *Observer* and the *Sunday Times* were patronizing—"A brave try but unsuccessful" (Symons 1958)—whereas the boulevard press were irritated by the very seriousness of the tale: "Too much moralizing and too little plotting" (Klein 1958). On the other hand, Howard Spring, who had criticized the weaknesses of *Dance of the Years,* wrote perceptively that Marge was: "A writer who . . . realizes that crimes are committed by and upon human beings, and that human beings constitute the circle of affected lives. . . . This is one of the few novels that permit their readers to enjoy the best of two literary worlds" (Spring 1958).

The British critics may have irritated Marge by their obtuseness, but in June the *Reader's Digest* took up its option on the novel, which resulted in a payment of $29,000. She was further gratified when in the following January, she learned that the Crime Writers' Association had placed *Hide My Eyes* second in their list of the best crime stories of 1958. Marge must have felt a sense of poetic justice in the fact that the chairman of the Association was the same Julian Symons who had been so cool in his review.

It was time for her to get down to a new book. Under the heading "C. Governess," she began to make notes, lists of characters, and scraps of narrative in her notebook. However, in September 1958 Marge admitted to Reynolds: "I haven't got on with the new book at all. I was working it out and it seemed it was a bit too like a detective story, if you follow me? I was wondering if perhaps I should concentrate on another of these suspense yarns" (Letter, 02.09.1958). She was determined to make no compromises in her conception of the crime novel, but she did very much want to retain her audience. This was largely composed of respectable middle-class readers, who demanded more sympathetic feeling in their reading and less out-and-out violence and wickedness. "I'm planning a more simple and 'heartfelt' story," she told Mrs. Taylor. "I think that having captured the 'Auntie' public we should consolidate the position if possible" (Letter, 26.01.1959).

In February 1959, acknowledging the waste and futility of the effort, Marge gave up her attempt to share Pip's London life. Instead, she now tried to inveigle Pip back to D'Arcy, seeking his active participation in the planning of the new novel. In June she wrote to Mrs. Taylor: "All goes well with us. The old art and fiction factory looks as if it is going to come into being again after all these years. . . . Pip and I are both working on the synopsis of the new book and we haven't done that since 1939" (Letter, 08.06.1959). An important step in consolidating the position at D'Arcy House was the decision to convert the old stables into a studio. The final result was one immense open room, about a hundred feet long, with a gallery at the west end which was reached by a concealed staircase. The richly carved balustrade and some of the panelling beneath was taken from from a vast Victorian-Flemish sideboard Marge had bought years earlier from St. Osyth Priory near Clacton. The whole room was painted white, giving an impression of lightness and air. It was furnished largely with antiques that Marge had picked up at auctions and dealers around the county. Pride of place was given to a refectory table with seating for sixteen, which took up half the room. Marge and Pip now had working quarters separate from the house, where they could write and paint. The small room off the gallery served as an office where Mrs. Greci took care of the paperwork, and beyond that was a well-equipped dark room for Joyce's photography. P.& M. Youngman Carter, Ltd. were now totally self-contained.

For some time Marge had been growing increasingly dissatisfied with the way in which her British agents, A. P. Watt, had been handling her affairs, but had been unable to decide on a move. She had a very well-defined conception of what she expected: "a good agent treats his author with the passionate indulgence of a dog fancier dealing with a difficult pet and is quite fanatical in his loyalty." His chief function should be to act as a buffer between author and publisher, and to be "dedicated and long-suffering" in his efforts on the author's behalf (Letter to M. E. Barber, 22.05.1962). In mid-September 1958 she finally wrote to Peter Watt that she was leaving his firm. A month later she moved to Curtis Brown. Watt wrote somewhat sadly to Marge: "I am extremely sorry that your Company should have felt compelled to take the step it has, particularly as we have had the privilege of looking after your literary work ever since you first started to write, and brought your first book to Uncle Hansard." (Letter, 01.10.1958).

Graham Watson of Curtis Brown's—who represented John Steinbeck, William Faulkner, and Gore Vidal in Britain—became Marge's new agent. He has recalled her as being a first-rate business woman, who always got her own way in the drawing up of contracts. One of Watson's chief tasks was to ensure that Penguin kept Marge's books in print. In his view, she was almost unique for the sheer number and extremely long life of her books in paperback, comparable in this respect only to Evelyn Waugh and Graham Greene (Interview with G. Watson, 04.01.1984).

Another conflict was also about to be solved: 1960 rang down the curtain on the almost endless tragicomedy of Marge and the tax inspectors. In January the Carters again had a meeting with the Inland Revenue Enquiry Branch. It now emerged that the reason for the latter's suspicions arose from the double taxation convention between Britain and the U.S., which exempted literary profits earned by British citizens in America from U.S. tax, and also provided for a free flow of information from American publishers and agents to the Inland Revenue. The information in the inspectors' possession suggested that Marge's U.S. income was larger than had been previously declared. The meeting broke up inconclusively. Then at the end of March the local Inspector at Witham wrote asking for an interview; the sort of questions that were bothering him reveal both the farcical and the irritating elements in the whole enquiry: "Is your client a successful writer because she lives well, or does she live well because she is a successful writer?" (Letter to Christlieb, 29.03.1960). A final meeting in London resulted in Marge's complete exoneration: "You will be glad to hear that our Inland Revenue ... have reluctantly decided that I seem to be completely and utterly blameless.... The inquisition is quite an experience ... the citizen has no rights apparently and is guilty until he proves himself innocent.... Possibly they were getting their own back for *The Beckoning Lady*" (Letter to I. Taylor, July 1960).

After a troublesome and nomadic old age, Marge's mother, Emmie Allingham, died on March 5, 1960. She had always been a very difficult woman with a totally undisciplined tongue; she said exactly what was on her mind, even if it was deliberately unfair or unkind. Her children found her vulgarity and lack of sensitivity particularly painful. One of the main causes of friction between her and Marge had always been a temperamental affinity, which led to quarrels ending not so much in animosity, as in exasperation. After Em's death, Marge wrote to William McFee: "She was a remarkable person and she died in a typically thorough and impulsive way. One day she complained of a pain in the chest and went to hospital for an X-ray. She had cracked a rib somehow and when I went in to see her she said suddenly, 'You know, Marge, I should let me *go* if I were you.' And go she did, quite suddenly, two days later after Phil had spent the afternoon with her and Joyce had just left" (Letter, 19.05.1960). Her death left the Forge in the hands of Aunts Maud and Grace, who, although attended by a trained nurse, still kept the family busy—Marge quite consistently referred to them in letters as "our naughty old ladies." Two weeks after Em's death, Maud had a heart attack and Grace Russell a fall in the bath. When they were in better health, they quarrelled and complained until Joyce was quite exhausted. Marge described the latent humour of these trials to Mrs. Taylor: "At 89 Aunt Grace . . . just won't have it that anyone has died and we are always being called upon to prepare for visits from either of her husbands (deceased), her Papa (Grannie's elder brother) or the full caste of 'Floradora' with whom she appeared nightly in 1889 . . . disconcerting perhaps but full of *joie de vivre*" (Letter, 29.08.1960).

Grace Russell died on November 2, leaving Maud in sole possession of the Forge for the next nine months (although she, too, was weakening rapidly). In January 1961 Marge told Reynolds that "the ultimate aunt has reached the penultimate stage when she requires all hands to augment the nursing staff, but nothing goes on for ever" (Letter, 12.01.1961). The truth of that final statement was brought home to Marge twice that year: on August 13 her friend Lavinia Davis suddenly died in her sleep, and two weeks later Aunt Maud finally died "after lingering since Christmas" (Letter to I. Taylor, 29.08.1961). It must have seemed as though links with the past were being remorselessly severed, and that the oft-observed principle of change could not be halted.

Since the beginning of the year, Marge had been attempting to get down to concentrated work on the *Governess*, but progress tended to take the form of a series of stops and starts. "I am pressing on with the book," she told Reynolds, "amid a catastrophic time with our old folk, who are passing out one by one amid flurries of nurses and doctors" (Letter, 04.01.1961). In May she reported to her BBC producer, Audrey Cameron, that she was "chained to the desk trying to finish a book which ought to have been published months ago" (Letter, 24.05.1961). Quite apart from the interruptions, Marge's concern for the new novel, which she wanted "to be the best ever and a little happier than *Tether's End*" (Letter to I. Taylor, July 1960), was forcing her to work with patient care. By the beginning of November she was struggling with the final chapters and wrote to Ian Parsons of Chatto's that she felt that the book was somewhat more "adult and convincing than the other two of its type (*The Tiger,* and *Hide My Eyes*)" (Letter, 08.11.1961). It is interesting to note her insistence on the continuity of these three books, even though the *Governess* is a much milder and more obviously social novel. The fact that she pointed out the connection confirms that Marge's production was much more organic than one might at first sight think. She was also concerned that Chatto's should advertise the new novel correctly, and, probably with their mistake of pinning the label "thriller" to *Hide My Eyes* in mind, pointed out: "I have put the word 'A Mystery' under the title because my last few books have been thrillers, which is to say that there has been very little mystery in them. Many people prefer the 'mystery' or 'detective' story which is, as a rule, a more serious minded piece of work than the thriller . . . so I thought I might as well get the label right from the beginning" (Letter to Parsons, 13.11.1961). There is a certain element of tongue-in-cheek about these remarks; Marge's use of the word "label" should be taken at face value—she was concerned here with the selling strategy, the marketing of her novel, or how to satisfy the customers. She most certainly did not think of her last few books as thrillers, and for her the *Governess* was only a "mystery" for the sake of those readers who needed familiar packaging.

It was characteristic of Marge's extraordinary professionalism that she interrupted work on the *Governess* one last time when she was asked to write a Christmas short story for the *Sunday Telegraph*. "It's worth it" she wrote to Mrs. Taylor, "and will stop me 'rushing' the finish—one of my bad habits" (Letter, 04.12.1961). The result was "Happy Christmas," which Marge thought was "the best Xmas story I've ever done," even "the best short story I've done for years" (Letters to Reynolds, 01.01.1962, and Dudley Barker of Curtis Brown, 20.03.1962). However, the *Telegraph*'s editor rejected the story for its lack of excitement. Marge immediately agreed to write another one, which was completed in three days, "The Snapdragon and the C.I.D.," a swift-moving Campion and Oates mystery reminiscent of the prewar *Strand* stories. It is symptomatic of Marge's awareness of the twin threads of continuity and change in her recent work that the denouement of the story takes place in a hotel for the elderly, where Campion "saw face after familiar face. They were old acquaintances of the dizzy nineteen-thirties whom he had mourned as gone forever when he thought of them at all" (1969, 218).

No sooner was this brief interlude over, than Marge, in a final burst of energy, set out to complete the *Governess*. On January 5 the first version was finished, so that the familiar routine of preparing the manu-script for the publishers could begin: "I clean it up, typing the whole thing out with one finger. After that it gets knocked around and pulled apart by the family. Then, with the structure complete, all that's left is the literary polish. I do this by dictating the whole manuscript to an old friend" (Duncan 1960). Grog was indeed called into action once more, spending the last weekend of January in yet another mammoth session at D'Arcy. As always, Marge was unsure about the book: "Dear me! I do hope the Governess suits after all this," she wrote to Watson. "I hope she turns out a nice girl. I'm no judge of a book at this stage" (Letter, 23.01.1962). A month later this diffidence had worn off and she could report confidently to Reynolds that "the fact that it has 'come off' restores my faith in pure homework. I feel I'm getting the hang of the job at last" (Letter, 26.02.1962). The reference to homework is a re-minder that Marge researched all her books with great care; she pos-sessed a comprehensive working library of law and criminology books, and always made a point of consulting whatever experts in medical, legal, and other fields she could get hold of.

Most of February was spent in bed, the annual bout of influenza having laid the entire household low. It was, therefore, a somewhat weakened Marge who received the glad tidings that Mary King, fiction editor of the *Chicago Tribune-New York News* syndicate had offered $6000 for the serial rights to the *Governess*. Serialization had always been an important element in Marge's publishing strategy; in her eyes the suc-cessful disposal of serial rights was always a barometer for the potential success of a book. Thus the purchase of the British serial rights for £2500 by *Woman's Own* delighted her: "It's going down most satisfactorily over here you'll be glad to know. Our top (paying!) magazine is serializ-ing it so I feel very happy" (Letter to I. Taylor, 16.03.1962).

Marge was now feeling full of energy once more. She and Pip were even contemplating the madcap scheme of turning *More Work for the Undertaker* into a play. But then began the dreary business of abridging the *Governess* for serialization. She did not feel that the drastic cutting improved the tale but, as she wrote to Dudley Barker, who was han-dling the matter for Curtis Brown, "the guts are all there and it's fairly smooth." She suggested that the missing "colour" might be filled in by letting the illustrator have a copy of the uncut version (Letter, 23.05.1962). For Marge the whole point of the undertaking was that it would probably promote sales of the hardcover edition of the book. Some more cheering news came from Mary King in a letter announcing her imminent arrival in England: "There is a new big help-yourself paperback shop in the Grand Central Railroad Station here and my sister Lulu is one of its regular customers. When she was looking at the shelves one day recently, the young man in charge said to her, "We have a treat for you Allingham fans—eleven new titles." (Letter, 04.06.1962)."

Never content to rest on her laurels, Marge revealed in an interview that she was already planning a new book that was to be "a thriller, but it will be constructive." She went on to reflect upon the function of the crime novel in an age in which nuclear weapons were threatening the destruction of the entire human race: "When all the awfullest things have been said—you tell people they're going to be annihilated any minute at the push of a button—then people become slap-happy. Now you've got to think about what happens next, chum." The interviewer concentrated on the expression "slap-happy" to accuse Marge of escapism, to which she retorted: "The whole of life is about escape. My garden is an escape. As long as you face every problem presented to you, it's not wrong to escape a little. After all you only escape from insanity to sanity, and that's a very good idea" (Pottersman 1962). It is important to note that she included in her defence of this position the proviso, "as long as you face every problem presented to you." Her attitude, and the attitude expressed in her fiction, was not to ignore the difficulty and challenge of reality, but to acknowledge their presence and importance and then seek an escape in the saner world of fictional narrative.

In the late summer Marge and Pip entertained a number of guests including Ken McCormick of Doubleday's and his wife. The long-established August Bank Holiday cricket party had given way, with the increasing age of the players, to a party held on the day of the children's gymkhana and pony show ("it's brighter than it sounds," Marge wrote to McCormick, 17.06.1962). Then in early September Pip left for a motoring trip through France to Andorra and back, tasting wine and capturing his impressions in drawings and notebooks on the way. It was this trip that he later turned into the delightfully readable travel book, *On to Andorra* (1963).

Pip's career had been developing steadily during the years since he left the the *Tatler*. Among other things, he had drawn a most successful series of pencil and chalk portraits of well-known personalities, including the Duke of Edinburgh and Charlie Chaplin. His literary ventures were also gaining recognition. Between spring 1959 and autumn 1962, Pip published a dozen short stories in *John Bull*, *Argosy*, and other magazines, which Marge—not entirely out of loyalty—found "very good indeed" (Letter to McFee, 19.05.1960). Domestic relations had be-

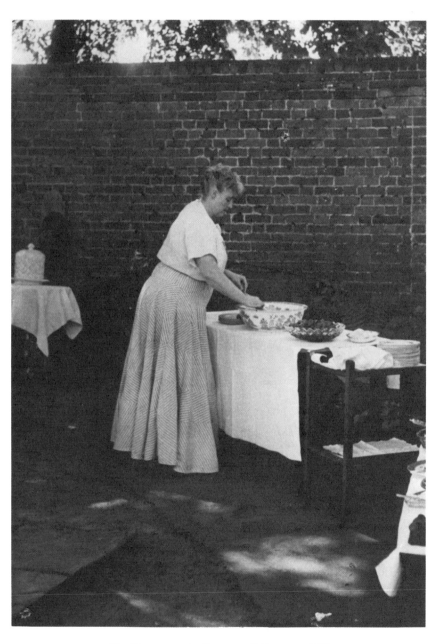

The Hostess on the Terrace at D'Arcy, ca. 1957

come peaceful, even emotionally satisfying. On their thirty-fifth wedding anniversary Pip sent a telegram from France: *"Tout mon amour à vous aujourd'hui—Philipe"*; one wonders whether the formality of the "vous" had a particular significance, or was due to the proprieties of the French postal authorities, who must have been responsible for Frenchifying the name.

At the end of February 1963, *The China Governess* was "off to a flying start with a reprint before publication" (Letter to I. Taylor, 12.03.1963). Within two weeks over 10,000 copies had been sold. The reviews ranged once more from lukewarm to downright negative, but as Marge wrote to Watson, "I am at that state of authorship when it's fair game to wallop Auntie" (Letter, 11.04.1963). Julian Symons was in the forefront of the critical attack again—"a deplorably silly story" (Symons 1963)—closely followed by Maurice Richardson in the *Observer*: "Miss Allingham has plenty of gas but she seems to be running short of blood" (Richardson 1963). Only the *Sunday Telegraph*'s reviewer showed any understanding of the novel, which he felt was "pointedly contemporary in its social comment," and also "a brilliantly effective thriller" (Mason 1963).

By now Marge had a clear idea of the ideal audience for whom she was writing: like her they would share the conviction that the detective story "with a serious undertone" was the most exciting new development in the genre. Or as she stated more simply in an interview, she felt that her books were "for people who want more than crime" (Meras 1963). She was optimistic, too, about her future career: "I am 58 rising 59," she wrote to Reynolds, "and my books are getting better as they should for a year or so. My bet is that some publisher is going to make a lot of money out of me in the next 10 to 15 years" (Letter, 25.01.1963). She felt, too, that age offered her more rather than less freedom to write about anything she wanted to: "As you get older, if you don't know about something and you want to write about it, you give your mind to finding out about it. You're not really frightened of writing anything. . . . You don't have to imagine the lot when you get older" (Meras 1963).

Apart from the occasional favoured visitor to D'Arcy—Paul Reynolds, Robert Lusty, Lee Barker of Doubleday's, the Gregorys—life in the country now knew few interruptions. The first Saturday in July was still Flower Show day, with fourteen guests to dinner, and September saw further guests arriving for the Horse Show party. In between Marge concentrated on the new novel, which she admitted to Reynolds was "not much like the others but you may like it" (Letter, 26.08.1963). At this stage its provisional title was "The Quiet Children," but Marge, true to her principles, was keeping very quiet about its subject matter. The only hint she let out that year was in a postscript added to a business letter to Lee Barker: "ESP has me enthralled" (Letter, 11.11.1963).

At the same time as she was confiding to Watson that she was "hovering on the brink" of getting down to the actual writing of the new novel, she came up with the idea of an omnibus volume of Campion tales: "One prints three books (or two and some shorts) and makes a nice fat volume designed to sell 5000 copies at 25/- as Christmas presents. The author receives a modest royalty . . . and it bridges the gap between his old and new books" (Letter, 11.04.1963). Marge always kept a shrewd eye on the necessity of keeping her name in the public eye. Chatto's approved of the plan, which resulted in *The Mysterious Mr. Campion*, containing *Dancers*, the *Tiger*, *The Case of the Late Pig*, a short story, and the long introductory article, "Mystery Writer in the Box." The omnibus volume came out in late October with a subscription of over 4,000 copies; "I hope," wrote Ian Parsons, "you'll think this a satisfactory kick-off" (Letter, 24.10.1963). Marge did, and regarded an invitation to attend a Foyles Literary Luncheon in November as a sign that her stock as a writer was high. The omnibus volumes (*Mr. Campion's Lady* appeared in 1965) not only served the purpose of bridging the gap between new novels, they also underlined her position as an established popular writer: "My whole idea has been to get them given as Christmas presents to young people with whom they are fast becoming standard favourites. Modesty forbids me to say that I am the present day Robert Louis Stevenson but I don't see why I should not be considered a runner-up in a bad period" (Memorandum to Milton Runyon of Doubleday's, 28.07.1965).

For some time Marge had been becoming increasingly irritated by Doubleday's. As early as January 1960 she had complained that "good books come from contented authors and not from those who always have to keep wondering where the next pound and the next publisher is coming from" (Letter, 18.01.1960). To Reynolds she had protested, "It doesn't sound to *me* as if they regard me as a valuable author" (Letter to I. Taylor, 25.01.1960). Towards the end of 1963, it seemed that there was not even "a strong publishing brain in charge" of the firm; this Marge found extremely disturbing: "I have now reached the stage when I don't feel I have a publisher so much as a capricious headmistress, who may humiliate me, or beat me down, or just not try to sell my work in order to get it into my head that I am not very important" (Letter, 26.11.1963).

Reynolds suggested moving to either Norton or William Morrow, but Marge hesitated, unwilling to leave a publishing house many members of which had become close personal friends. When she heard that Milton Runyon—"my favourite among the Doubleday boys" (Letter to Reynolds, 20.01.1959)—was planning to visit her in February, Marge wrote to him that she was proposing to find a new publisher. At D'Arcy, they talked the matter over in detail, but Marge's mind was made up. The next day she sat down to write letters to Doubleday explaining that she felt she needed a change (Diary, 24.02.1964). In retrospect, it seems that at the heart of Marge's dissatisfaction was a basic inability to communicate with Mrs. Taylor: "The problem between Isabelle Taylor and Miss Allingham was the failure of a meeting of the minds. Mrs. Taylor was very demanding and pretty sure she was always right. Miss Allingham was light years more sophisticated" (Letter from K. McCormick, 27.03.1984).

In the lengthy memorandum Marge prepared for Runyon later in the year, she presented the conflict as essentially one between Reynolds and Isabelle Taylor, with herself as the innocent, misunderstood victim. This version seems unfair on Reynolds, but whichever explanation is correct, what mattered at the time was that Marge did finally make up her mind to move to Morrow's.

The new novel, however, was what really concerned her most throughout the year. Joyce reported that Marge was "full of enthusiasm and certainly has a very fresh and up-to-date idea in the book now on the desk" (Letter, 07.01.1964). Bernard Levin has said of the sixties that "there was a restlessness in the time that communicated itself everywhere and to everyone" (Levin 1970, 9). Marge's enthusiasm was very much in accordance with the spirit of the times, and she felt confident that her fortunes would hold through the decade. She wrote to Winifred Nerney, now living in retirement, "My belief has always been that the sixties were the great years for adventure story writers" (Letter, 25.02.1964).

Marge experienced moments of frustration with her progress on *The Mind Readers*, due both to her own slowness, and to the usual inroads that unexpected interruptions made on her time. Leslie Cresswell, who was now nearing seventy and getting cantankerous and difficult to handle, having decided to move to D'Arcy, took possesion of the Wheatsheaf cottage, one of several properties in the village that Marge had bought and renovated. When he moved in at the end of March, she helped him with decorating and arranging his belongings. No sooner was this done, than poor health forced her to stop work: "Not at all good. Had to lay off and rest. This spring trouble is a mixture of suppressed sinusitis and ordinary glandular heats at pre-menopause

Marge with Leslie Cresswell in the Late 1950s

period times. I think the flushes send the toxic sinusitis matter into the brain and make one dizzy" (Diary, 16.04.1964). Whether or not this was an accurate diagnosis—the symptoms have a disturbing similarity to those of hyperthyroidism—matters cannot have been improved by Marge having, the very next day, to fulfill an obligation to Penguin Books. A Southampton bookseller had just opened a new paperback bookshop and Penguins were anxious to send some of their top authors to a "major multiple signing party" there (Letter from P. Buckman, 01.01.1964). Marge travelled to Southampton in the company of Monica Dickens and Keith Waterhouse and did her best to do what was expected of her. Although she claimed to have enjoyed it enormously, it was an exhausting ordeal. Monica Dickens has written: "My memories of that day are that she was extremely stout and unwieldy. . . . We had quite a long walk from the hotel to the bookshop along the sea front and I remember that we lugged her along in the cold sea wind with great difficulty" (Letter, 31.01.1984). Nevertheless, on return to D'Arcy, Marge went straight back to work on the new novel, revising, rewriting, and slowly getting ahead. Then in mid-May came the death of another link to the past, Winifred Nerney. Marge sadly put her book on one side and wrote a short tribute to her friend: "Her whole life was spent reassuring writers that their calling has dignity and value and in presenting them in the best possible light to the people for whom they worked" (1964a). Nerney, as she was called by all who knew her, had been Arnold Bennett's secretary until his death, before becoming Doubleday's representative in London. She was a person of endearing character; as Marge wrote to Runyon, "she was . . . one of those rare people who just make a splendid job of whatever it is. . . . She always made one rather pleased and proud to be an author" (Letter, 29.05.1964). Marge was saddened by the lack of official tribute to Nerney in the usual journals, and wrote saying as much to the editor of *The Author*: "there can be few writers who met her who did not receive some help or civility from her" (Letter, 04.06.1964).

A few days later, Marge wrote in mock desperation of her painstaking labour on the new novel: "The work I put into these things you'd think they were Holy Writ!" (Letter to Pauline Meiggs, 10.06.1964). Slow as she may have been, the multiple interruptions which still dogged her did not help. "I am having one of those exasperating summers," she told her German translator, Peter Fischer, "in which I'm trying to finish a book and the painters are trying to do up the house and all my overseas friends and relations think it's a good time to come to England" (Letter, 28.07.1964). However, by early August the last chapter but one was complete and, rather as in former times, Marge read it to Pip, "who is gratifyingly impressed" (Diary, 03.08.1964). When it was finished a month later, Pip helped her with the revising and correcting, and then took the manuscript with him to London to deliver to Chatto's. It really seemed as though he and Marge were at last finding encouragement and support in each other's company again. Marge certainly regarded *The Mind Readers* as something of a joint venture in an old familiar mode. For her it was "the first of the new AAA (Allingham Adult Adventure) books," which she saw designed to act as a counterblast to the established pontificators of the crime fiction world. She suggested to Watson that with Chatto's help she might be able to "bust out of this AWFUL Gollancz-Symons-Mystery Writers Association stale blood and fumbling-sex blanket-bath and have fun again" (Letter, 29.10.1964). If this sounds as though she was adopting a deliberate lowbrow stance, it can only have been out of pure naughtiness and irritation with the crime establishment, who would not take her seriously.

Resumption of creative partnership with Pip created a nostalgic mood, in which Marge reflected that between them the Carters and old Doctor Salter had now occupied D'Arcy House for a hundred years. Her home and her garden had become very much symbols of the continuity which she knew it was an escape and an illusion to pursue, but found a comfort to imagine. Perhaps for the very same reason she preferred the idea of a Conservative victory in the approaching General Election, fearing the centralist control she was convinced a Labour government would bring. She admitted to having a soft spot for the Conservative leader, Sir Alec Douglas-Home, who, in a newspaper interview, had confessed to a weakness for mystery stories and for Allinghams in particular. It is not surprising that Marge wrote of him as her "favourite man," although the revelation that "he *looks* like Campion," is certainly unexpected (Letter to I. Taylor, 06.07.1964).

Marge's agents and publishers on both sides of the Atlantic were unanimous in their admiration of *The Mind Readers;* she was particularly delighted by an enthusiastic cable from Lawrence Hughes of Morrow's, as she had looked forward to a successful start with her new publishers. The novel, which is concerned with the potential of Extra Sensory Perception in a military or secret service context, is dedicated "To my technical advisers." In a memorandum for Reynolds, Marge noted that these "were the newspapers . . . whenever I saw a mention of the subject in the press I made a note of it." She goes on to explain that she was no stranger to ESP, having grown up believing quite firmly in thought transference. Marge recalled childhood card games when she expected to be able silently to persuade her neighbours to discard the cards she needed. She had never queried the reality of the phenomenon, but had concentrated on trying to discover how it took place: "I observed that it was a little overspill of casual emotion which seemed to 'power' the operation" (undated manuscript). Any actual effort to transmit or receive thoughts was, in Marge's experience, a hindrance to communication. She wondered whether an advance co py of the novel might be sent to the leading authority on ESP in the United States, a professor at Duke University, in order to obtain expert approval.

The new year found Marge's mind working overtime and filled with plans for the future. In one letter to Watson she discusses the possible future of books on tape, author's rights, and the new omnibus, *Mr. Campion's Lady*, for which she had written both a long preface and new introductions to the novels it contained: *Sweet Danger*, *Traitor's Purse*, and a revised, shortened version of *The Fashion in Shrouds*. As if this were not enough, she touched on a short book she had written during the autumn of 1964 describing her own schemes for the care of the aged. Based on experiences at the Forge, *The Relay* (which neither Morrow or Chatto were interested in) was frankly uncommercial. Marge finally proposed "another small book-on-the-side" about Dr. Salter and his garden. However, she did admit: "The first consideration must be the new book. It is to be a proper murder mystery with a good romance in it, plenty of action and 'situation' and a London and coastal setting with barges. I am also going to have a treasure hunt and a much lighter atmosphere than I have had lately. (Mr. Lugg will positively appear!) When I get it into some sort of shape you shall have a brief synopsis" (Letter, 07.01.1965).

Marge's plans for getting down to the new book were rudely interrupted by a sudden request from the *Ladies Home Journal* in New York for an interview article about John Le Carré (David Cornwell). Marge, intrigued, accepted. A thirteen-page telegram arrived from Peter Wyden, the *Journal's* editor, explaining procedure: Le Carré was staying in Austria, where he was being interviewed by a freelance journalist, Leslie Hannon, who was to furnish Marge with transcripts of the interview. "What we seek," Wyden cabled, "is the Allingham touch applied to the combined insights of yourself and Cornwell into the motivations, personalities, atmosphere of people who live lives in which secrecy is a vital element" (Telegram, 21.01.1965). The transcripts of Hannon's tapes arrived on January 25; the next day Wyden sent another seven-page telegram informing Marge of Cornwell's response to detailed questions about women's reactions to James Bond, which she was expected to incorporate in her article. She finished the piece the next afternoon. Joyce and Marge drove to London that evening and posted copies of the article from the Central London Post Office by midnight. Not unnaturally Marge was surprised when no acknowledgment followed. Then on January 30 a cable came for Hannon, closely followed by Hannon himself. Wyden was not completely satisfied: "Allingham marvellous but greatly repeat greatly underplays herself. She great writer when Cornwall still washing elephants. Crave her corresponding experiences and personal reactions as mystery expert (not just mystery writer) especially her views wherever men women concerned. Want semblance of equal discussion not merely interview. This is vital" (Telegram, 30.01.1965).

Wyden followed his cable with a telephone call to Hannon at D'Arcy giving him until the next day to complete the article. Hannon asked Marge a number of superficial questions about her life and then went off to the studio to complete his assignment. He returned at 11 P.M. having written nothing. Marge then insisted on dictating her answers to Wyden's queries. By two in the morning Pip was getting restless, so everyone went to bed. However, Marge was worried and could not sleep: "so I got up around 5 A.M. and went down and completed the interview on the typewriter . . . not caring as long as what was sent was sound, relevant stuff" (Letter to M. Reiss of P. R. Reynolds, 01.02.1965). When Hannon came down to breakfast, he was relieved that the work had been completed, and after cabling the additional text to New York, departed leaving an exhausted Marge longing for sleep.

The resulting article, "My Love Affair with the World of Spies and Spying," was still mainly about Le Carré; it gave the impression that over the tea cups at D'Arcy House, Marge, in a somewhat brittle, chatty manner, was doing her best to bring out the salient features of Le Carré's writing and personality. Only at one point did she really appear to express her own opinions. The talk turned to women and James Bond, and Cornwall suggested that as a lover Bond was essentially therapeutic, being shown as a violent cure for all sexual problems. Marge commented: "It was good to hear the Bond style of sex dismissed so deftly. I mentioned to Le Carré that I first heard the theory that the main purpose of sex was to do one good . . . when I was in high school . . . and that it seemed to me as dull an idea then as it does still. 'I hope James Bond will forgive me,' I said, 'if I say that I think young men often overestimate the gratitude women feel toward them for their attentions'" (1965b, 118). She gained a favourable impression of David Cornwall from the tapes and his books; he reminded her of the young Graham Greene, though "not so miserable" (Letter to Reynolds,

27.02.1965). Marge seems to have found the whole experience stimulating and the final result—even if the article as published was not what she had written, but rather a processed product—pleasing.

It was not until April that Marge was able to get down to sketching a final outline for the new book, *Cargo of Eagles*, which, as she told Hughes, was to be a "piece of 'plugged-in' adult adventure which will move as fast as I can make it" (Letter, 10.05.1965). Work on the book went very slowly throughout the year, which seemed to have almost more than the usual share of interruptions: photographers, publishers, agents, interviewers from the BBC, the Conservative Party, the flower show, researchers, and Anglia television all combined to prevent Marge from having any continuous period of undisturbed time to work on her novel.

At the end of June, *The Mind Readers* was published in the U.S. to a very mixed critical reception, but with greater commercial success than most of her previous books. An advance sale of over 8,000 resulted in the first edition of 10,000 being swiftly sold out, so that Morrow had to issue a second printing. While the *Wall Street Journal* and the *New York Herald Tribune* dismissed the book, most of the other major American newspapers were friendly; the *Chicago Tribune* found it "thoughtful and engaging" (Anon. 1965a), and in the *St. Louis Post Dispatch*, the reviewer praised Marge's "sly sense of humor" and "fertile imagination" (Schwartz 1965), while a new champion, Charles Champlin of the *Los Angeles Times*, commented on the "wide variety she achieves within a presumably standard formula" (Champlin 1965).

When the British edition appeared after several postponements at the end of October, "the old 'dyed-in-the-wool' reviewers, or rather 'thriller' reviewers, found it obscure" (Letter to Hughes, 07.06.1966). Both the *Observer*'s critic and Julian Symons in the *Sunday Times* complained about the obscurity of the narration—"I don't know what can be done about J. Symons. I seem to get in his paper despite him" (Letter to Norah Smallwood of Chatto's, 03.11.1965). The only wholly positive reviews appeared in the odd trinity of the conservative *Daily Telegraph*, the communist *Daily Worker*, and the provincial *Midland Chronicle*, which regarded *The Mind Readers* as Marge's most remarkable book to date and praised the brilliant reasoning and convincing narration (Moore 1965).

The mixed reception of her books by the reviewers, and the continually improving sales, particular of the Penguins and American paperbacks, led Marge to reflect critically upon her achievement. She felt that she had broken into the "good family reading" field, which transcended generation, age, and even class. She was, however, aware that it was a very difficult image of herself to maintain "because what the reader really wants is 'the same but different' every time" (Letter to Reynolds, 13.07.1965). Nor had she really sought the role of supplier of goods which would satisfy the broad middle range of customer. Marge was too much the conscious writer, the ambitious novelist, to be satisfied by simply commercial success. She was also very much aware of changes that were taking place both in popular taste and in modes of perception:

> The gulf between the old popular fiction . . . and the new, is the gulf between Sherlock Holmes . . . and the space age tales of science fiction. At best they both attempt a factual everyday picture of their eras; but new horizons, not only in the universe but *in our own minds*, have opened up in the interval, and I think my own slightly off-beat approach may turn out to be merely the new viewpoint. (Letter to Reynolds, 09.09.1965)

Marge repeated this idea to Runyon, pointing out that in the last ten years her early books had started to sell well again, and seemed "to appeal to the new generation *and their children*" (Letter, 13.09.1965). She felt that she was very much a part of this new world, and that she had been conditioned for it by her parents, both of whom, in their individual ways, had been ahead of their time. She claimed this quality for herself, too, and even for her writing: "I don't know that I'm a particularly good writer, but I think I might be an *advanced* one in my own line" (Letter to Reynolds, 24.09.1965). It was this aspect of her work which cut her off from those critics, the crime and thriller establishment, who were unable to accept the innovations and literary quality which she had brought to the genre.

That summer, Marge described herself and Pip as "free, white and only sixty-one!" (Letter to Reynolds, 09.06.1965) and ready to get down to work together, if only to defy approaching old age. Marge told an interviewer, "We are getting light-hearted again because Tonker just simply hates old age. He refuses to grow old. I suspect my next book will be Marge with Pip's help again" (Wallace 1965). Then quite suddenly she went through "a dreary patch" of illness in early July, due to an overdose of thyroid extract. By the end of the month she was working again and feeling fit. Whatever the subjective impression, this brief illness seems to have had lasting effects which were noticeable to others. Her natural obesity had increased, and her movements were slower and more laboured, symptoms typical of an underfunctioning thyroid. When, in December, the novelist Hammond Innes met her at a party given by the Carters' friends, the Reids, he noted:

Marge in the Studio with Her Sister, Joyce, and Pip in the Mid-1960s

Illness had made her very large so that movement was difficult. It was very sad, yet that is not all I remember of her. It was her voice I remember, a very youthful, almost girlish voice. And I shall always remember her leaving. She had a scarf—grey chiffon, I think—and she put it over her head and tied it under her chin, and suddenly her face looked so young . . . the impression was very vivid, a cumbersome body and a sparkling personality. (Letter, 17.02.1984)

In the middle of February 1966, Marge fell seriously ill and took to her bed in a highly excitable state. She spent part of the time talking aloud to herself or those around her, very lucidly analysing her own condition. One afternoon Mrs. Greci, who was keeping her company, transcribed her remarks in shorthand. Marge talked of herself in the third person as the "Queen Beetle," whose social position was akin to that of a queen bee supported by her swarm. She felt that she was experiencing a heightened change of life, which would be a rejuvenation for all around her. After a number of perfectly sane comments on her physical condition, which corresponded very largely to that of someone suffering from hyperthyroidism (alternating high and low blood pressure, sweatings, convulsions of the muscles, and a need for cool drinks and light meals), Marge suddenly remarked that she was frightened of approaching death; but almost immediately a reaction set in, and she said that she should pull herself together and live. A constant note in her wanderings was the feeling that she was stretching and growing and getting slimmer, and she recalled that her grandmother had appeared to go through a similar process shortly before she died.

Marge's condition did not improve, so that she was finally taken to Severalls Hospital in Colchester. Her behaviour was certainly induced by her thyroid condition, which often results in the impairment of intellectual functions, personality changes, or severe emotional disturbance. Mistakenly diagnosing her problem as mental rather than physical, the medical authorities detained Marge for observation, invoking the law whereby, in the interests of their own health, patients may not be discharged for twenty-eight days without the consent of the supervising doctor. Once again, as in 1955, the age-old conception of female madness dominated over accurate and thoughtful medical diagnosis. On a scrap of paper Marge scribbled a pathetic note to Pip: "Oh Tonker save poor Marge . . . *try* try try again. I am ill not at all balmy. All my love. Marge." A few days later there was a slight but definite improvement in her mental state, and the doctors wanted to remove some tissue from a growth in her neck and chest for examination. However, her condition improved sufficiently for them to abandon this and to attempt immediate therapy. The treatment that was chosen was radiation with radioactive cobalt, a common but extremely uncomfortable method at the time for dealing with cancerous tumours. Marge does not seem to have had any clear idea what was the matter with her; she wrote to Runyon: "I'm in the doctor's hands ... a strictly non-malignent, non-painful lump in my chest, but the cure (which appears to involve a sort of hygenic flame thrower) is unamusing. Still, I progress and everybody says how lucky I am to be so 'big and strong'" (Letter, 06.04.1966).

A week later thoughts of writing were once again uppermost in her mind when she reported the excellent progress she was making to Reynolds, "apart from having to have a few weeks holiday afterwards, which will make the new book later than ever, I am almost as good as new" (Letter, 14.04.1966). Marge was discharged from hospital in time to be back at D'Arcy for her sixty-second birthday, but was certainly in no condition to start work again. To make life easier for the household, she was brought downstairs to the outside washhouse, which was fitted up as comfortably as possible as a bedroom. It was here that she received the news of Mary King's approaching visit to England. In her letter, regretfully declining an invitation to meet Mrs. King in London, Marge made light of her illness and the restrictions of convalescence: "We decided that this was the rainy day we had long had in mind and it seemed the ideal time to have a sabbatical year. So that is what I am doing. I am sure you will be hearing of me again. Now that I am not working the ideas seem to be flowing again" (Letter, 13.06.1966).

12

The New and the Strange

*The purely material aspect of crook adventure has been beaten to
a pulp in the last thirty years and I, for one, am getting bored
by it. I want the* new *and the strange.*

Margery Allingham

In her final years, Marge pushed the development of the multilevelled
crime novel about as far as it could go without rendering the story itself
unreadable. While *The China Governess* is in many senses a throwback
to the sort of social investigation she had pursued in *Death of a Ghost* or
the novels of the late thirties, the other two books of the period are
conscious attempts to integrate story, theme, and discourse. *Hide My
Eyes* is about the unwillingness to see evil in those one wants to love,
and it is a reflection on the effects that a limited perspective can have
upon narrative. Similarly, *The Mind Readers* is a novel about the transference of information in a gadget-prone age, *and* a study of the process
and forms of linguistic and literary communication. At the same time
all three novels are related to earlier works and to each other, thus
emphasizing the organic nature of Marge's fiction. *Hide My Eyes* continues the study of evil begun in the *Tiger;* its intrepid young people,
Richard Waterfield and Annabelle Tassie, look forward to the young
sophisticates of the *Governess,* Julia Laurell and Timothy Kinnit. Both
the *Governess* and *The Mind Readers* open with a contemplation of the
changing London skyline, and are social investigations of the second
decade of postwar England. As in previous novels, characters are rein-
troduced not merely as trademarks or simple reminders of earlier books,
but also as measures of social, intellectual, and moral change. Thematically all three novels are concerned with the use and misuse of human
intelligence; furthermore, all three confirm the necessity for hope and
confidence in the powers of a new generation to rise to the demands of

the future. Each book, in its own way, is an illustration of what Marge wrote to Reynolds in 1962: "I think we've come to the end of the period when the popular writer kept saying 'There are no answers' and are sailing into a time when he'll find he's got to give a few and pretty clearly and firmly" (Letter, 19.02.1962).

Chapter 14 of *Hide My Eyes* is entitled "Hide My Eyes" and appropriately enough begins in a cinema. Annabelle has arrived in London in response to a mysterious letter from a Mrs. Polly Tassie, promising to do something for her husband's niece should she turn out satisfactorily. It is implied that Polly hopes to use the young girl as a possible steadying influence on the unreliable young man she and her late husband befriended, Gerry Hawker. Later that first day together, Polly invites Annabelle to an evening at the movies followed by a meal in her favourite restaurant. By the time of this cinema visit, the reader has been offered sufficient information and clues to know that Gerry is a multimurderer. Although Polly suspects that he is dishonest, she has no idea that he is a real criminal. As Annabelle settles into her seat, she says, "It's like settling down to dream in a great State bed. Flicks are rather like dreams, aren't they?" To which Mrs. Tassie replies, "I suppose they are. That's why I like them best without colour" (1958b, 133). The limited, and, in a sense, deliberately unreal perspective of the black-and-white film is a multiple sign: not only does it place Mrs. Tassie in an older generation with a different cultural tradition, it also underlines her need for a unity of impression (if something is a dream then it must look like a dream), and emphasizes her need to create her own conditions of perception. From then on the chapter proceeds ruthlessly to expose the unreliability and danger of her point of view.

She begins by asking Annabelle about Mr. Campion, who, together with Superintendant Luke, paid her a routine call earlier in the day, alarming Mrs. Tassie with questions about a glove which in fact she once bought for Gerry and which the reader knows as "the glove left behind in the Church Road shooting" (23). As Polly begins to gain knowledge, so her manner changes in an "abrupt cessation of goodwill" (134); it is at this point that the film begins. Preoccupied with her disturbing thoughts, Polly pays no attention to the screen. The contrast between the perspectives of the two women is underlined when Annabelle bursts out, "This is terrific fun, Aunt Polly. You don't know how I love it" (135)—the use of "know" only emphasizes Polly's ignorance. Having thus established the discrepancy, Marge goes on to show that Annabelle, young as she is, still knows more than Polly whose limitation of vision is chronic. The girl innocently refers to the circumstances surrounding the first murder of the book, linked in the reader's mind with Gerry and some waxwork figures from the late Mr. Tassie's collection, and adds brightly, "I wonder what happened in that case. . . . We ought to have asked Superintendant Luke. . . . He's on the murder squad" (136), which naturally only serves to alarm her aunt further. They then arrive at the restaurant, and a long interlude follows, with which Marge deliberately retards the tempo of events. Polly is anxious to telephone her solicitor, Matthew Phillipson, who had an appointment with Gerry that afternoon, to confront him with Polly's knowledge of his having forged a cheque. Unbeknown to Mrs. Tassie, Gerry has already planned and carried out Phillipson's murder. Before telephoning, she talks with Sybille Dominique, the restaurant proprietor; Polly harps back to the glove and to a scene with Gerry in that same restaurant. Mrs. Dominique recalls a newspaper cutting Polly had shown them with a picture of a glove—"it was something a murderer had left behind" (142). It is essential to this process of the unwilling accumulation of knowledge that Polly resists acceptance of the obvious. The conversation between the two women culminates in Mrs. Dominque's advice, linking the willing nonconformity of affection with the desirable security of knowledge: "When one is fond of a son, real, adopted or step, one has no rules. . . . One forgives. That is all there is to it, and the whole nature of the attachment. That's life. But, dearest, one still ought to *know*. One should take common precautions, both for his sake and for one's own" (143). She goes on to lead Polly to the realization that they know nothing about Gerry "that he has not told us himself" (143). The Gerry Hawker they know is a creation of words, a self-made construct; the figure he has chosen as their image of him is nothing but a useful fiction. Once this has been established, Marge has Polly telephone and learn about the solicitor's murder.

I have chosen to begin my discussion of *Hide My Eyes* by dealing with this one chapter in order to indicate how a theme that begins as an essential feature of the plot comes to dominate the narrative technique. The relation between the limited perspective and the acquisition of knowledge is continually present in the novel, as too, is the exploitation of the restricted viewpoint as a narrative strategy. It is through the limited insights of Mr. Vick, the barber, that Richard Waterfield gains his first intimations of Gerry Hawker's personality. At the end of the novel, Polly Tassie's neighbour, Miss Rich, a retired schoolteacher, is able to help the police because she "was in the habit of deriving what light she needed during the night from the street lamp outside" (199). Although the view from her basement window must of necessity be partial, the one thing she can see clearly is Polly's house and everything that happens there. Again, when the clues he has gathered lead Richard to Rolf's Dump in Limehouse, he is met by a semiblind night watchman whose information, since he "had not the evidence of his own eyes . . . could only come from one source" (127), namely Gerry Hawker. In this instance, limitations guarantee accuracy and not the opposite.

It comes almost as a surprise when the theme of restricted vision is also applied to Superintendant Luke, who, although on Gerry's trail, is unable to accept his possible involvement in the world of Mrs. Tassie and Annabelle: "I may be hiding my eyes," Luke is made to say, " but I just cannot see either of them involved in anything of this sort" (177). The limited perspective that interests Marge is not so much that which is imposed from without, but the limitation which is an integral part of personality, or which is deliberately self-imposed. Luke, as a policeman acutely aware of his point of view, cannot bring himself to transcend a perspective which he acknowledges is potentially limited. It is significant that it is Gerry who, with ruthless clarity, recognizes the true nature of the phenomenon. In the scene in which he is planning to eliminate Polly, whose knowledge has made her a potential danger, he points out her own blind complicity in his wrongdoing: "If you knew, you connived, you approved . . . you hid your eyes. You're like that. You deceive yourself very easily. . . . Anything goes if it's done by someone you're fond of, that's your creed" (191).

Of all Marge's novels, *Hide My Eyes* is perhaps the most carefully structured; at a first reading one is only partly aware of diffuse items of information gradually coming together to hint at patterns behind the action. Lavinia Davis noticed this and wrote to Marge that the pattern of the novel "is very properly concealed until a second reading by the story, the background and the characters" (Letter, 29.08.1958). The familiar features of an Allingham novel—meticulously observed details of character and setting—are so very much present that they easily distract from the pure technique of the narration. Among the many possible examples there is first of all Polly Tassie herself—"her kindly face wore the solemn preoccupation of a child's" (133)—and her kitchen with its "red linoleum on the floor patterned like a Turkey carpet" (57). The novel has its fair share of typical Allingham minor characters; Dickensian in their vividness and vitality, their essential traits are caught in an economy of telling phrases. There is, for example, the hairdresser, Mr. Vick—"a dark pale-faced cockney, womanish without being emasculated"—who speaks "as if each word was some nice little gift which he felt sure the recipient would appreciate" (49). The cavernous Tenniel Hotel, doomed to make way for reconstruction, is personified in an aged waiter—"to look at he was remarkably like a toad and moved with some of that pleasant creature's spry difficulty" (107). Not only do such neatly caught personalities and scenes conceal the structural workings of the novel, they also tend to prevent the first-time reader from realizing that he is put in possession of all the major clues in the first forty-five pages.

This information is carefully distributed; we learn that one of the witnesses in the first murder case, saw, in an old-fashioned bus near the scene of the crime, an elderly couple whom he knew he had seen before, "and he was certain it was through glass" (22). The second clue comes fifteen pages later, when the local police constable recalls this statement and links it to his memory of the Tassie museum. When Annabelle enters Mrs. Tassie's house through the exhibition, her attention is caught by a large glass case with a painted backcloth and a small but empty double seat in the foreground. Almost immediately she is confronted with Gerry who speaks to her in a "deep and pleasant" voice (40), reminding the reader of the anonymous murderer in the opening chapter, whose voice was twice described as pleasant. The connection is established beyond doubt by Gerry's heavy neck muscles, which were again part of the earlier description. Mrs. Tassie then supplies a necessary clue when she describes the missing figures to Annabelle in such detail that the reader can have no doubts that they were identical with the figures seen in the bus. Only then are they explicitly linked with Gerry, when Polly admits that "he took them to have them renovated for me, and of course that's the last I heard of them" (45). This way of offering information to the reader simply obviates any necessity for later authorial comment. We now "know" that Gerry and the anonymous murderer are identical.

In contrast to the knowledge that is based on a limited perspective, we are presented with the fact that Luke, without ever having met Gerry, without knowing the identity of the murderer for whom he has painstakingly been searching, has by means of deduction built up an accurate picture of him: "This man is different. He's almost refreshing. He's got a brain and he's got nerve and he's not neurotic. He's perfectly sane, he's merciless as a snake and he's very careful. . . . He's a crook. He makes a living by taking all he needs from other people. The really unusual thing about him is that he kills quite coldly when it's the safest thing to do" (28). Gerry's coolness and certainty only begin to collapse under the pressure of the revelation of Polly Tassie's accumulated knowledge of him, knowledge which she would prefer not to have and which only towards the end is freed from the distortions of her limited viewpoint. In chapter 19, Gerry, realizing the potential danger she poses, is planning to drug her and then let her be gassed. As the careful preparations for her murder proceed, she gains the courage to reveal her knowledge. The five major steps that Polly takes are spaced over the whole chapter and it is their accumulated significance that is so overwhelming for Gerry. She begins by informing him that she understands why he is trying to burn his coat in the kitchen stove, "There was blood on it" (190), and goes on to disclose that she knows about Matthew Phillipson's murder. She then calmly tells him that she has at last accepted the evidence of the glove, "You shot those people in Church Row" (191). Shortly after, she adds that she is now convinced that he placed the wax figures in the bus on the night of the first murder: "I thought that when I first read it," she admits candidly, "but I shut my eyes to it" (193)—emphasizing the subjective nature of limited vision. Her final statement appears to be the expression of conventional wisdom rather than a revelation of knowledge: "Murder will out, Gerry" (194), but for her, as ultimately for the reader, it is the logical conclusion drawn from the sum of her knowledge derived from the accumulated evidence.

It is significant that this devastating series of statements is framed between Polly's remark about Gerry: "when you look like that there's nothing there" (190), and her final words before succumbing to the chloral he has put in her hot milk: "If . . . you . . . kill me, . . . there'll be nothing . . . to keep you alive" (196). Not only do the excitement and tension of the chapter depend largely upon the device of the limited perspective, which produces only partial knowledge, but Marge also demonstrated that, by structuring the isolated observations of her restricted perspective, Polly can perceive Gerry for what he is: a creature of words, a hollow fiction who lives only in her love-enriched vision of him. Yet when Gerry has at last been arrested, Luke answers his sergeant's question about whether Polly will "stick by him when it all comes out" with the words: "She'll forgive him without question, whatever he's done to her and however high we hang him. . . . She can't help herself. She's only a vehicle. That's Disinterested Love, chum, a force, like nuclear energy. It's absolute" (218). After the sophisticated interweaving of plot, narrative strategy, and theme, this explanation appears to be too easy and too conventionally moralising. Yet taken in the context of the concerns of the novel, what emerges is Marge's drastically honest and consistent explanation that Christian love, human love, and love of one's neighbour are all ultimately products of a limited perspective, and in fact depend upon that limitation for their very existence. So, too, is the device of the restricted point of view as essential to the mystery of crime fiction as the proliferation of clues. Such limitation of vision is usually an attribute of the investigator, who, like the reader, moves from partial to total knowledge by way of a viewpoint strictly limited by his task. In *Hide My Eyes*, Marge simply universalizes the phenomenon, so that it dominates both plot and narrative, story and discourse. Just as we have come to distrust the godlike knowledge of earlier novelists, and to prefer the limited or biassed vision of imperfect narrators, Marge transfers this condition to a wider plane by suggesting that only a divine being such as the Christian God is capable of *both* omniscience *and* disinterested love.

There is every temptation to regard *The China Governess* as continuing another Allingham tradition which had been partially abandoned after the *Undertaker:* the novel which exploits the confrontation with violence and crime to reveal and examine the strengths or weaknesses of society. It was this aspect of her fiction which prompted Charles Champlin, arts editor of the *Los Angeles Times,* to write that Marge's mysteries "revealed the social history of England over a 40-year period as clearly as many more earnest works" (Champlin 1971). At the same time it is quite possible to classify the *Governess* simply as a serious story of mystery and suspense, and still to have caught something of the essence of Marge's work, rather as the London *Times* in its obituary notice did: "She ranked with Dorothy Sayers and Agatha Christie, but, unlike most of her contemporaries, she was able to adapt her style with notable success to the more sophisticated suspense genre which became fashionable after the war" (Anon. 1966). The phrasing of this tribute, suggesting as it does that Marge adapted to a new fashion, misses the point that it was she who was largely responsible for its very creation.

Marge herself viewed the *Governess* from quite a different angle; she wrote to Ian Parsons that she felt it was probably "a trifle more adult and convincing than the other two of its type, the *Tiger* and *Hide My Eyes*" (Letter, 08.11.1961). At first sight the book seems to belong to a totally different category; unlike the two earlier works there is no concentration upon the criminal mind, nor is there a balancing pole of goodness such as Canon Avril or Polly Tassie. Admittedly the plot of all three books is concerned with increasingly younger women of unusual innocence (Meg Elginbrodde, Annabelle Tassie, and Julia Laurell); admittedly, all three are set in a contemporary London which Marge herself, in the blurb she wrote for the *Governess,* described as being "as colourful, as mysterious as, and even more cosily sinister" than the London of Charles Dickens. What, however, did she mean by "its type"? It is only possible to repeat what has been said already of the earlier books, and of *Hide My Eyes* in particular: they are crime novels which transform a central element of plot and theme into a dominant narrative mode. Paul Reynolds instinctively recognized this in the *Gov-*

erness when he wrote to Marge that "This beautifully integrated plot with grand atmosphere and written so well makes a very grand book" (Letter, 13.02.1962). What in older criticism were two distinct elements—plot and atmosphere on the one side and fine writing on the other—cannot, in Marge's best work, be usefully separated. At the heart of the *Governess* is the insistence that each human being is the story that he has to tell, and that this story must be told—and read—correctly. As Superintendant Luke tells Councillor Cornish, "There's only one really impossible thing about the truth and that's how to tell it" (1963, 172), or as Timothy Kinnit, the young man in search of his identity, tells Julia Laurell: "I'm the continuation of an existing story" (129).

Apart from the dynamic Councillor Cornish, with his social conscience and confused private allegiances, and the thoroughly embarrassing and coy Nanny Broome, a relic from a past world of superior servants, the characters in the *Governess* are not as impressive or as completely presented as in many of the earlier books. Compared with either the *Undertaker* or the *Tiger*, even the London setting is not as forcefully vivid, apart from the opening panoramic characterisation: "The great fleece which is London, clotted and matted and black with time and smoke" (9). On the level of plot and characterization, the relation of the *Governess* to the *Tiger* and *Hide My Eyes* is that of a fragile and somewhat insipid porcelain figure to a monumental marble statue. The major link, however, is to be found in the thematization of fictional narration.

Like so many literary works of the early sixties, the *Governess* is a novel which centres upon the search for identity, and the question about the factors which define it. Timothy Kinnit is suddenly faced, at the age of twenty-two, with the fact that he is not who he thought he was—the adopted natural son of Eustace Kinnit, a refined and gentle art expert—and could perhaps be the child of a mentally defective woman from the slums of the East End. He attempts to trace his true identity back through the chaos of twenty years, by way of the postwar reconstruction of east London, the Second World War, the London blitz, and the evacuation of mothers and babies to the countryside.

In the background to Timothy's twentieth-century search for identity lies the sinister story of the nineteenth-century Kinnit governess, accused of murdering her lover, acquitted, and forced into a senseless suicide, which was followed by the revelation of the identity of the true murderess—the elder Kinnit daughter. This tale, so very much a part of the plot, is linked to the major theme when Mrs. Broome, showing Julia round the Kinnits' country home at Angevin, assures her, "It's not *the* room, you know, miss. . . . This isn't the one the tale is about" (38).

The action of the *Governess* unfolds in a context of narratives in which everything, or more important, everyone, becomes a story and part of a story. When Basil Toberman (the arrogant underdog of the Kinnit household, who as a self-styled art expert is reminiscent of Max Fustian in *Death of a Ghost*) arrives at Angevin to discover that Julia is in hiding there, he bursts out, "Well this is fascinating! It's going to be a better press story than I thought" (60). Toberman's concern is not for facts or empirical reality, but for the potential narrative, a version of the truth, a fiction. Again this is an implicit comment on the crime fiction genre, which relies for its full impact upon versions of events, happenings, characters, and structures.

When the two stories of Timothy's search and Councillor Cornish's past begin to approach one another and then to coincide, so, too, do the worlds of the self-made man and the quasi-aristocratic aesthete start to clash. In conversation with Cornish, Eustace Kinnit invents his version of what Timothy has been going through—a story which, like all fictions, reflects the teller's personality as much as it attempts to present facts: "When one is a child one gathers scraps of information about oneself, little pieces of embroidery from nurses and so on, and one weaves perhaps a rather romantic story until the time comes when cool reason demands facts which are dull and even a trifle drab compared with a tale of fancy, all moonshine and romance." To which Cornish replies: "Romance! . . . My God, if you want romance you must go to reality! The things she thinks up take the shine out of any old invention" (153). This is not simply the cliché theme of "life is stranger than fiction," but, in the way in which it is presented, something far more subtle. Eustace's imagined account of what has been happening to Timothy proceeds from the weaving of a story to the destruction of a "tale of fancy" by "cool reason." That is, Marge deliberately focusses on the fictional process as escape—a favourite theme—and does not, as Cornish does, suggest that reason (reality) is superior to fiction, but simply that they are mutually antagonistic. Eustace/Marge presents the point of view of the experienced artist, whereas Cornish counters with the conformism of the self-styled realist. There can be no doubt in the reader's mind which attitude leads to true knowledge; particularly when, only a few pages later, Julia, who has begun her own line of investigation, is described as being "in that strange mood when hypersensitiveness reaches the point almost of clairvoyance" (160). Sensitivity and the irrational are presented as surer roads to truth than pure reason—a theme that Marge took up again in *The Mind Readers*—so that when Cornish finally comes to relate *his* story to Luke, he says of the nuns who brought him his supposed son, Barry: "The story they told me was so damn silly I knew it must be true" (173). Storytellers are notoriously aware that they may not be believed, nor is it necessarily important that they should be, except upon their own terms. Thus Cornish reports that the nuns, in their turn, were sceptical of his account of how his first wife died in childbirth, "All the story of my first wife could have been a fiction" (175). The choice of the word "fiction," as a synonym for lie, emphasises once again that Cornish speaks in the persona of the simple, rational, no-nonsense man-in-the-street.

The foregrounding of human existence as narrative, human beings as stories, and individual fates as fictions, reaches its climax and most explicit moment when, at the very end of the novel, Campion acts as the controlling perspective of the narration. He observes the interior of the Kinnits' home, the Well House, which is a series of galleries built round a central staircase. This construction enables him to observe all the major characters of the tale simultaneously: "Mr. Campion was comforted. It was a picture of beginnings, he thought. Half a dozen startings: new chapters, new ties, new associations. They were all springing out of the story he had been following, like a spray of plumes in a renaissance pattern springs up from a complete and apparently final feather" (266). Marge presents Campion as the ideal attentive reader, who shares the authorial view of a story in which developments in human relations are the chapters, and the essential structure (pattern) is inherent in the isolated detail. The employment of an extended metaphor which leads the reader to define his own reading as the interpretation of evidence leaves no doubt about the essential latent literariness of the crime novel.

Marge's desire for the new and the strange is most apparent in *The Mind Readers*. Just after the novel's publication in the United States, she wrote to Reynolds, "I am convinced that detective novels have got to have a plus element to keep ahead nowadays" (Letter, 16.07.1965). She felt that in order to ensure favourable reception and consistent sales she would have to keep up with what she called in her letter "the gadget age." In so far as the new novel was largely set at a secret research establishment, dealt with ESP, reflected on the military use of communication without instruments, and made use of computers, transistors, and the power of the media, Marge was fulfilling her programmatic aims. She wanted more than just this, however. In a letter to one of her academic correspondents, Professor Oliver Ellis, she wrote that her intention was "to give an impression of the communal mind at work, or the hand-of-God or evolution in action" (Letter, 12.08.1965). That is, the gadgets and paraphernalia of technological and electronic media society are, to a large extent, so much window dressing. At the heart of the novel are more traditionally human concerns. As in the case of *The Beckoning Lady*, which gave Marge, as a writer, so much pleasure, *The Mind Readers* departed from the pattern set by its immediate predecessors. She admitted as much to Reynolds when she told him: "*The Mind Readers* is a more individual piece of work than I've done for some time. I didn't bother about pleasing editors and concentrated on the reader" (Letter, 08.12.1964).

The plot of the novel is almost frighteningly complex, and for that reason I shall once again attempt a brief summary. At Godley's research establishment on an island off the Essex coast, scientists are working on the communication potentialities of telepathy. Although they have had only limited success, Sam Ferris, the eight-and-a-half-year-old son of one of the researchers, and his twelve-year-old cousin, Edward Longfox, have been experimenting successfully with the very same phenomenon. The boys have discovered that a Japanese transistor containing the new element nipponanium has remarkable amplifying properties. With the help of their so-called iggy tubes they are able to receive the thoughts and emotions of others with remarkable accuracy.

Sam and Edward spend half-term at the home of Canon Avril, to whom they are distantly related. Luke and Campion, who are investigating a leak of information from Godley's island, meet the boys, discover the iggy tubes and temporarily take charge of them. When Paggen Mayo, the chief of Godley's establishment and the boss of Sam's father Martin Ferris, hears about the iggy tubes, he wants to try them out. He is overwhelmed by the experience, takes possession of the devices, and departs in a hurry for an unknown destination. Rumour has it that Mayo has defected, but the next day his body is discovered in the back of a lorry involved in a major road accident. Before Campion can leave for the island to carry on his investigations, Edward Longfox disappears, further confusing an already complicated situation.

On the island, Campion meets an associate of former times, Thos. Knapp, now codirector of a firm specializing in electronic bugging devices. Knapp helps Campion to obtain information which leads him rapidly closer to discovering the identity of the murdering spy. This turns out to be the canteen manager, Fred Arnold, who is not only a recent recruit to the British Secret Service, but also an agent of an anonymous enemy power. He now attempts to get rid of Campion but is thwarted, and accidentally killed by his own weapon. Meanwhile Edward Longfox carries out a convincing experiment in thought transference with a schoolfriend in Paris. The experiment is monitored at the orders of Lord Ludor, the ruthless tycoon owner of Godley's. However,

Ludor is frustrated in his attempt to gain possession of the boy and the invention. Edward has already contacted a scientific magazine for boys which is connected with the vast media empire of Ludor's rival Lord Feste. His representative, the editor of the *Daily Paper*, uses Feste's television network to announce the discovery and to state that he has engineered the buying up of all available transistors of the special type. This has been done to ensure people's privacy by preventing the commercial exploitation of the iggy tube.

There are many familiar elements in this brand-new story. Godley's island, surrounded by grey mudflats, and the presence there of Thos. Knapp, takes the reader back to the first true Campion novel, *Mystery Mile*; Lord Ludor can then be seen as a latter-day Ali Fergusson Barber, or better still a revamped Brett Savanake from *Sweet Danger*, with the modern refinement that he no longer needs to take to crime personally since the advance of technology and the sophistication of business practice have made that unnecessary. The family connections of the two boys to Amanda and Campion—Sam Ferris is the grandson of Mary Fitton and Guffy Randall, and Edward's mother was the Earl of Pontisbright's daughter (*Sweet Danger*)—are clear indications that Marge intended the reader to think back to the earlier fictions. It is as though she was determined that *The Mind Readers* should be understood as a conscious effort to span the time gap in order to use an earlier age as a yardstick to measure the progress—scientific, social, moral, and literary—of the present. Similarly, the reappearance of Canon Avril (*Tiger in the Smoke*) establishes a relation between scientific progress and ethical standards. Jokingly, Avril suggests that the iggy tubes could potentially be used to grant his helper and friend, Miss Warburton, instant omniscience. She objects that that is a wicked idea; Avril immediately pounces on the word: "That dreadful old question. Can advance be wicked?" (118).

The Mind Readers is fundamentally a novel about communication, which serves as an element in the plot, as a theme which runs through the novel, and, finally, as an essential aspect of the writer/reader relationship. On the one hand there is Paggen Mayo's strictly scientific view which relies on empirically testable evidence: "Before I'm convinced that a message has passed, I want something which *someone else* . . . can see, hear or taste" (31). Then there is the intuitive view, equally based on experience, that is characteristic of Canon Avril: "An infant can listen for his mother's voice in a babble and never miss it. It's the only one which makes any sense" (62). Applied to the reading of crime fiction, this refers to the necessary ability to follow the essential clues and to identify them amid the interference of the mass of other information that the language of the text generates. Another aspect is embodied by Lord Ludor, whose brain Campion describes as a computer: "In goes the data and out comes the answer in flat, inhuman terms, absolutely correct if everybody concerned happens to be made to one of the half-dozen patterns which he has found most common. A terrible and terrifying chap" (150–51). What is horrifying about this form of communication is not that it is based on machines and technological know-how, but that it relies on cold generalizations about human beings. Campion finds Ludor terrifying because he is someone who has eliminated risks in judgment by insisting on a standardized view of human nature.

It comes then as no surprise that Campion finds himself unable to share the pure scientist's enthusiasm for the potentials of Edward's discovery. When Martin Ferris says "It's a genuine breakthrough, but it doesn't alter any of the essentials," Campion deliberately misreads the final statement, taking it to cover experience beyond the concerns of theoretical science: "The snakes and the angels remain but it is another skin off the onion" (225). Marge is both fascinated by science and frankly sceptical about its claims; to describe the pushing back of the frontiers of ignorance as simply peeling off the skins from an onion implies the ultimate revelation of a void. Whereas to insist that in spite of the progress of scientific enquiry, evil and good remain rejects any claim that science is capable of significantly improving mankind.

Successful communication depends on the encoding and decoding of information. If the encoding processes are correct, a clear and meaningful structure should emerge. This is demonstrated in the novel by Campion's telephone calls to his security chief, L. C. "Elsie" Corkran, which are carried out in the form of a lighthearted chat with a vivacious girlfriend. The significant aspect of these conversations is that they are so encoded that the reader, who has absorbed the clear information of the text up to that point, has no difficulty in decoding them, and thus finds enjoyment in the process rather than in the already familiar message. An essential aspect of the coding process is touched on by Amanda when she comments on the clumsy experiments in telepathy being conducted at Godley's island: "The link is not between intelligences, but each intelligence does its own decoding" (105). This can also be understood as a direct observation upon the reception—both by critics and readers—of Marge's fiction. The relationship between author and reader is not one of total correspondence and identification; each reader will respond to the text according to his or her own abilities or "intelligence." Once again Marge takes a thematically central element of the plot and utilizes it to comment on the process of the writing and reading of novels.

That which successful coding and communication reveal is the pattern, the linking structures, of information. Campion refers indirectly to this shortly after Avril gives Mayo the iggy tubes: "Ever since he had first encountered Longfox's Instant Gen he had been aware of a sense of inevitability concerning it, and he found himself wondering if this most unlikely intervention was part of the pattern of the phenomenon" (84). The answer to this speculation only comes near the very end of the book, when the pattern begins to emerge more clearly. Campion has been closeted with Thos. Knapp, obtaining from his communications network information on the progress of the investigation. He steps outside into the cool morning air and, we read, "stood back from the main history and looked at it" (198). The establishment of a structure demands the interpretation of information, which in turn has to be carried out from a position of objective distance. Campion observes that "two designs were sharply differentiated"—the use of the word "design" is important—"the main sweeping curve of the break-through," the dominance of the scientific discovery; and "his own preoccupying pattern," the knowledge of the identity of Paggen Mayo's murderer. It is, however, a member of the Special Branch—a representative of institutionalised intelligence—in a chapter significantly entitled "The Official View," who baldly announces: "There's a pattern in these things, and once you've seen it, you've seen it" (129), which is not only true of the events of the novel, or of its thematic elements, but, above all, of the crime fiction genre itself.

Part of Albert Campion's—and, presumably, Marge's own—alarm at the behaviour of scientists is contained in the observation of "the ease with which they accepted their own wonders once they were in existence." The moral centre of the book seems to be located in this remark. What Campion finds even more alarming is, however, a curious ability which Marge associated with the scientific mind: "they were able to look at truth in the nude . . . with the dispassionate interest of medicos" (112). The implied unadornment of scientific truth is poles apart from the literary experience. In fiction truth is always adorned, never nude— the nudity is arrived at in private after the reader's decoding has been completed.

Epilogue

A month after returning to D'Arcy, Marge had made no progress, she even seemed to be weakening. She was taken back to Severalls Hospital, where she expressed the wish to see a Church of England priest. The next day, June 30, 1966, Joyce Allingham and Christina Carter went to visit her. From the end of the corridor they saw her being taken on a stretcher to the X-ray department. Marge died on the way. What she had thought was a benign growth proved to be multiple malignant tumours on the lungs, as well as cancer of the breast, which, aggravated by an attack of pneumonia and abnormally high blood pressure, proved fatal.

The funeral took place in the late fourteenth-century church of St. Nicholas at Tolleshunt D'Arcy five days later; the order of service included all the simple classics of the Christian religion: the twenty-third psalm, the thirteenth chapter of St. Paul's first epistle to the Corinthians, the children's hymn "All things bright and beautiful." After a brief address, Marge's body was buried, a few yards from Dr. Salter and quite close to her grandmother, in the small hedged graveyard across the road from the church.

Of all the tributes and letters of sympathy which arrived at the house, the one which, perhaps most nearly summarised them all came from Lee Barker of Doubleday's: "She was always so full of the joy of living, so full too of warmth and vitality and humour. She's one of the really great people I've known in forty years of editing and publishing" (Letter, 01.07.1966).

Marge left the manuscript of *Cargo of Eagles,* which she had been dictating to Pip before she fell ill, unfinished. He was finally persuaded to complete it. Pip went on to write two further Campion novels—*Mr. Campion's Farthing* (1969) and *Mr. Campion's Quarry* (1971)—based on ideas he and Marge had discussed together, before he died on November 30, 1969 after an operation for lung cancer.

Friends, relatives, and acquaintances looking back on their experience of Marge pick out so many aspects of her personality: her rippling laugh, her energy, her sense of fun, her generosity, affection and companionship, her capacity to laugh at herself, her happiness, her adaptibility, integrity, loyalty, and understanding. In a letter to Meiggs in December 1937 she wrote: "I, Marge, am a composite thing. . . . I am made up of millions of loosely related things. . . . These things are all *mortal,* and by that I mean not only capable of dying but capable of being *reproduced.* . . . For me it is everything and nothing that dies."

Allingham Family Genealogy

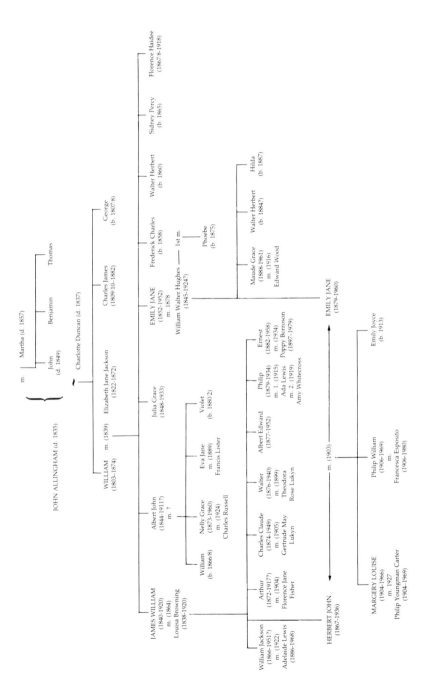

Allingham Family Genealogy

Bibliography

Agate, James
1934   Review of *Death of a Ghost*, *Daily Express*, 22.03.1934.
1936   Review of *Flowers for the Judge*, *Daily Express*, 27.02.1936.
Allingham, Margery
1923   *Blackkerchief Dick*, London (Kaye & Ward) 1974.
1928   *The White Cottage Mystery*, Harmondsworth (Penguin) 1978.
1929   *The Crime at Black Dudley*, in Allingham 1982.
1930   *Mystery Mile*, in Allingham 1982.
1931   *Look to the Lady*, in Allingham 1982.
1931a   *Police at the Funeral*, Harmondsworth (Penguin) 1978.
1933   *Sweet Danger*, Harmondsworth (Penguin) 1959.
1934   *Death of a Ghost*, Harmondsworth (Penguin) 1966.
1935   "Meet Albert Campion" (broadcast talk), 17.06.1935, unpublished typescript.
1936   "Is Golf a Menace to Marriage?" *Daily Mail* (Scotland), 10.04.1936.
1936a   *Flowers for the Judge*, New York (Doubleday, Doran).
1937   *Dancers in Mourning*, Harmondsworth (Penguin) 1958.
1937a   *The Case of the Late Pig*, Harmondsworth (Penguin) 1961.
1938   "Practising to Deceive," *Time and Tide*, 05.11.1938.
1938a   Speech given at Foyle's Literary Luncheon, 25.08.1938, Unpublished typescript.
1938b   "New Novels" (Review article), *Time and Tide*, 05.03.1938.
1938c   "Billeting in Villages" (Letter to the editor), *The Times*, 13.10.1938.
1938d   "New Novels" (Review article), *Time and Tide*, 02.04.1938.
1938e   "New Novels" (Review article), *Time and Tide*, 24.12.1938.
1938f   *The Fashion in Shrouds*, Harmondsworth (Penguin) 1961.
1939   "New Novels" (Review article), *Time and Tide*, 25.02.1939.
1940   *Black Plumes*, Harmondsworth (Penguin) 1966.
1941   *The Oaken Heart*, London (Hutchinson) 1959.
1941a   *Traitor's Purse*, Harmondsworth (Penguin) 1961.
1941b   "New Novels" (Review article), *Time and Tide*, 16.08.1941.
1941c   "New Novels" (Review article), *Time and Tide*, 25.10.1941.
1942   "Changes in the English Village" (Broadcast talk), 24.03.1942, Unpublished typescript.
1943   *The Galantrys* (U.S. edition of *The Dance of the Years*), Boston (Little, Brown & Co.).

1945   *Coroner's Pidgin*, Harmondsworth (Penguin) 1957.
1949   "Mystery and Myself," *Town and Country*, August 1949.
1949a   *More Work for the Undertaker*, Harmondsworth (Penguin) 1971.
1949b   "The Thriller," Unpublished typescript.
1950   "Mysterious Fun for Millions of Innocent Escapists," *New York Times Book Review*, 04.06.50.
1950a   "Letter to a Goddaughter," n.d., Unpublished typescript.
1952   *The Tiger in the Smoke*, Harmondsworth (Penguin) 1961.
1953   "My Family Thought It Silly to Stop Writing," *World Books Broadsheet*, November 1953.
1955   *The Beckoning Lady*, Harmondsworth (Penguin) 1978.
1958   "Crime for Our Delight," Talk given at Harrods, 14.11.1958, Unpublished typescript.
1958a   "Profile: Margery Allingham" (Interview with John Sherwood, BBC European Division), 19.03.58, Unpublished typescript.
1958b   *Hide My Eyes*, London (Chatto & Windus) 1969.
1961   "Crime Writer," *Reynolds News*, 01.10.61.
1962   *The China Governess*, Harmondsworth (Penguin) 1971.
1963   "Mystery Writer in the Box," in *The Mysterious Mr. Campion*, London (Chatto & Windus).
1963a   "A Medal," *Homes and Gardens*, June 1963.
1963b   "London My Market Town" (Broadcast talk), 06.04.1963, Unpublished typescript.
1964   "A Note on *The Mind Readers*," Unpublished typescript.
1964a   "Winifred Nerney," written 26.05.1964, Unpublished typescript.
1965   *The Mind Readers*, New York (William Morrow).
1965a   Preface to *Mr. Campion's Lady*, London (Chatto & Windus).
1965b   "My Love Affair with the World of Spies and Spying," *Ladies Home Journal*, April 1965.
1968   *Cargo of Eagles*, New York (Macfadden) 1969.
1969   *The Allingham Case-Book*, New York (Morrow).
1982   *The Margery Allingham Omnibus*, Harmondsworth (Penguin).
Anon.
1930   Review of *Mystery Mile*, *Record* (Philadelphia), 12.04.1930.
1931   Review of *Police at the Funeral*, *The Lady*, 05.11.1931.
1934   Announcement of *Death of a Ghost*, *Bookseller*, 02.02.1934.
1934a   Review of *Death of a Ghost*, *Glasgow Herald*, 08.03.1934.
1934b   "Another Good Novel" (Review article), *The Tatler*, 25.04.1934.
1941   Review of *Black Plumes*, *New Statesman*, 01.02.1941.
1941a   Review of *Traitor's Purse*, *Christian Science Monitor*, 09.08.1941.
1943   Review of *The Galantrys*, *New Yorker*, 16.10.1943.
1954   "From the 'Tatler' to Tolleshunt D'Arcy," *Essex County Standard*, 01.10.1954.
1955   Review of *The Beckoning Lady*, *Times Literary Supplement*, 01.01.1955.
1961   "Our Maudie," *The Record* (Fleetway Publications House Magazine), September 1961.
1965   "When Clues Give Way to Clobberings," *Times Literary Supplement*, 08.04.65.
1965a   Review of *The Mind Readers*, *Chicago Tribune*, 04.07.1965.
1966   "Miss Margery Allingham. Sophisticated Suspense" (Obituary), *The Times*, 01.07. 1966.
1979   Obituary notice for Leslie Cresswell, *Essex County Standard*, 11.05.1979.

Auden, W.H.
1948   "The Guilty Vicarage," in *The Dyer's Hand*, London (Faber) 1963.
Barzun, Jacques
1961   *The Delights of Detection*, in Winks 1980.
Becker, Jens-Peter
1975   *Sherlock Holmes & Co.*, Munich (Goldmann).
Benham, Hervey (ed).
1945   *Essex at War*, Colchester (Benham).
Benney, Mark
1966   *Almost a Gentleman*, London (Peter Davies).
Bentley, E.C.
1934   "Three Detective Novels" (Review article), *Daily Telegraph*, 16.03.1934.
Bishop, George W.
1941   Review of *Traitor's Purse*, *Daily Telegraph*, 01.03.1941.
Blake, Nicholas
1936   "Going Too Far" (Review article), *Spectator*, 28.02.1936.
1942   "The Detective Story—Why?" in Haycraft 1946.
Boileau, Pierre B. and Narcejac, Thomas N.
1969   *Der Detektivroman*, Neuwied & Berlin (Luchterhand).
Bowen, Elizabeth
1955   Review of *The Beckoning Lady*, *The Tatler*, 25.05.1955.
Bremner, Marjorie B.
1954   "Crime Fiction for Intellectuals," *Twentieth Century*, September 1954.
Buchloh, Paul G. and Becker, Jens
1973   *Der Detektivroman*, Darmstadt (Wissenschaftliche Buchgesellschaft).
Caillois, Roger S.
1941   "The Detective Novel as Game," in Most and Stowe 1983.
Calder, Angus
1969   *The People's War: Britain 1939–1945*, London (Granada) 1982.
Carr, John Dickson
1935   *The Hollow Man*, Harmondsworth (Penguin) 1954.
Carter, Philip Youngman
1941   "Nothing Can Change"(Poem), *The Egyptian Gazette*, Oct./Nov. 1941.
1969   Preface to *The Allingham Case-Book*, New York (Morrow).
1982   *All I Did Was This*, Nashville (Sexton Press).
Champlin, Charles A.
1965   "Early Day 007 Still at Work," *Los Angeles Times*, 22.08.1965.
1971   "Final Chapter of Albert Campion," *Los Angeles Times*, 05.02.1971.
Chandler, Raymond
1962   "Casual Notes on the Mystery Novel," in *Raymond Chandler Speaking*, ed. D. Gardner and K.S. Walker, London (Hamish Hamilton).
Chesterton, G.K.
1901   "A Defence of Detective Stories," in Haycraft 1946.
1964   "How to Write a Detective Story," in *The Spice of Life*, Beaconsfield (Darwen Finlayson).
Christie, Agatha
1968   "Margery Allingham—A Tribute," *Penguin News*, March 1968.
Craig, Patricia and Cadogan, Mary
1981   *The Lady Investigates*, London (Gollancz).

Dolland, John
1937   Review of *Dancers in Mourning*, *Woman's Own*, 10.07.1937.
Dove, N.D.
1977   "The Criticism of Detective Fiction," in Winks 1980.
Driberg, Tom
1978   *Ruling Passions*, London (Quartet).
Du Bois, William
1952   Review of *The Tiger in the Smoke*, *New York Times*, 30.08.1952.
Duncan, Sylvia
1960   "Profile: Margery Allingham," *Modern Woman*.
Eco, Umberto
1965   "Narrative Structures in Fleming," in Most and Stowe 1983.
Ekwall, Eilert
1960   *Concise Oxford Dictionary of English Place-Names*, Oxford (Oxford University Press).
Eliot, T.S.
1951   "Wilkie Collins and Dickens," in *Selected Essays*, London (Faber).
Fischer, Peter
1969   "Neue Häuser in der Rue Morgue," in Vogt 1971.
Freeling, Nicholas
1965   Letter to the *Times Literary Supplement*, 20.05.1965.
Freeman, R. Austin
1924   "The Art of the Detective Story," in Haycraft 1946.
Gilbert, Michael (ed.)
1959   *Crime in Good Company*, London (Constable).
Gillett, Eric
1933   Review of *Sweet Danger*, *Sunday Times*, 17.03.1933.
Graves, Robert and Hodge, Alan
1940   *The Long Week-End*, Harmondsworth (Penguin) 1971.
Hamilton, K.M.
1953/54 "Murder and Morality: An Interpretation of Detective Fiction," *Dalhousie Review*, 33.
Hare, Cyril
1959   "The Classic Form," in Gilbert 1959.
Hartman, Geoffrey
1975   "Literature High and Low: The Case of the Mystery Story," in Most and Stowe 1983.
Haycraft, Howard
1941   *Murder for Pleasure. The Life and Times of the Detective Story*, New York (Biblo & Tannen) 1968.
1946   (ed.) *The Art of the Mystery Story*, New York (Simon & Schuster).
Heissenbüttel, Helmut
1966   "Spielregeln des Kriminalromans," in Vogt 1971.
Hill, Christopher
1971   Article on Alexander Dunlop Lindsay, in *Dictionary of National Biography 1951-1960*, Oxford (Oxford University Press).
Hind, Jean Macgregor
1955   "The Women who Make Crime Pay," *Evening News*, 19.09.1955.
Hopkins, Harry

1963   *The New Look. A Social History of the Forties and Fifties in Britain*, London (Secker & Warburg).

Hoskins, Percy
1938   Review of *Dancers in Mourning*, *Evening Standard*, 11.04.1938.

Iles, Francis
1955   Review of *The Beckoning Lady*, *Sunday Times*, 01.05.1955.

Irvin, Kay
1937   Review of *Dancers in Mourning*, *New York Times*, 12.09.1937.

James, P.D.
1978   "Dorothy L. Sayers: From Puzzle to Novel," in Keating 1978.

Jefferies, Cyril R.
1935   "Your Essex," No.6, *Essex County Standard*, 26.10.1935.

Keating, H.R.F. (ed.)
1978   *Crime Writers*, London (BBC).

Klein, Rudolf
1958   Review of *Hide My Eyes*, *Evening Standard*, 23.09.1958.

Krutch, Joseph Wood
1944   "'Only a Detective Story'," in Winks 1980.

Lejeune, Anthony
1984   "Lady Rhondda: Founder of *Time and Tide*," *Time and Tide*, Summer 1984.

Levin, Bernard
1970   *The Pendulum Years. Britain and the Sixties*, London (Cape).

Lewis, Peter
1978   *The Fifties*, London (Book Club Associates).

Lofts, W.O.G. and Adley, D.J.
1970   *The Men Behind Boys' Fiction*, London (Howard Baker).

McCarthy, Mary
1936   "Murder and Karl Marx," *Nation*, 25.03.36.

Mann, Jessica
1981   *Deadlier Than the Male. An Investigation into Feminine Crime Writing*, London (David & Charles).

Marsh, Ngaio
1934   *A Man Lay Dead*, Glasgow (Fontana) 1984.
1938   *Death in a White Tie*, Glasgow (Fontana) 1985.
1981   *Black Beech and Honeydew. An Autobiography*, Auckland and London (Collins).

Marwick, Arthur
1982   *British Society since 1945*, Harmondsworth (Penguin).

Mason, Howard
1963   Review of *The China Governess*, *Sunday Telegraph*, 03.03.1963.

Masterman, J.C.
1933   *An Oxford Tragedy*, Harmondsworth (Penguin) 1939.

Maugham, W. Somerset
1952   "The Decline and Fall of the Detective Story," in *The Vagrant Mood*, London (Heinemann).

Meras, Phyllis
1963   "Miss Allingham Loves to Write," *Providence Sunday Journal*, 03.03.63.

Moore, Henry
1965   Review of *The Mind Readers*, *Midland Chronicle*, 26.11.1965.

Most, Glenn W. and Stowe, William M. (eds.)
1983   *The Poetics of Murder*, New York (Harcourt Brace Jovanovich) 1983.

Mowat, Charles Loch
 1965   *Britain between the Wars 1918–1940*, London (Methuen).
Murch, A.E.
 1958   *The Development of the Detective Novel*, London (Peter Owen) 1968.
Nicolson, Marjorie
 1929   "The Professor and the Detective," *Atlantic Monthly*, April 1929.
Page, Norman (ed.)
 1974   *Wilkie Collins: The Critical Heritage*, London (Routledge).
Panek, LeRoy L.
 1979   *Watteau's Shepherds. The Detective Story in Britain, 1914–1940*, Bowling Green
         (Bowling Green University Popular Press).
Partridge, Ralph
 1952   Review of *The Tiger in the Smoke*, *New Statesman*, 23.08.1952.
Pike, B.A.
 1975–76 "Margery Allingham's Albert Campion: A Chronological Examination of the
         Novels in Which He Appears," *Armchair Detective*, 9.
 1977   Idem, Part IV, *Armchair Detective*, 10.
 1977a   Idem, Part VI, *Armchair Detective*, 10.
Porter, Dennis
 1981   *The Pursuit of Crime: Art and Ideology in Detective Fiction*, New Haven (Yale
         University Press).
Pottersman, Arthur
 1962   "Over the Edge," *Daily Sketch*, 31.07 1962.
Prescott, Orville
 1943   Review of *The Galantrys*, *New York Times*, 13.10.1943.
Proust, Marcel
 1920   *Remembrance of Things Past*, vol. 2, trans. C. K. Scott Moncrieff and Terence
         Kilmartin, Harmondsworth (Penguin) 1984.
Quick, Dorothy
 1952   Review of *The Tiger in the Smoke*, *East Hampton Star*, 28.08.1952.
Richardson, Maurice
 1963   Review of *The China Governess*, *Observer*, 10.03.1963.
Rodell, Marie F.
 1943   *Mystery Fiction: Theory and Technique*, London (Hammond) 1954.
Routley, Eric
 1972   *The Puritan Pleasures of the Detective Story. A Personal Monograph*, London (Gol-
         lancz).
Sayers, Dorothy L.
 1928   Introduction to *Great Short Stories of Detection, Mystery and Horror*, First Series,
         London (Gollancz).
 1931   Introduction to *Great Short Stories of Detection, Mystery and Horror*, Second Se-
         ries, London (Gollancz).
 1934   Introduction to *Great Short Stories of Detection, Mystery and Horror*, Third Series,
         London (Gollancz).
Schwartz, Beatrice A.
 1965   Review of *The Mind Readers*, *St. Louis Post-Dispatch*, 11.07.1965.
Segrave, Edmond
 1943   Review of *The Dance of the Years*, *John o' London's Weekly*, 22.10.1943.
Showalter, Elaine
 1977   *A Literature of Their Own*, Princeton (Princeton University Press).

1985   *The Female Malady: Women, Madness, and English Culture, 1830–1980*, New York (Pantheon).
Snow, C.P.
1932   *Death under Sail*, London (Heinemann) 1959.
Spring, Howard
1943   Review of *The Dance of the Years, Country Life*, 05.11.1943.
1958   Review of *Hide My Eyes, Country Life*, 02.10.1958.
Stevenson, John
1984   *British Society 1914–1945*, Harmondsworth (Penguin).
Storr, Anthony
1961   "A Black-and-White World," *Times Literary Supplement*, 23.06.61.
Strachey, John
1939   "The Golden Age of English Detection," *Saturday Review*, 07.01.39.
Straus, Ralph
1931   Review of *Police at the Funeral, Sunday Times*, 01.11.1931.
Strong, L.A.G.
1959   "The Crime Short Story. An English View," in Gilbert 1959.
Suerbaum, Ulrich
1967   "Der gefesselte Detektivroman. Ein gattungstheoretischer Versuch," *Poetica*, I.
Sunne, Richard
1933   "Men and Books," *Time and Tide*, 11.03.1933.
Swinnerton, Frank
1938   *The Georgian Literary Scene*, London (Dent. Everyman).
Symons, Julian
1958   Review of *Hide My Eyes, Sunday Times*, 28.09.1958.
1959   "The Face in the Mirror," in Gilbert 1959.
1963   Review of *The China Governess, Sunday Times*, 03.03.1963.
1965   Letter to *Times Literary Supplement*, 27.05.65.
1972   *Bloody Murder. From the Detective Story to the Crime Novel*, London (Faber).
Taylor, A.J.P.
1965   *English History 1914–1945*, Harmondsworth (Penguin) 1983.
Todorov, Tzvetan
1977   *The Poetics of Prose*, Ithaca (Cornell University Press).
"Torquemada"
1938   Review of *The Fashion in Shrouds, Observer*, 10.07.1938.
Vogt, Jochen (ed.)
1971   *Der Kriminalroman*, Munich (Fink).
Wallace, Edgar
1925   *The Murder Book of J.G.Reeder*, New York (Dover) 1982.
Wallace, Erica
1965   "The Woman with Murder on Her Mind," *Bristol Evening Post*, 12.07.1965.
Watson, Colin
1971   *Snobbery with Violence. Crime Stories and Their Audience*, London (Eyre & Spottiswoode).
Wheatley, Lola
1962   "The Professional Touch," *The Writer*, December 1962.
Winks, Robin W. (ed.)
1980   *Detective Fiction. A Collection of Critical Essays*, Englewood Cliffs (Prentice-Hall).
Wrong, E.M.
1926   "Crime and Detection," in Haycraft 1946.

Index

MA and PYC are used as abbreviations for Margery Allingham and her husband, Philip Youngman Carter. Names of fictional characters are in quotation marks.